Live Well in
MEXICO

HOW TO RELOCATE, RETIRE, AND
INCREASE YOUR STANDARD OF LIVING

KEN LUBOFF

John Muir Publications
Santa Fe, New Mexico

John Muir Publications, P.O. Box 613,
Santa Fe, New Mexico 87504

Printed in the United States of America
First edition. First printing October 1999

Library of Congress Cataloging-in-Publication data
Luboff, Ken.
Live well in Mexico : how to relocate, retire, and increase your standard of living / Ken
     Luboff.
        p.   cm.
Includes index.
ISBN 1-56261-432-0
1. Mexico—Description and travel. 2. Retirement. Places of—Mexico. I. Title.
F1216.L83 1999   99-24014
972—dc21   CIP

Editors: Peg Goldstein, Cathy Kingery
Graphics Editor: Bunny Wong
Production: Marie J.T. Vigil
Interior design: Marie J.T. Vigil
Cover design: Marie J.T. Vigil
Typesetting: Laurel Avery
Map illustration: Mike Hermann—Purple Lizard Maps
Printer: Publishers Press
Front cover photo: © Craig Raney/Photo Network (Guanajuato)
Back cover photo: *vertical*—© Francene Keery/Leo de Wys, Inc.
                  (Pinotepa Zapotec, Oaxaca)
              horizontal—© Larry Dunnire/Photo Network (Oaxaca shoreline)
Distributed to the book trade by
Publishers Group West
Berkeley, California

Contents

Acknowledgments

Special thanks to Barbara for her love and sense of humor throughout. She edited, criticized, and was a constant source of inspiration. Together we can do anything. Namaste!

Maureen Earl is a great friend and a truly fine writer. Her artful additions to the book are invaluable. Thank you, Moish.

The following friends made other important contributions: Kendal Dodge Butler, Izzy Flores, Beverly Hunt, Peggy Lee, Bill Reiner, Deborah Rubio, Raquel Settles, Sally Sloan, Bob and Lee Story, Gary Thompson, Hector Ulloa, Michael Veselik, and Carol Williams. My heartfelt thanks to you all.

Special thanks to all the wonderful expatriates and Mexican people we met in our travels. You shared your stories, directed us to "unknown" towns and hidden beaches, and offered important insights into the Mexican culture. We thank you all.

This book is dedicated to Liza.

Introduction

An ancient proverb says that you must first empty the cup before it can begin to refill. Retiring is the beginning of emptying the cup; living in Mexico is an exciting way to begin refilling it.

I was like most other people I knew—working hard in a stressed-out world while wistfully dreaming about the day I could stop and retire to some fantasy beach. In recent years, so many friends had become ill or died that I began having visions of a coworker entering my office to find me with my feet pointed straight up in the air behind my desk, the rest of me dead on the floor.

Finally, at the ripe young age of 52, the opportunity arose to sell the company stock I owned. The moment had arrived! With great fear and trepidation, my wife, Barbara, and I contemplated the reality of retiring with less money than we thought we would need. Would we have enough? We began asking each other questions: How will we keep from being bored? Where will we live?

We decided to give ourselves a month or two away from home as a period of transition into our new life. A friend, Eve Muir, kindly offered us her house in San Miguel de Allende. We accepted and moved to Mexico. Our two-month stay became four months, four became six, and so on. Now, five years later, we are still living in Mexico, in our own home, and loving every moment of it.

Mexico is one of the unknown wonders of the world—it is amazing how little people to the north know about their neighbor. In fact, people in the United States know more about Thailand than they do about Mexico. Most Americans think of Mexico as having a few palm-studded beaches lined with mega-hotels and resorts and a vast, scary inland of baking cactus with unfriendly, if not hostile, Pancho Villas.

This image couldn't be further from the truth. Mexico is filled with both natural and man-made wonders—hot rivers, snowcapped mountains, magnificent colonial towns, charming Swiss-style villages, indigenous people wearing flamboyant costumes, exotic coffee plantations, art deco fantasies in the jungle, and the generosity of a very warm people.

No other bordering countries in the world are as different from each other as Mexico and the United States. Mexicans think differently and view the world through a completely different set of lenses than Americans. You can see this contrast clearly as soon as you cross the border. Mexico's food, music, architecture—even the way the people look—are unlike our own. The differences in themselves are an attraction—in Mexico we are explorers discovering a new terrain as well as new ideas and points of view. A friend, Chris Smith, recently sent us a story that explains one of the differences in the two cultures beautifully:

An American businessman stood at the pier of a small coastal village in Mexico, when a small boat carrying a lone Mexican fisherman docked. Inside the small boat were several large yellowfin tuna. The American complimented the Mexican on the quality of his fish and asked how long it took to catch them. The fisherman replied, "Only a little while."

Sierra Gorda region in the state of Querétaro

Ken Luboff

The American then asked, "If it took only a little while to catch these fine fish, why didn't you stay out longer and catch more fish?" The fisherman explained that this catch was enough to support his family's immediate needs.

The American then asked, "But what do you do with the rest of your time?" The fisherman replied, "I sleep late, fish a little, play with my children, take a siesta with my wife, Maria, and stroll into the village each evening where I sip wine and play guitar with my amigos. I have a full and busy life, señor."

The American scoffed, "I am a Harvard MBA and could help you. You should spend more time fishing and with the proceeds buy a bigger boat. With the proceeds from the bigger boat you could buy several boats. Eventually you would have a fleet of fishing boats. Instead of selling your catch to a middleman you would sell directly to the processor, eventually opening your own cannery. You would control the product, processing, and distribution. You would need to leave this small coastal fishing village and move to Mexico City, then L.A., and eventually New York City, where you will run your expanding enterprise."

The fisherman asked, "But señor, how long will this all take?" The American replied, "Fifteen to twenty years."

"But what then, señor?" inquired the Mexican. The American laughed and said, "That's the best part. When the time is right you would announce an IPO and sell your company stock to the public and become very rich, you would make millions."

"Millions, señor? Then what?" asked the Mexican. The American said, "Why, then you would retire, of course—move to a small coastal fishing village where you could sleep late, fish a little, play with your kids, take a siesta with your wife, and stroll into the village in the evenings where you could sip wine and play your guitar with your amigos."

🐟   🐟   🐟

Obviously, retirement in Mexico is not for everyone. Mexico is a different country and takes some getting used to. But if you're adventurous and have a good sense of humor and a lot of patience, living in Mexico can seem like the next best thing to paradise!

And retiring in Mexico offers some obvious advantages over other countries. The foremost may be its location. Mexico is a breeze to reach from the United States. It has modern airports and a quickly developing four-lane highway system. The trip by car from the U.S. border to most central Mexican cities takes only a day or two. And once at home in Mexico, a good telecommunications network can keep you in touch with friends and family back in the States. Phoning the United States is easy, but we usually just turn on our computer and stay connected by e-mail.

Living in Mexico costs us about one-fourth of what it used to cost us to live in the States. Depending on where you make your home, it is possible to retire very well in Mexico on $1,500 per month—even less. After all, a pound of oranges costs about 15 cents, a dozen eggs 85 cents, a full-time maid $35 to $40 per week, and a dozen fresh long-stemmed roses $2! Sure, in the fanciest areas of towns like San Miguel, Cuernavaca, and Puerto Vallarta, higher rents will drive monthly expenses up. But outside the ritzy areas—in the countryside and the smaller villages—houses rent for as little as $200 a month.

Those interested in buying a house in Mexico will find that new laws make it easy for a foreigner to own property with a secure title. A few U.S. mortgage companies now offer mortgages on Mexican real estate at competitive rates. Real estate is appreciating in coastal areas, but bargains can still be found, and building costs are about one-third to one-half of those in the United States.

For the most part, Mexicans are sweet people who will go out of their way to help a friend or even a congenial acquaintance. We have gone into shops for the first time and, because the shopkeepers could not break our large bill, been told to return and pay later. Knowing at least a little Spanish, even if it is badly spoken, will make kindnesses like this more likely.

But can a country with a great sunny climate, friendly people, beautiful beaches, first-class recreational facilities, spectacular mountains, and low prices be perfect? It appears that that would be too much to ask. Like anywhere on earth, Mexico has its downsides.

Outdoor market in San Miguel de Allende

Among them are environmental degradation, poverty, and crime. Cultural differences are a source of frustration to some new arrivals. Government is not efficient by U.S. standards. Ever wonder where all the old typewriters and carbon paper have gone? When you're dealing with border crossings, immigration, the police, or the government, out come the forms with about 10 carbon copies.

We make no bones about it, living in Mexico takes adjusting to. For those of you who are stuck in your ways or not ready to experience some inconveniences, Mexico will be a real challenge. But if you are up for that challenge, you will meet amazing people with unique ideas. You will make good Mexican friends. You might even learn a new language!

With this book, we try to provide you with detailed information about health care, money, housing, and working in Mexico, so that you will have a good understanding of what it takes to make the move. Chapters on history and people will give you insight into the Mexican character and worldview.

Beginning with Chapter 13, we describe the towns and cities where most newcomers to Mexico will wind up living—towns that new arrivals can ease into relatively effortlessly. Each location has a large and well-established expatriate community. All have English-language libraries, volunteer organizations, and clubs, and all have high-quality health and recreational facilities. Each has a unique character and a different mix of foreign residents. These are the towns that we recommend to most people who ask us about living in Mexico.

But foreigners live in every corner of the country. The towns and cities described here are only the tip of the iceberg. We have arrived at the most remote mountain villages only to run into retiree residents from Europe, Canada, the States, and other parts of the world. We have a good friend, an American woman about 45 years old, who lives happily on a 20-acre farm in the state of Michoacan with her French boyfriend. Another old friend and his wife are building a house on a remote beach in the state of Jalisco.

In Chapter 18, we highlight Guadalajara, the city with the largest population of foreigners, and several very beautiful and remote towns and cities with small—sometimes very small—foreign populations. These descriptions may whet the appetites of the more adventurous among you.

Remember, retirement ain't what it used to be. It is no longer a bunch of little old women and men sitting on porches, smoking pipes, rocking, and discussing the weather. Retirees we meet are much too busy hiking, painting, playing golf, traveling, and getting on with their new lives to have much time left over for rocking.

A few notes: We occasionally use the word *American* to refer to people from the United States. The fact is that Canadians and Mexicans are Americans as well. All three countries are part of North America. But we use *American* because Mexicans commonly use the word to refer to people from the States and Canada. It would be more correct to refer to ourselves as a *Norteamericanos* (North Americans), *de Los Estados Unidos* (from the United States), or *Estadounidenses*—all of which are mouthfuls.

Also note that the Mexican economy is changing rapidly. In

some parts of the country, such as along the Pacific coast, a building boom is pushing real estate prices up like mad. In San Miguel, real estate sales are "soft." The country is also experiencing moderately high inflation, and the peso, which has been steadily devaluing against the dollar for years, has recently strengthened. Such changes can affect prices. The prices given in this book, therefore, are meant only as a guide. Unless otherwise specified, all prices are given in dollar amounts, for the convenience of the reader.

Finally, we would like your input. Send us an update (in care of John Muir Publications) about a city we have included in the book. Maybe a new English bookstore has opened or great new library. Tell us about towns you have visited with great retirement potential. Maybe you already live there!

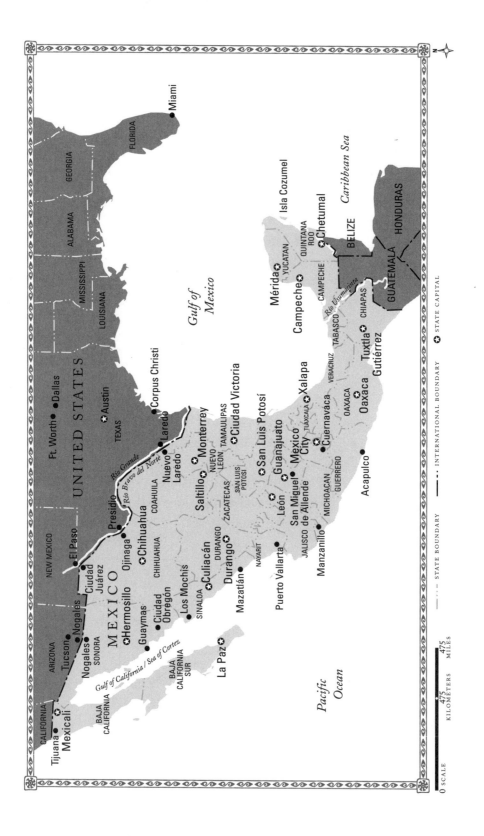

N

Caribbean Sea

Gulf of Mexico

Pacific Ocean

Gulf of California / Sea of Cortez

UNITED STATES

MEXICO

FLORIDA
GEORGIA
ALABAMA
MISSISSIPPI
LOUISIANA
TEXAS
NEW MEXICO
ARIZONA
CALIFORNIA

Miami
•Dallas
Ft. Worth •
☼ Austin
Corpus Christi
Laredo
Nuevo Laredo
Monterrey
Ciudad Victoria
Presidio
El Paso
Ojinaga
☼ Chihuahua
Saltillo ☼
☼ Durango
Culiacán ☼
Los Mochis
Ciudad Obregón
Guaymas
☼ Hermosillo
Nogales
Tucson
Nogales
Ciudad Juárez
Mazatlán
Puerto Vallarta
Manzanillo
La Paz ☼
Tijuana
☼ Mexicali
Acapulco
San Miguel de Allende
León ☼
Guanajuato
☼ San Luis Potosí
Mexico City ☼
Cuernavaca
Xalapa ☼
Oaxaca ☼
Tuxtla Gutiérrez ☼
Campeche ☼
Mérida ☼
Chetumal ☼
Isla Cozumel

BELIZE
GUATEMALA
HONDURAS

YUCATAN
QUINTANA ROO
CAMPECHE
TABASCO
CHIAPAS
VERACRUZ
OAXACA
GUERRERO
MICHOACAN
JALISCO
NAYARIT
DURANGO
ZACATECAS
SAN LUIS POTOSI
NUEVO LEÓN
TAMAULIPAS
COAHUILA
CHIHUAHUA
SINALOA
SONORA
BAJA CALIFORNIA
BAJA CALIFORNIA SUR
TLAXCALA

Rio Grande
Río Bravo del Norte
Río Usumacinta

0 SCALE

475 KILOMETERS

475 MILES

•–• INTERNATIONAL BOUNDARY

––– STATE BOUNDARY

☼ STATE CAPITAL

Overview of a Sweet New Life

Most tourists come to Mexico to lie in the sun on a tropical beach, whoop it up in a border town over the weekend, or see an archaeological ruin or cathedral. Foreigners living here, on the other hand, have the opportunity to slow down, tune in to the subtleties of the culture, and discover the wonderful diversity of terrain within Mexico's borders. As they meet and become friendly with Mexican people, foreign residents will be invited to weddings and other family celebrations, religious ceremonies, and community festivities. If they want, they can leisurely explore the country—canoeing through a lush jungle lagoon in the morning, then sleeping in a high mountain pine forest that night. They might attend a first-rate opera in Guadalajara in the evening and spend the night in a quaint fishing village just 45 minutes away.

The contrasts in Mexico are astounding: the Stone Age and high technology stand side by side. An old man rides along the highway on his burro—a huge General Motors plant his backdrop—as a new Mercedes whizzes by. Poor families live in tin hovels back-to-back with fancy cybercafés. Your experiences in Mexico will be just as varied and sometimes just as contrastive.

Topography and Population

The Rio Grande defines more than half the border between the United States and Mexico. West of El Paso, no natural boundary exists; only an imaginary line divides Mexico from New Mexico, Arizona, and California. The entire border is closely guarded by the United States.

Narrowing from its northern border of 1,600 miles, Mexico measures just 125 miles on its southern border at the Isthmus of Tehuantepec. The west and south coasts are bounded by the Pacific Ocean, the southeast bordered by Guatemala, Belize, and the Caribbean Sea, and the east by the Gulf of Mexico. The peninsula of Baja California, about 800 miles long, is separated from the mainland by the Gulf of California.

Mexico has more than 6,200 miles of coastline: 4,400 miles on the west and south coasts, 1,774 on the east coast. The country covers an area of 760,000 square miles. More than two-thirds of Mexico is mountainous, ranging from 3,000 to over 18,000 feet in altitude. The two principal mountain ranges, the Sierra Madre Occidental (West), running along the Pacific coast, and the Sierra Madre Oriental (East), join together as the country narrows south of Mexico City. This is an area of spectacular mountain peaks—many of them extinct volcanoes—with more than 22 rising to 10,000 feet or higher. The two most famous peaks are Popocatepel (gushing smoke these days) and Iztaccihuatl. Both are over 17,000 feet and straddle the states of Mexico and Puebla. The highest peak of all is the majestic Pica de Orizaba, standing at 18,855 feet in the state of Veracruz. Between the two Sierra Madre ranges lies a vast high plateau, home to the majority of Mexico's 97.5 million inhabitants. The plateau itself is crisscrossed by a series of valleys and mountain slopes.

Mexico is the world's most populous Spanish-speaking country,

> *In Mexico, the Stone Age and high technology stand side by side.*

with a rapidly expanding population. More than 50 percent of its people are under 20 years old. The overall population density is about 125 people per square mile, compared to the United States with an overall density of about 70 people per square mile. However, the countryside feels empty because Mexicans tend to live close to family and friends in villages and cities. Mexico City, with a population of about 26 million, is the world's largest city. In some areas its population density reaches more than 40,000 people per square mile. The second largest city in Mexico is Guadalajara, with 5 million inhabitants. In area, Mexico is the world's 13th largest country, slightly less than three times the size of Texas.

Attitude toward Foreigners

The United States of Mexico (Los Estados Unidos Mexicanos) has 31 states, plus the federal district (Mexico City), commonly called D.F. or Distrito Federal. Like the United States and Canada, Mexico is part of North America, a fact that makes it difficult for us "foreigners from North America" to find a unique name for ourselves in Mexico. *Los Estadounidenses* (people from the United States) would probably be the most politically correct name—if we could even pronounce it. Some Mexicans call us *de Los Estados Unidos* (from the United States). But, for the most part, Mexicans call us *Norteamericanos*, or just *Americanos*. On occasion we will be called *gringos*, a term for Anglos who come from (or just look like they come from) the United States or Canada. In the past, this was a more derogatory term, but these days many Mexicans use it to describe people from the north. *Gringa* is used affectionately to describe a young Anglo girl.

In general, Mexicans are polite and reserved when dealing with foreigners from the north. Newcomers from the States often take this treatment as friendliness, but it is far more complicated than that. Mexicans and other inhabitants of Latin America often wear masks that cover their true feelings (see Chapter 3: "Mexico's People"). Nevertheless, common courtesy is part of every interaction in Mexico, as is formality. This formality appears unexpectedly at times. For instance, you will get used to being greeted with *"Buenos dias"* or *"Buenas tardes"* by the gas station attendant or a stranger on the street and to being called *Señor* or *Señora* by a shopkeeper, but it will surprise you when a total stranger in a restaurant says, *"Buen provecho"* (good appetite) or *"Con permiso"* (excuse me) when passing your table. It is a good idea to learn as many of these formal expressions as possible. Using them will bring you a new measure of respect in the eyes of Mexicans. And, with time and some effort, they will help you to make good Mexican friends.

Economy

After the devaluation of the peso in 1995, it looked as though Mexico was being thrust into the Dark Ages economically. The devaluation had devastating effects. The budding and optimistic middle class had discovered credit during the years of Salinas de Gortari's presidency. Many people now had mortgages, car loans, and high credit-card bills. The devaluation caused interest rates in Mexico to soar as high as 150 percent, creating economic chaos. People lost their homes, businesses, and cars. The change wiped out many gains made by the middle class and created hardships at all levels of society. People were gloomy and angry.

The economy has begun to improve, and international loans have been repaid. Mexico has been registering fairly high growth rates since the second quarter of 1996, and employment rates are rising slowly. The purchasing power of the peso is stabilizing, and high inflation rates are dropping to levels that help lighten the debt burden for middle-class individuals and corporations. Many Mexicans are once again beginning to feel guardedly optimistic about their economic future.

Nevertheless, there is vast poverty in the country. Mexicans complain bitterly about how hard it is to make ends meet. Wages for most people are still very low. The minimum wage in the country is less than $120 a month, and almost half of the working population earns less than $240 a month. Even with relatively low inflation, prices are still rising, keeping a large mass of the population poor. However, the income levels that make life difficult for much of the Mexican population, along with the continued slow devaluation of the peso, are an advantage for retirees living on dollars in Mexico.

Mexico's economy is driven by tourism, industrial production, oil and gas production, textiles and clothing, and agriculture. Mexico has 20 percent of the world's oil reserves. It produces and exports a wide selection of agricultural goods. Just about every kind of fruit and vegetable is grown here, both on giant, modern, irrigated farms and on small family plots. Hundreds of North American companies have built factories here to take advantage of low-cost labor and NAFTA rules.

Environmental Issues

Mexico is rich in silver, copper, gold, lead, zinc, natural gas, and timber. It is the sixth largest oil producer in the world. But in exploiting its resources, Mexico has wreaked havoc on its environment. Overgrazing, poor crop choices, and inefficient farm management have led to the deterioration of the topsoil. Forests have been hacked down, lakes and rivers polluted, and air quality in some areas has deteriorated badly. The fires of 1998 were started in the slash-and-burn tradition and whipped by the winds of El Niño. A catastrophic environmental disaster, they wiped out portions of the rain forest in the state of Chiapas. Air quality in Mexico City is very poor. Not long ago, Barbara and I visited some of the city's great museums, including Frieda Khalo's house and Leon Trotsky's house and museum. We had to cut our visit short and escape the city because our throats hurt and our eyes watered and burned after just a few days.

When Barbara and I first began visiting Mexico in the late 1960s, plastic was not yet in heavy use in the country. Before venturing into the market to shop, we had to have, at the very least, a large shopping bag and a bottle or two. Oil and honey were sold only in bulk. We also brought along a specially designed wire basket for eggs. When something needed to be wrapped, the shopkeeper used old newspaper.

Now, plastic and other types of packaging materials have caused many of the same environmental problems in Mexico as they have in the States. Unsightly plastic bags are strewn along highways, and plastic bottles litter many rivers, streams, and hundreds of impromptu roadside dumps.

In response to continuing environmental degradation, grassroots groups have sprung up around the country and have begun reforesting, cleaning up rivers and streams, and reeducating people about environmental issues. Some more enlightened state governments have also begun to recognize the problem and have funded local environmental departments or matched funds with independent organizations. Still, Mexico's environmental movement is perhaps at least 25 years behind that of the United States. Even with the efforts of dedicated and hardworking people, without economic growth there will not be any significant improvement.

Crime

For those contemplating retiring in Mexico, the issue of crime is an important one. One of the long-lasting, egregious effects of the 1995 devaluation and the poverty it brought was an increase in crime, especially theft. Official statistics show a 24 percent increase in crime between 1994 and 1996. The highest crime rates are in the big cities. In some parts of the country, especially in northern Mexico, crime is related to drug trafficking—but few tourists or foreign residents are affected. Political violence plagues some remote areas in the states of Guerrero, Oaxaca, and Chiapas.

We foreigners who live in Mexico learn to take reasonable precautions against crime, as we would in the United States, then we get on with our lives. Crime is a fact of life, but it does not overshadow the wonderfully enriching qualities of retiring here. In most small towns and rural areas of Mexico, crime takes the form of robberies and burglaries. This is especially true in small retirement communities like San Miguel de Allende and Ajijic and in mid-sized cities like Puerto Vallarta, Mazatlán, and Oaxaca. For this reason, many new retirees are now buying homes in gated developments. For our part,

Bob and Marybeth Macy

A portion of Mexico's 6,200 miles of coastline at Punta del Pescadero

we make sure that our home (not in a gated community) is secure when we go out of town by hiring a house sitter or arranging for someone to check the house each day. We know our neighbors and have good sturdy locks on our doors and windows. We don't leave packages or items that might look interesting to a thief in our cars on the street overnight. We usually don't walk home alone late at night.

In general, crime in small Mexican towns is far less violent than crime in comparably sized U.S. cities. Most violent crimes occur in Mexico City. When we travel there, we become super-conscious of our surroundings. We try not to be flashy, and we don't pull out great wads of cash in public. We take only official taxis and don't walk alone at night. Sound familiar? These are more or less the same types of precautions people should take in any large city in the world.

Politics

Friends have expressed concern that living in Mexico may be dangerous because the country could descend into political chaos. To this we answer that Mexico is one of the most politically stable countries in the hemisphere. Its constitution is based on democratic principles, such as freedom of speech, religion, and the press. Mexico also has highly developed legal and judicial systems. On the other hand, almost every Mexican institution has long been rife with corruption and payoffs. The country clearly has political problems, with extremists operating at both ends of the spectrum. Nevertheless, in many ways politics in Mexico are in their best shape in years, with a good variety of political parties available to voters.

For the last 70 years, since the end of the Mexican Revolution, the Revolutionary Institutional Party (PRI) has dominated the political scene. The PRI always handpicked each president and controlled Congress, creating a one-party system. In recent years, Mexican government has begun to change. Two strong opposition parties have emerged—the conservative, pro-business National Action Party (PAN) and the left-leaning Party of the Democratic Revolution (PRD). Each party made strong showings in the 1997 midterm federal elections, leading for the first time ever to a federal Chamber of Deputies in which no party has an absolute majority. Such changes have begun to convince many Mexicans that they are in the process of transition to a more democratic political system.

The multi-party system appears to be working in Mexico. Opposition leaders have claimed governorships in several important states, and Cuauhtemoc Cardenas, the son of one of Mexico's most beloved presidents and a member of the PRD, is now the mayor of Mexico City. Nevertheless, the PRI is still extremely strong, and the two opposition parties are underfunded and fractionalized. The PRI, though it may continue to lose power, is likely to be the dominant political party in the foreseeable future.

For foreign residents interested in politics, following the political scenes in both Mexico and the United States is like reading two overly dramatic tragicomedies. Most of the characters are full of themselves and uninteresting and more often than not act like kids squabbling over toys. Discussing Mexican politics with friends is one thing, but loudly expressing a political point of view is another. Mexican immigration law prohibits foreigners from engaging in political activity.

Education

For the majority of Mexicans, education has historically been of little or no importance. Until this century, education was not available to the masses, and even if it were there would have been almost nowhere to make use of it. Even today, there are more educated Mexicans than there are jobs. By law, children must attend school from the ages of 6 to 14. But the government doesn't spend as much money or place as much value on primary education as it does on university programs. Though most children do attend school for at least a few years, it is not unusual to see very young people working at menial jobs during the day. In 1989 official government sources put the literacy rate at 87 percent, but it's unknown how accurate this number is.

Cuisine

If you think the food in Mexico will resemble the fare at Taco Bell or a Mexican restaurant in the States, you're in for a wonderful surprise. Sure, there are tacos, enchiladas, and fajitas in Mexico, plenty of them, but the cuisine of Mexico has so much more. There are regional specialties and sauces that would make any gourmand's head spin, but what makes Mexican cuisine stand out is the great variety of fresh fruits, vegetables, and fish.

> *We once found an outstanding Japanese restaurant halfway between nowhere and outer nowhere.*

A common myth is that the food is hot, hotter, or hottest, but in fact most of the food is mild. On tables in restaurants, along with the salt, pepper, and napkins, you'll find different types of bottled hot sauces and a bowl or two of homemade picante sauce (salsa).

From an eating point of view, traveling in Mexico is a joy compared to the United States. Even in the middle of nowhere, you can find a good homemade meal, and you won't have to resort to McDonald's or Denny's. As a rule, you'll find more varied menus and international specialties in the tourist areas and large cities—just as in the States. But Mexico is full of surprises. We once found an outstanding Japanese restaurant on a hill overlooking a spectacular beach halfway between nowhere and outer nowhere. On our last trip to the coast, we found a Polish restaurant in the small beach town of Bucerias!

Occasionally, restaurants along the roads and in small towns don't have menus. When you ask what's available, the staff will usually ask you what you want. Be careful! Ask for something simple like eggs. Once in a small restaurant, after going back and forth through the "What would you like?" "What do you have?" dance, we decided on chicken. A short while after ordering, we saw a small child run out of the back of the restaurant. A half hour later, the small child ran back clutching a squawking chicken. Need we go on? The chicken was delicious and, of course, very fresh! But eating in that restaurant was an all-day affair.

Most restaurants want very much to please their customers and will bend over backward to do so. A short time ago, in a lovely mid- to upscale restaurant in San Miguel, I ordered lasagna, which I wasn't happy with. I asked Barbara to taste it, but before she could, two waiters descended on me. They had seen the sour look on my face when I first tried it. They took the lasagna away and brought the specialty of the house, a delicious *arrachara*-style steak (marinated in a special slightly hot sauce).

In Mexico, unless you are in areas where there are lots of gringos, you are going to have to change your eating habits. The most important thing to remember is that the main (and heaviest) meal of the day, the *comida*, is eaten between 2 and 4 p.m.—a most sensible custom in our opinion. Whenever we visit the States, it takes us a few days to adjust. We walk into restaurants at 2:30 and hear: "Sorry, folks, we are closed until 6 p.m." and are forced to go to a Denny's or McDonald's for our comida. For the evening meal, many people just snack at home or buy a couple of tacos at a stand. Many poor Mexican women set up little taco or *gordita* stands in their doorways in the evening (especially on weekends), where strolling neighbors can pick up a fresh, usually deep-fried, goody.

Generally speaking, the average restaurant outside of tourist areas will serve the following breakfast: fresh-squeezed orange or carrot juice, eggs any way you like, and either fresh hot tortillas, *bolillos* (bo-lee-yos, crusty French bread–style Mexican rolls), or *Bimbo* (white bread). Usually, we opt for tortillas. But if we're in the mood for bread we're sure to ask for bolillos. Coffee is often instant, but for some reason Nescafé in Mexico tastes about 100 times better than Nescafé in the States. Some restaurants serve *café de olla*, a delicious home-brewed coffee made with cinnamon. Black tea and *te de manzanillo* (chamomile) is always available. If eggs aren't your thing, usually oatmeal (*avena*) is available, or pancakes from a mix.

For your comida, if you are not looking for anything fancy, we recommend the *comida corrida* ("running meal"), or special of the day. It is the cheapest meal on the menu, you don't have to think about what you want, it's easy to order if you don't know Spanish, and it will be served fast. It usually consists of a soup—generally a cream-based vegetable soup—a main course of simply prepared chicken, beef, or pork, steamed fresh vegetables, rice, beans, and sometimes a small "salad"—a couple slices of tomato and onion and a few lettuce leaves. Dessert is generally flan, Jell-O, or pudding. The meal is served with a refreshing homemade *agua* (water-based fruit drink), and tea or coffee is served afterward. This meal will put you back $3 to $5 and will rarely be memorable, but it should be quite satisfactory and filling. If you want a soft drink or beer with your comida, you will have to pay a bit extra. *Cena*, the light evening meal, often consists of things like tacos, tostados, or fajitas. But if you're hungry, restaurants also serve a wonderful variety of entrées.

Don't be afraid to experiment. Restaurants serve many wonderful dishes that you won't find anywhere but in Mexico, and you don't have to worry about getting anything weird or disgusting like sautéed chicken eyeballs or stewed puppy stomach. To us, the most disgusting item on the menu is tripe, which in Mexico is called *menudo* and which quite a lot of people actually like. Some of the strangest (but most delicious) things we've eaten are tuna (not the fish but a type of cactus fruit) ice cream, *huitlacoche* (a black fungus that grows on corn) crepes, and *cabrito* (baby goat). One fabulous Mexican specialty, *chiles en nogada*, is a green chile stuffed with ground beef and smothered in a tamarind-walnut cream sauce with pomegrante seeds sprinkled on top. *Sopa Azteca* (Aztec soup) appears on almost every menu. It is prepared in several ways, but usually is a clear tomato- or chicken-based broth with crisp tortilla strips, avocado, onions, cheese, *chipotle* chile (a smoky, not-too-hot chile), and chicken. At the beach be sure to treat yourself to fresh fish.

Some of the best meals we've had anywhere in the world have been at beachfront *palapas* (palm-frond shacks with no flooring). There's nothing like digging your feet into the sand, watching waves pound the beach and palm trees sway in the breeze, and eating fresh fish with garlic-butter sauce running down your chin—or maybe shrimps *a la diabla* (smothered in a hot sauce). Add a hot tortilla or two and a cold beer, and you know you've landed in paradise. In the

Ken Luboff

A street in Ajijic decorated for a celebration

state of Nayarit (north of Puerto Vallarta), fish is barbecued *sarandeado* style. We took some New York friends there, and they said they could not get fish at *any* price in Manhattan that would compare. We paid about $20 for the four of us.

If you're a vegetarian or a vegan, unless you're in a large town, tourist area, or place with lots of expats, your choices will be limited at restaurants. But don't worry—you won't starve. Keep in mind that the markets are full of incredible vegetables and fruits. And, as we said before, most restaurants want to make their customers happy, and many will gladly fix you something special—like a plate of rice (*sopa de arroz*) with steamed veggies. Or ask for rice and some veggies in a fresh, piping-hot tortilla with a little hot sauce sprinkled on top. Voilà—a wonderful vegan taco! All restaurants serve quesadillas (cheese-filled tortillas), many serve sautéed mushrooms in garlic sauce, and there's usually guacamole. The beans are usually, but not always, cooked with a bit of lard—ask to be sure. Granola and yogurt are available everywhere, as well as nuts and seeds. There are many fruit and juice stands, so you can always get a *licuado*, basically a smoothie with any combination of fruits and water or milk. (Just point to the fruits you want if you don't know the Spanish words.)

Please note: Most restaurants in cities serve only purified water and ice cubes. They usually wash their vegetables well. In the country, sanitation is more hit-and-miss. *Absolutely* wash your hands before eating, and if you want to take a little extra precaution, squeeze lemon juice (a natural disinfectant) over your food. Usually, a small plate of halved lemons is served with every meal. If not, ask the waiter for *limones*.

Cultural Oddities

The unique Mexican world view can produce some funny, bizarre, and Felliniesque experiences. I can't tell you how many times we see or hear something that causes us to shake our heads in amazement. These phenomena are wonderful because they remind us just how foreign the Mexican culture is—and enhance our sense of adventure in such an exotic land.

As you may know, Mexicans love a fiesta. It may take the form of a party, parade, celebration organized by the town, or impromptu gathering. Mexicans have a saint for every day of the year and one for every neighborhood. They celebrate major religious holidays like Easter (Semana Santa), Virgin of Guadalupe Day, and Christmas. They hold dozens of political rallies and observe national holidays like Independence Day and El Cinco de Mayo. All of these events are celebrated in their own way, some more strangely than others. You never know when you are going to encounter something really odd. We have gotten used to rounding a corner and bumping into a crowd of costumed dancers in absurd homemade chicken or who-knows-what masks, or in store-bought rubber heads of Laurel and Hardy, Bill Clinton, Carlos Salinas de Gotari, or Mickey Mouse. We have seen parades of Aztec Indians walking shoulder to shoulder with soldiers in Civil War dress, priests, and guys in space suits—all preceded by an oompah band. We have seen decorated taxis parading on their saint's day and somber funeral processions through the streets.

On Day of the Dead (around Halloween), people visit cemeteries with flowers and candles. They bring food, wine, and booze or wear a dead loved one's favorite hat. Some stay all night talking to the dead, playing music, singing, and not paying too much attention to the priest chanting in the background. Mexicans say that on this night the veil between the living and the dead is at its thinnest, and the dead can hear and appear to their loved ones. The day before the Day of the Dead is dedicated to young children who have died. For a week or so leading up to these days, stands around town sell sugar candy shaped and painted like skulls, skeletons, and caskets. Some candies are exquisitely "carved." Many people set up altars in their homes—some quite large and elaborate—dedicated to one or more dearly departed. The altars hold flowers, candles, and photos of the dead, of course, but also anything else that the dearly departed might enjoy, like a pack of cigarettes, a bottle of tequila, guitar strings, paintbrushes, or a hammer and nails.

It is not unusual to be startled awake at 5 a.m. by the sound of rockets exploding in the sky. Then there are the ubiquitous church bells, roosters, barking dogs, and loud truck mufflers. On weekends and holidays, a neighbor may decide to play his stereo at full volume, or music at the city park may be loud enough to cause a mild earthquake. Most incomprehensible to non-Mexicans are the occasional town celebrations in which two bandstands are set up next to each other with speakers the size of Buicks. Two bands then play simultaneously—completely different ear-shattering music until late into the night. Meanwhile, the crowd in the street below dances, seemingly impervious to the noise, loving every high-decibel moment of it.

Mexican shops can and do sell many strange combinations of goods. Imagine a small store in the United States that carried booze alongside children's toys! We've seen shops that sell both jewelry and Tupperware and a Laundromat selling souvenir masks and crosses. "No way!" you might say. But in Mexican shops, anything goes.

Be aware that Mexicans are reluctant to say, "I don't know." When you ask for directions you will most certainly be given directions—although the direction-giver may have no idea where the street or town you seek is located. When you ask what day a job will be completed, you will always get a specific completion date. The plumber will say, "I will be there tomorrow at 10 a.m." Whether or not he comes is up to the gods. You are likely to be told what you want to be told. Such responses stem from the fact that Mexicans sincerely want to help and oblige—not from meanness.

Mexicans really mean it when they say *mi casa es tu casa*. One day Barbara was walking our dog in the country and encountered a poor woman who, without too much ado, asked Barbara how old she was and if she had knee problems (which, it turned out, the woman had). After a little chat, the woman gave Barbara directions to her home and said she should visit any time—that her home was always open.

Mexico is one of the most biodiverse countries on earth, with more reptiles and amphibians than any other country and an estimated 30,000 species of plants.

She said she was poor and that her house was very humble, but she would be honored by Barbara's visit. Another time, in San Miguel, we were invited to a Christmas posada at a Mexican's home. The party spilled out into the street, where a piñata for the children was strung between two houses. A couple of American tourists wandered down the street to see what the commotion was. The hostess happened to be outside and asked them if they had eaten or had a drink yet. They kind of sputtered, "Well...we were just passing by, we weren't invited." The hostess looked at them like they were half crazed—she had just invited them! To be asked into a stranger's home is not out of the ordinary.

One of Mexico's more endearing attractions, as far as we're concerned, is the element of surprise. The culture and people forever fill us with wonder. There is an innocence in the way teenagers giggle together, or play with their families unembarrassed, and in the way lovers kiss in doorways. It makes us want to kiss too! We can't wait to find out what we'll stumble upon next here.

Mexico's History

A ncient Mexico may have fallen, but it is not buried. Even today it is evident in almost all aspects of contemporary society. Prehistoric and ancient Mesoamerica remain very much part of the heartbeat of the twentieth century, a profound ingredient of Mexico's soul. The past is fused inexorably with the present, for Mexico's most ancient inhabitants have left a legacy that continues to contribute to the art and characteristics of this country.

One of the oldest societies on earth, Mexico had established several great civilizations long before the appearance of modern people in Europe. Archaeologists have identified over 10,000 ancient Mesoamerican building sites and cities. Evidence indicates that this land may have been populated for more than 30,000 years. The most widely accepted theory is that nomadic tribes from Asia crossed into the Western Hemisphere before or during the last ice age, via a land bridge that connected Siberia to Alaska. The tribes migrated south through Alaska, Canada, and the United States into what is now the Republic of Mexico.

Fishermen, hunters, and gatherers of fruits, the tribes remained nomadic until they discovered wild corn. At that time, the small plant's one meager ear contained just a few grains, but between 5000 and 3000 B.C., farmers improved this primitive plant, producing corn as we know it today. With the advent of cultivated corn, wandering prehistoric tribes were able to settle in scattered communities.

Pre-Columbian Residents

The most acclaimed pre-Columbian tribes included the Olmecs, Toltecs, Teotihuacanos, Zapotecs, Maya, Mixtecs, and Aztecs. The powerful Olmecs, who lived in the dense jungles of southern Veracruz and northern Tabasco, can be traced to 2000 B.C. Although they left few architectural remains, a great wealth of their stone sculpture and pottery has survived. These artifacts show us the astonishing extent of the Olmecs' cultural evolution. They originated a numbering system, hieroglyphics, an almost perfect calendar, and astronomical observations that are amazingly accurate. They were adventurous, colonizing many areas and widely influencing other tribes.

The Olmecs contributed to the development of other civilizations, especially the Teotihuacanos, who erected the imposing Pyramids of the Sun and Moon in their vast city of Teotihuacan, 25 miles northeast of what is now Mexico City. These pyramids took 10,000 people a period of twenty years to construct. Talented urban planners, the Teotihuacanos continued to build until around A.D. 650, when they began to decline, eventually abandoning their city some 150 years later (some archaeologists claim that the Toltecs destroyed Teotihuacan). As Teotihuacan began to fall, the Zapotecan cities of Monte Alban and Mitla were becoming prominent in Oaxaca. Again, the Olmec influence can be seen in the Zapotecs' hieroglyphs, their sophisticated 52-year calendar, and their bar-and-dot mathematical system.

In Oaxaca, where both Zapotecs and Mixtecs developed large urban centers, archaeologists are still uncovering abundant and wondrous artifacts. Oaxaca is one of Mexico's principal crafts centers, and although many materials have been modified and modernized, many crafts found in the region are a continuation of ancient traditions.

The Mayans, in southeastern Mexico and reaching into Guatemala and Honduras, were also influenced by the Olmecs.

Ron Mader

Mitla ruins near Oaxaca City

Architectural geniuses, the Mayans built some of the greatest cities in the southern regions, including Palenque, Yaxchilan, Chichen Itza, Uxmal, and Tikal. A mind-blowing fact: These enormous cities were built without the aid of the wheel. Contrary to popular belief, the Mayans knew about the wheel, but they refused to use it because they had no animals large enough to pull it and they would have been degraded by pulling it themselves.

The Mayans refined the Olmec calendar further. Based on the solar year of 365.242 days, it was more accurate than the calendar used in Europe at that time. It was the Mayans who introduced the mathematical concept of zero—unknown even to the Roman Empire. Their mathematical system was based on the number 20 rather than 10, and through advanced calculations the Mayans were able to pinpoint eclipses with remarkable accuracy.

The great Mayan cities, for still-obscure reasons, were abandoned beginning in the fifteenth century, about 50 years before Columbus set out from Spain. Rebellion against ruling priests, natural disasters, and the forecasting of intrusion by barbarians from the north are some of the reasons put forth to explain the decline of this incredible civilization.

Astronomical observations played a pivotal role in Mesoamerican life. Astrology and religion were firmly linked, and the sun and moon were worshipped as deities. Almost every Mesoamerican city was built in strict accordance with celestial movements, and ceremonies and sports were planned around the activity of stars and planets. Rituals to appease the gods were performed to prevent droughts, floods, and earthquakes. Gods of the sun, moon, wind, rain, fire, and earth predominated, and human sacrifice was considered absolutely vital—especially with the Aztecs, who believed that without sacrifices the sun would be extinguished and all life would perish. This belief would ultimately cause the Aztecs to lose their country to a handful of invading Spaniards.

The Aztecs and the Spanish Invasion

It was the Aztecs whom Hernán Cortés and his men discovered in November 1519. Some historians claim that the Aztecs were called Mexicans, thus the name Mexico. But whatever their name, this tribe was the fiercest and most powerful of all. The Aztecs arrived from the north and invaded the Valley of Mexico toward the end of the twelfth century. A series of islands on a vast lake, the region was then divided into several city-states, none of which were dominant. At first the Aztecs exercised little power. It was not until a priest saw an omen—an eagle perched on a cactus with a rattlesnake in its beak—that the Aztecs began to overthrow the smaller cities and build the mighty city of Tenochitlan, now Mexico City.

Ancient Mexico may have fallen, but it is not buried.

They built causeways to link their capital on the largest island with the mainland. They planted gardens on floating reed islands, which provided both food for the city and safeguard from attacks.

As they grew in strength and numbers, the Aztecs forged alliances with the powerful states of Texcoco and Tlacopan and began to conquer and brutally suppress other tribes. Each conquered tribe was heavily taxed. Increasingly, the only way these vanquished tribes could pay was in human life—sacrifices that the Aztecs needed to keep the sun rising. Hundreds of thousands of captives were sacrificed. The Aztecs' city flourished rapidly. By the time the Spaniards arrived, the Aztecs, although relative newcomers, were undoubtedly the most authoritative and feared of all tribes.

In April 1519, just 27 years after Columbus reached the New World, Hernán Cortés and about 700 men dropped anchor off the coast of Veracruz. Cortés, on horseback, had no trouble overpowering the Indians. Horses were unknown in the New World, and the sight of fair-skinned beings astride these huge beasts terrified all those who encountered them. Cortés enlisted the aid of Jeronomo de Aguilar to act as an interpreter. A Spanish priest shipwrecked several years earlier, he had been living among the Indians in peace. Cortés was quick to advise the Indians about the importance of Christianity and the greatness of King Carlos V of Spain. The Indians of that region were peaceful, and they listened attentively.

Cortés and his expedition searched for the city they were told was filled with "towers floating on water." When they arrived at the pass between the mountains of Popocatepetl and Iztaccihuatl, they were not prepared for the astounding sight that lay below them in the Valley of Mexico. Tenochitlan, home to 100,000 people, was at the height of its glory. Given that it was also at the height of its barbarous power, it is amazing how quickly the Aztecs succumbed to Cortés and his men.

According to Aztec belief, 1519 was the very year in which the god-king Quetzalcoatl, disguised as the plumed serpent, was to return to claim his throne. Legend has it that the night Cortés arrived, a brilliant comet appeared in the sky and at the same time lightning struck a temple. Moctezuma, the Aztec emperor, instantly mistook the white men on horseback for gods—heralded by the comet and the flash of lightning. Having never seen horses before, the Aztecs thought each animal and rider were one unearthly being. In fact, there were only 16 horses with Cortés, but that was enough to awe the Aztecs.

When Cortés rode down into Tenochitlan, he was greeted as a god and housed in the former palace of Axayacatl, Moctezuma's father. Soon the Aztec emperor began having doubts as to Cortés's godliness, and for a few months Moctezuma kept his distance, keeping Cortés virtually imprisoned in the palace. Pressured by his people, who insisted that Cortés was indeed a god, Moctezuma finally agreed to meet him. Cortés, a fearless and a masterful organizer, tied the emperor in psychological knots and ended by saying, "Either we take you prisoner, or you die by your own sword." Moctezuma, now convinced Cortés was a god, willingly became a prisoner.

Soon after, the Spaniards began the wholesale destruction of the city. Aztecs watched in horror as the Spaniards destroyed their temples and idols. Moctezuma, from his luxurious prison, could do nothing. The Aztec bows and arrows, clubs, stones, and darts were no match for the Spaniards' steel, artillery, and muskets. Within a short time, Cortés and his force of less than 700 men were in full command of the immense city. When Cortés heard that a second Spanish fleet, led by Panfilo de Navaez, had arrived on the coast, he left 140 men under the command of his lieutenant, Alvarado, and raced off to meet the fleet.

During Cortés's absence, Alvarado had 200 Aztec nobles killed. When Cortés returned with an enlarged army, the city was rioting and Moctezuma was once again in command. While trying to pacify the city, Moctezuma was killed by one of his own men when he stepped onto the roof of his palace to address the people. With no leader to control them, the Aztecs rose up fiercely against the Spaniards, who were forced to flee the city. It is said that the Spaniards escaped by using bridges comprised of the dead and dying between the causeways. They found safety at Tlaxcala, where the tribal leaders had been impressed by the Spaniards' bravery against the Aztecs.

The battle continued. The Aztecs' Indian enemies joined Cortés, swelling the ranks of the Spaniards. Now reinforced, the Spaniards steadily managed to obliterate Tenochitlan with canons. By August 1521, the defenders were worn down and resistance ended. Spanish rule began, and Mexico was declared a territory of Spain. By 1575 there were 60,000 Spanish in Mexico. While as a group they were the elite, not all were powerful or rich. Some even resorted to begging.

Spanish Rule

The administration of New Spain was a hodgepodge of powers and subdivisions, with much infighting. Spain's two main objectives were to convert every last Indian to Catholicism and to appropriate the riches of Mexico, notably gold and silver, which were discovered in unimaginable quantities. To eliminate pure Indian races, impregnation and intermarriage were encouraged. Catholicism was enforced—often brutally. Hundreds of thousands of Indians died of smallpox, and the tribes managed only sporadic opposition to the Spanish, who had already spread and conquered territories from the Gulf of Mexico to Guatemala, the Yucatan, and Honduras.

From 1570 to 1821, silver was mined in Mexico in such vast amounts that the world supply doubled. One-fifth of all silver mined belonged to the Spanish Crown, but much of it never reached Spain. This was the era of pirating, and British and Dutch pirates even won titles for preying upon the treasure-laden Spanish galleons. For 200 years the escapades of Walter Raleigh, Francis Drake, Thomas Cavandish, and other celebrated pirates made them heroes in their homelands, fiends abroad, and objects of romantic fiction. Greed was rampant, and the beginning of Mexico's continuing acquaintance with corruption was founded.

By 1800 education was completely dominated by the Catholic Church and was the exclusive property of the privileged classes. The masses were deliberately denied education, impoverished, and taught to fear the church. With these conditions, revolution was an inevitability, although the elite didn't imagine that the downtrodden would even entertain such a notion. The *ejido* system, whereby families were granted small holdings of land, was failing as large haciendas absorbed the small farms. The church was the biggest landholder of all; at the close of the colonial era, it owned over half the land and buildings of Mexico and was exempt from taxation. Spain had forbidden Mexico to trade with any other country other than itself, bringing to near collapse an economic system that could no longer survive the rage of the people.

The American Revolution of 1776 had started the first small

rumblings, but it was the French Revolution shortly afterward that brought Mexicans to the point of actually discussing revolution against Spain. Subversive talk and the distribution of revolutionary literature were swiftly and cruelly punished, but as conditions for the vast majority grew steadily worse, there was no stopping the inevitable.

Independence

On the night of September 15, 1810, Father Miguel Hidalgo y Costilla, a lowly parish priest in the town of Dolores, Guanajuato, joined by Ignacio Allende, commander of the local militia, rang the church bells to assemble the villagers. There he raised his famous cry, *El Grito*, the shout that is reenacted all around the country each year on September 15, Mexican Independence Day. Hidalgo was not a military man, and no preparations had been made to arm or feed the 50,000 Indians and mestizos who arrived within the first week alone. Armed only with machetes, slingshots, clubs, crude spears, and a terrible rage against the Spanish, the ragtag army swept

Brad Wetzler

In small towns, Catholic churches still dominate the scene.

through the countryside looting, burning, and acquiring large numbers of enthusiastic recruits. On November 2, they won their greatest victory at Las Cruces in the state of Mexico. The revolution was under way. The battle was gory, drawn out, and bloody, lasting until 1821, when Colonel Agustin Iturbide finally took the capital. Mexico, after terrible bloodshed, had won its independence. The Spanish flag was taken down forever, and the Mexican flag—with an eagle on a cactus devouring a serpent—was erected.

With the advent of independence, Mexico was in complete chaos. No native-born Mexican had experience in government, and during the war a new class, the military, had come into being. Military generals, virtually all corrupt and caring nothing for the lower classes, ran the country for the next hundred years. With the leaders' exorbitant payrolls, the national treasury was in constant bankruptcy. During this period, Mexico had two self-proclaimed emperors—including Colonel Augustin Iturbide and Maximilian of France—40 presidents, the 35-year dictatorship of Porfirio Diaz, and a number of provisional governments. Between 1830 and 1850, Mexico lost Texas, Arizona, New Mexico, and California to the United States and was invaded by the French and the Americans 14 times.

Nothing changed for the lower classes, who were as repressed and destitute as before independence. Large landholdings were given to preeminent families and friends of presidents. By 1910, one thousand families owned 90 percent of the country, and 95 percent of the rural population was landless. Ferocious bandits roamed the hills inciting riots, and Mexico had again arrived at a state of insurrection. "Land for the landless" was one of the most stirring cries of the era.

Revolution

In 1910 violent revolution started. There was no one leader. Instead, many factions fought with and against each other, depending on their needs and position at the time. Never had a more confusing battle taken place. Pancho Villa and Emiliano Zapata admired each other and often helped one another, only to then fight against each other. Presidents came and went, political assassination was rife, the church was forcibly closed then reopened. Intellectuals joined in the struggle ostensibly to help the workers and downtrodden, but often worked only to forward their own ideals. Promises were made then broken, bills were drawn up, signed, and then ignored. Censorship became a way of life. Hundreds of thousands of civilians were killed, and priests and nuns went into hiding. The battle seemed to take on a murderous lifeblood of its own. Mexicans had started something they could not control, let alone stop. The conflict would have a lasting effect upon the working and farming classes; to this day most are reluctant to protest against inequitable conditions.

Although a new constitution in 1917 declared an end to the hacienda system and returned land to the people, little changed. Modern Mexico is said to have started in 1921, when General Obregon, then president, finally took decisive steps to put the constitution into effect. Although people got their land back, political havoc continued, with presidents and other leaders being assassinated, including Obregon.

The 1920s brought a certain amount of peace and economic recovery to the devastated country, but until 1934, when General Lazaro Cardenas took office, Mexico was governed by veterans of the revolution, all power hungry and all well entrenched in corruption. Although a veteran of the revolution himself, Cardenas recognized that unless the needs of the people were met, another battle would ensue. He took education and land distribution seriously and also nationalized the petroleum industry, announcing to the nation and the world that Mexico, and Mexico alone, was the sole owner and leader of its oil industry. All foreign interest in this enterprise was expelled, and the country lauded him. The world was impressed with Mexico's authority.

Mexico entered the twentieth century as a country in disarray. As it moves into the twenty-first century, despite economic and political problems, modern Mexico has a more stable identity. Much of this stability is due to the Mexican character and its people's ability to live in the present while embracing the ways of their ancient ancestors. Were the Mexicans less cheerful and quixotic, it could be a very different story.

Mexico's People

Perhaps more than any other country, you have to study the history of Mexico to begin to grasp the Mexican character. The combination of Indian and Spanish blood resulted in a highly complex caste system. During the second century of Spanish rule, authorities counted a total of 16 different racial categories, classifications that helped solidify a distinct class system. At the lowest end of the social ladder were the Indians; at the top were the pure Spanish. Those in between ranged from various mestizos (of mixed blood) to Mexican-born Spaniards. The system was further complicated by the importing of black female slaves, who produced yet another class of people. Today, over 80 percent of Mexicans are mestizos, with skin color ranging from light to quite dark. For Mexicans, class remains an important social issue, built into their psyche and reflected in every aspect of society, from marriage to hiring.

It was not until the end of the Mexican Revolution of 1910 to 1921 that the mestizos recognized that they were the overwhelming majority. They were even advanced as a new race by philosopher-writer Jose Vasconcelos, who became education minister in the new revolutionary government. He named mestizos as *la raza*, "the race," and asserted their superiority based on their blend of the best qualities of Indians and Spanish.

Ken Luboff

**Women from the *campo* (countryside) relaxing
in San Miguel de Allende**

The mestizos are simply and proudly Mexicans, all of them. However, even today most Mexicans carry self-doubt as to their ancestry and status. Many families, usually those living in Mexico City, will proudly tell you that they have pure Spanish blood, going back seven generations with no intermarriage with anyone of mixed blood. Rather than questioning this claim, foreigners should nod or smile with respect and not start a discussion on racism.

The subject of race is a sensitive one, and foreigners cannot easily ask Mexicans about their racial heritage. At a dinner party we once had, a friend visiting from the States asked another friend, a Mexican lawyer and a man of sophistication, what percentage of Indian blood he had. For just a moment we saw our lawyer friend's protective facial cloak—his mask—come down. Knowing he had lost face, he reached for a bottle of wine and replied in a forced, offhanded manner that his family was old and pure Spanish. But a palpable heaviness hung over the table, and as soon as was decently possible, the Mexican left. When we saw each other a few days later, the incident was not mentioned, and our friendship remains intact.

In many ways, Mexican and Asian cultures are similar. Both groups are skilled at wearing masklike expressions, making it difficult for newcomers to understand what people are really thinking. Often, how Mexicans react inside to a situation or statement is sharply incongruent with their outward response. Newcomers usually find Mexicans to be polite, formal, congenial, and even friendly. They mistakenly believe that what they see is what they will get. Only with time do foreigners begin to understand that the Mexican character is subtle and complex. In time you will begin to understand Mexican etiquette. Until then, just be polite. Mexicans are gracious, aware that foreigners don't understand their ways, and they will forgive many of our transgressions as long as we are polite.

Mexican friends explain that Mexicans are fatalistic, remarkably patient, proud (often to the point of arrogance), mystical, strangely evasive, and impassive. At the same time, Mexicans display a love of music and dance, a readiness for a fiesta, and a warm and extraordinarily cheerful disposition. All these traits are coupled with a machismo that goes way beyond the machismo displayed in other countries. One thing few Mexicans—even the most humble and illiterate of *campesinos*, man or woman—will tolerate is loss of face. Foreigners have to learn this fact immediately. For many generations, Mexicans were subjugated and had control over only their personal dignity. For this reason they have developed a sense of pride that can be formidable and is not something to be messed with.

Rules of Etiquette

Coming from a relatively classless society, certainly a country of less rigid or conspicuous classes, we Americans are often bewildered by the overt class structure in Mexico. And it takes time to learn the finer points. Just accept that the system exists and treat all Mexicans with respect, including the bus driver and the checkout person at the grocery store. Use *usted* (the formal *you*) until a Mexican uses *tu* (the informal you) with you. Note that people who work for you will never use tu when addressing you, and you should not encourage this practice—to do so would make them extremely uncomfortable.

Our neighbor's gardener, Arturo, is an immensely likable man. Each day he travels many miles on a rickety bicycle to town, where he takes care of several gardens. And each year he announces that the rains will start on May 28. That they usually start before or later, but never on this specific day, doesn't faze him one bit. This year, after May 28 had come and gone and still the rains had not arrived, I teased him. He shrugged, then grinned and said the rains were late because it was raining heavily in a faraway country called Turkey. He had seen this news on television.

Arturo is an unusual campesino. Two of his brothers died of alcoholism and three of poverty-related illnesses. So he allows himself just one beer each Saturday after work and plans to have no more than three children. It's unlikely his wife will disobey him in this matter, even though the church and her family might not approve of so few children.

Arturo is deeply loyal to our neighbor because he sees that she respects and trusts him totally. She can joke with him about his ways and he about hers. Recently, Arturo made a mistake, feeding the roses too much fertilizer and killing them. He took full responsibility and asked to have his pay docked. Instead, our friend told him that the fertilizer was *basura*, "rubbish," and that she wouldn't buy it again. He looked at our friend, then grinned and said, "Well, it's made in the United States and therefore not correct for Mexican soil."

"What about me?" our friend asked. "I was made in the United States. Does that make me not fit for Mexican soil?" "You, señora," replied Arturo, doffing his hat, "you are an honor to have in our country."

To unknowingly treat an equal as an inferior must be carefully avoided. Hence, until status is firmly established, Mexicans are formal with each other—to a degree of politeness that has long disappeared from the United States. Always address people with respect. Use titles in formal circumstances: *licenciado(a)* for lawyers or anyone else with a university degree, *doctor(a)* for doctors, *arquitecto(a)* for architects, and *profesor(a)* for all teachers. Address a plumber, electrician, carpenter, or other skilled tradesman as *maestro*. Adding *Don* or *Doña* to a first name is useful, such as Don Pedro, Doña Maria, or Don Alberto. You will be addressed as *Señor* or *Señora*, and you should use these titles with everyone you meet—until or unless they invite you to use their names.

If you ever need to correct a Mexican—the most humble of workers included—never do it in front of anyone else. Take the worker aside, explain that you're not satisfied with his or her work, and suggest a different way. Stress that a misunderstanding has occurred, that it is not the worker's fault (unless it blatantly is), and that you are used to different methods. The more educated the Mexican, the easier this situation will be, but even so, handle it with tact. Sometimes the problem can be greater, and the worker less agreeable, if you are a woman and he is an uneducated man.

If you retire in a city rather than a small pueblo, you will inevitably meet many middle- and upper-class Mexicans. Ultimately you will make some good friends among them. Here, too, be sure to follow proper etiquette: Always use *usted* until they use *tu*. Even if you are with good Mexican friends, don't criticize the politics of their country, even though they may criticize it loudly themselves. (Many Mexicans are perplexed to hear gringos criticize the United States. They find it greatly disloyal, even if they themselves have little love for the States.) Once you have lived in Mexico for a while, you may feel comfortable enough around friends to add your opinions on Mexican politics. But, until then, be prudent. Also realize that some Mexicans—often academics and intellectuals—have a longstanding gripe with the United States and are not eager to mix with gringos. But they are well worth getting to know, if you can, for they have long and lively debates on all subjects, including literature, the arts, politics, religion, sexual conventions—just about everything. Most speak several languages.

Here is yet another dichotomy in the culture: Mexicans, usually the men, can curse like no one else can. And they do. Perhaps only Arabs can rival them in their almost poetic cursing (remember the strong strain of Moorish blood in Spaniards from hundreds of years ago). However, this habit doesn't mean that we foreigners can take up cursing—although it's tempting, as many curses are quite funny and colorful. Our advice is to avoid imitating Mexican profanities until you are really a part of this country. Cursing will not make you "one of the boys." Rather, it will shock Mexicans profoundly.

A small but important point that can be startling to people from the north: The formal Mexican handshake is not strong like the hearty American grasp. The first time I shook a Mexican's hand, it kind of freaked me out. It felt like shaking a moist towel. Except when dealing with well-traveled businesspeople, you will find yourself shaking rather limp hands. Accept this fact and make your handshake equally sensitive. It's the Mexican way.

Mexico's Poor

The birth rate in Mexico has fallen significantly recently, from an average high of 3.2 percent between 1950 and 1970 to 2.1 percent between 1990 and 1995. In the villages, however, the campesinos (farmers and country folk) continue to have extremely large families. Often, 12 or more children, many ill, live with their parents in a one- or two-room shack with no running water or electricity. Many of these children don't go to school and continue the cycle of poverty and illiteracy. The church still has a stranglehold on the campesinos, instilling in them a curious blend of fear and comfort.

Thousands of campesinos, in a desperate endeavor to better their living conditions, move to Mexico City, usually with disastrous results. The city is now the largest in the world and cannot support more people fleeing the campo. The influx is a growing problem, and one for which no one has managed to arrive at a realistic solution.

According to the World Bank, some 20 million Mexicans subsist on less than a dollar per day, and 42 million live in extreme poverty. Poverty is a state of life here, despite the fact that Mexico also has a disproportionate amount of enormously affluent people by world standards.

Getting the Job Done

Too often, poverty is mistakenly attributed to laziness—in almost a hackneyed joke. Mexicans are not lazy; in fact, many are very hard workers. However, their work ethic is different from ours, and this situation is slow to change (except among professionals). For many generations, Mexicans were ruled by brutal and authoritarian bosses, and they were not encouraged to think for themselves. Today, if a group of workers are not well supervised, they will all work on their own without consulting their fellow workers. The result is a completely disorganized job that will take forever.

Then there is their concept of time. Mexicans view time as circular, not linear. Keeping a precise time schedule is not viewed as important—work can always be done later, *mañana*. Besides, working like a robot or adhering to a rigid schedule is seen as taking the spice out of life. We have witnessed this attitude clearly with our excellent carpenter, Gabriel. He will agree to a job, like building a door by the first of the month. He intends to finish the door on

FOOD FACTS

- Mexicans love eggs and eat about 16 percent more than their neighbors in the United States. Average annual per-capita consumption is about 17 kilos—or one egg every day.
- In general, Mexicans are thinner than people from the States. One reason may be Mexicans' low ice cream consumption. At 1.5 liters per year per person, Mexican ice cream intake lags behind Western Europe at 10 liters per year and way behind the United States at 23 liters per year.

time, but other jobs will come his way. He will take on each of them and work on them all at the same time. When we ask about our door, he will put it on top of the pile and move ahead with it. But when we ordered it, we already accepted the fact that the door would not be built on time.

If a plumber or any tradesman says he will be at your place tomorrow morning, never take that as a given. He may arrive in the morning, or he may not. Believe us, you'll get used to it, and if you don't, then Mexico is not for you. For most of us who have moved here, the mañana attitude has entered our thinking, too. Often when we return to the States, we have to snap to and get back into the routine of punctuality.

Mexicans live and work in the here and now, not for tomorrow or the day after—which is the distant future for most of them. Foreigners usually learn the hard way. You may invite some Mexicans to dinner at 7:30, only to have them roll up at way past 9, by which time the dinner is spoiled. You can try saying "7:30 gringo time" or 7:30 *en punto* ("on the dot"), but even that is usually ignored. Or your

Ken Luboff

Making friends in Mexico helps teach you about its culture.

guests may not arrive at all. When Mexicans receive an invitation, they will always accept, even if they know they will not be able to make it. To say no would be an insult. We have learned to do the same thing. On occasion, when invited to a party at a Mexican's home, we have accepted graciously, then not shown up.

We have a friend, José, a highly successful businessman, who arrives not just a few hours late but days late. In business, he is on time; socially, rarely. When we first moved to Mexico, José said he would take us out for dinner to celebrate Barbara's birthday. We asked what time to expect him, and he muttered eight o'clock. At eight we were ready. No José. At nine o'clock, hungry, we had a snack. At 10, Barbara had another snack, then went to bed. Around 11, José arrived. Barbara came out with her arms folded in mock anger. José laughed. "Excuse me, but that's how it's done here. Go on, get dressed." We did, and had a wonderful evening, during which José went to great lengths to explain to us this manana concept. On another occasion, he said he'd arrive on Friday to take us to an old Spanish hacienda. In fact, he arrived the following Tuesday, four days late (this is extreme, even for Mexico).

So, you may ask, isn't that downright rude? What's all this about Mexican politeness? But being late in Mexico is not considered rude. The exceptions to the lateness are flights and buses. Flights always depart on time, and buses almost always depart on time. Professionals such as doctors and lawyers also expect you to arrive on time for your appointments.

Finding Your Niche

Life is not dull in this country. It is sometimes highly frustrating, but never dull. And it does teach you to live in the here and now. Spontaneity is a way of life here, both in social situations and at work, and offers a good lesson to most Norteamericanos. You learn to loosen up and live in the moment. If you don't, you're not too likely to make many Mexican friends or, for that matter, make it in Mexico at all. However, don't worry too much about fitting in. You are likely to live among many other foreigners, and Mexicans who live around large numbers of gringos are more likely to be on time. More or less—you never know.

Reading some of the very rich literature of Mexico will give you good insight into the Mexican character. Laura Esquivel's novel *Like Water for Chocolate*, and the movie of the same name, will probably give you more insight into the Mexican character than hours of studying nonfiction. That the book is set in another era means nothing; the same psychology prevails today.

Sure, modern Mexicans wear jeans like their American counterparts, but they are not the same as Americans. They adhere to family and ancestral traditions deeply, some are extremely influenced by the church, they are fiercely patriotic, and while many may outwardly emulate Norteamericanos, most have absolutely no aspirations to be like us. We have heard Mexicans express pity for us—that our family structures are so weakened, that we must follow a strict schedule, that we place far too much importance on money and too little on spiritual matters, that we are not able to enjoy life or be spontaneous, that the clock is such a tyrant in our lives . . . the list is long.

The Mexican people have been downtrodden for centuries, have been ruled by many cruel dictators, and have lost much to invading forces—including the United States. Yet they are warm and loving to foreign residents. Once you have made friends with some Mexicans, and you have gained their trust and respect, you will find that they will turn themselves inside out to help you, make you laugh, and comfort you when you are sad.

¿Se Habla Español?

Most foreigners who retire to Mexico don't speak a word of Spanish, except maybe to name a few Mexican foods such as chiles, enchiladas, and tacos. The lack of Spanish is one reason most new arrivals start out living in major retirement communities where English is commonly spoken.

Almost everyone born in Mexico speaks Spanish as a first language. The only exceptions are a few remote Indian groups who still speak one of fifty remaining Indian dialects. Increasing numbers of Mexicans speak English, especially those working in business and tourism. Even in more remote cities, lawyers and doctors usually speak at least a little English. However, even in a town loaded with your countrymen, it is unlikely that the woman behind the counter at the grocery store, your maid or gardener, or even your landlord will speak English. It quickly becomes clear that learning some basic Spanish and, in time, improving to a conversational level will make life in Mexico much easier.

Spanish schools and tutors are plentiful in areas where foreigners live; individual instruction costs about $8 to $10 an hour. Group lessons are less expensive and often just as effective. A combination of private and group lessons is recommended for faster learning. Although learning Spanish can seem daunting at first, it's worth every minute. The ability to speak and understand a second language is immensely empowering.

Aside from the obvious frustrations of not being understood, to live in Mexico without speaking Spanish is to miss out on a great deal of fun. Spanish is a multifaceted and deeply poetic language, with a great many nuances. Not to understand it is to miss out on the very psyche of the country and its people. For those who want to understand the complexities of Mexican culture, learning to speak Spanish is an absolute prerequisite, and learning a few simple phrases can immediately create a surprising amount of goodwill.

Most Mexicans have a wonderfully droll sense of humor and a rather delightful—almost whimsical—outlook on life. They deeply appreciate foreigners who make the effort to learn their language, no matter how badly they slaughter it at first. Unlike many other nationalities, most Mexicans are patient and helpful to a foreigner learning Spanish. Occasionally, if a Mexican is trying to learn English, he or she will playfully swap words with you.

A bulletin board like this one in Mazatlán may point you toward a house rental or valuable language classes.

Ken Luboff

At first a newcomer to Spanish can make some extremely funny mistakes. A friend of ours, after her third Spanish lesson, went home and began boiling a large pot of water. The young maid, who was used to purifying the water with *gotas* (iodine drops), asked what she was doing. Our friend turned to the maid and, taking great care, said in Spanish, "I am boiling the water because it has germs in it, and I am going to kill you." The maid fled. Only later did our friend realize that she had used the wrong pronoun, *you*, instead of *them*.

Some words have double meanings, and if used in the wrong way they can be an embarrassing. For instance, *huevos* means eggs, but it can also mean balls (as in testicles). A big *chile* can mean a large penis, and the verb *coger*, which means to grab or grasp, also means to fornicate. The Spanish word for handcuff offers insight into the Mexican character. The word is *esposa*, which also means wife! We'll let you interpret that one.

> *To live in Mexico without speaking Spanish is to miss out on a great deal of fun.*

Spanish can be a formal language, but it is far less brusque or curt than English. For instance, in Spanish one rarely gives a direct order, and for a foreigner to do so is to invite offense. However, it is easy to avoid this practice.

The very psychology of Mexicans is expressed in their language. Little, if indeed anything, is a certainty in Spanish. For instance, the phrase "when I arrive" is expressed in the subjunctive *cuando llega*, which actually means "I may arrive." If you drop and break something, you don't usually say "I dropped it." You say, "It dropped itself." If you crash the car: "The car crashed itself." Barbara and I have avoided spats about missing keys because they always lose themselves. And, of course, you are never late—something made you late. This language pattern came about from the Indians' terror at being reprimanded by their Spanish conquerors.

Over the centuries, words from other cultures have insinuated themselves into Spanish, as they have into most languages. Often,

Useful Spanish Expressions

Hola—Hi
No hablo español—I don't speak Spanish
Habla Ingles?—Do you speak English?
No entiendo—I don't understand
Como esta usted?—How are you?
Muy bien, gracias, y usted?—Very well, thanks, and you?
Buenos dias—Good morning
Buenas tardes—Good afternoon
Buenas noches—Good evening
Mucho gusto—Pleased to meet you
El placer es mio—The pleasure is mine
Como le va?—How's it going?
Adios—Goodbye
Hasta luego—See you later
Por favor—Please
Si—Yes
No—No
Que hora es?—What time is it?
Donde esta?—Where is the?
Quien?—Who?
Por que?—Why?
Cuanto cuesta esto?—How much is this?
Es mucho—Too much

Keep in mind that in most Spanish words, the accent is placed on the next-to-last syllable. If not, then an accent mark will appear on the syllable that is to have the emphasis. A common gringo mispronunciation, because it is an exception to the accent rule, is saying farm-a-CI-a instead of far-MAH-cia.

Ken Luboff

Knowing Spanish proves useful; this sign reads "Phone Cards Sold Here."

you will hear the word *ojala* (OH-ha-la—God willing), which is actually a shortened form of "may Allah hear." The word has Moorish origins. Very few people probably give any thought to what it means; they just use it.

The histories of Mexico and the United States are so intertwined that many U.S. cities have Spanish names, such as Chula Vista (pretty view), Las Vegas (the flat lowlands), and Los Alamos (the aspens). Likewise, hundreds of Spanish words share roots with an English equivalent. For example, *observar* is to observe, *aplaudir* is to applaud, *adoptar* is to adopt. Many English and Spanish words share the same spelling but are pronounced differently, including *simple* (SEEM-play), *mediocre* (may-dee-OH-kray), *material* (mah-tay-REE-al), and *hospital* (ohs-pee-TAL). Sometimes if you add an *o*, *a*, or *e* to a noun and speak with a Spanish accent, you may be pointed in the right direction: *farmacia*—pharmacy, *banco*—bank, *restaurante*—restaurant, and so on. Once in the farmacia, you can ask for *aspirina*, the banco will cash your *cheque* (check-ay), and the restaurante will serve *coca*.

You needn't always puzzle over a translation, however. Once at a pharmacy, Barbara made a long, convoluted request in Spanish for panty liners. She had just about exhausted herself when the pharmacist said, "Oh, Always Panti Liners," implying, "Why didn't you just say so?"

Money Matters

Before our move to Mexico, we spent many hours crunching numbers, determining whether or not we could afford to retire. We spoke to experts, who assured us gravely that we would need many hundreds of thousands—even millions—of dollars to retire and live well for the rest of our days. The discussions were disconcerting, to say the least.

Then we took a trip to Mexico and talked to retirees there. We found that many were living well on $800 to $1,500 per month. What gives, we asked? What gives is that almost everything in Mexico costs 25 to 75 percent less than it does in the United States, depending on your U.S. location. A decent lunch in Mexico, for example, might cost around $5, while the same lunch would cost $12 in Houston and $20 in San Francisco. Prices also vary from place to place within Mexico. An elegant meal for two in a restaurant in Mexico City can easily cost more than $100, while the same meal in San Miguel de Allende will cost only $50. And if you retire in a city with few or no other foreigners, the most expensive restaurant in town might set you back only $20 for two. And no matter where you are in Mexico, two people can always find a delicious meal for under $6.

Housing costs vary the same way. In Chapala, a six-room, two-bedroom house in a nice neighborhood costs about $450 a month to rent. That same house in San Miguel de Allende might rent for $600 a month, and in Mexico City $1,000 a month. In any out-of-the-way Mexican village, you could rent that same house for almost nothing (if you could find it). Friends of ours rent a house for about $500 a month and live well for about $1,200 per month total, including the cost of a part-time maid and gardener. Barbara and I own a house and live a more luxurious lifestyle for less than $20,000 a year.

Our guess is that almost anyone reading this book can afford to retire in Mexico. Begin by examining your resources. Do you have money flowing in each month from Social Security, a pension, a part-time job, royalties, investments, or inheritance? Would you consider selling your business or home or renting your home to free up enough cash to help fund your new lifestyle?

Estimating what life below the border will cost is tricky. Even if you intend to maintain the same lifestyle you have in the States, your life is likely to change in unknown ways. For example, Barbara and I never imagined that after only one month in Mexico we would have a maid and cook coming in for a few hours each day. In the States, only people with big bucks can afford such luxuries. But in Mexico, where the wage is about $1.50 to $2 per hour, almost anyone can.

We estimate that you will live an equal, if not more gracious, lifestyle in Mexico for about 25 to 50 percent of what it costs in the United States, depending on where you live. But don't forget that even when you live in Mexico full-time, you will still have some ongoing expenses in the States. Add to your estimated Mexican cost of living U.S. mortgage payments, life and auto insurance, car registration, college tuition, loans, and so on. Once you are settled in Mexico, you can reduce many of these expenses. For instance, we were able to reduce the cost of health insurance by replacing a high-cost U.S. policy for Barbara with an international policy of equal quality, including coverage in the States, for about half the price. Whether you're insured or not, medical costs in Mexico can be as much as 75 percent less than they are in the United States.

A much-talked-about issue in Mexico is inflation. While high inflation—almost 20 percent—makes life very difficult for Mexicans, we who are living in Mexico on dollars are insulated against the effects of inflation. But this is not always the case. The peso, which has been steadily devaluing against the dollar (almost 15 percent in 1998), has been stable for most of 1999.

Many foreigners claim that their cost of living in Mexico actually goes down each year. The longer they live in the country, the more they learn to live in a peso-based economy. They begin viewing costs in a more Mexican way. When they first arrive, an item costing 100 pesos seems cheap: "It's only $10, let's buy more!" But after a few years the price of the same 100-peso item seems steep: "100 pesos, you've got to be kidding!" This fact is certainly true for us; we live on $5,000 a year less than we did five years ago.

We expatriates in Mexico have come to realize that less is more.

We began tracking all of our expenses soon after we arrived in Mexico. Every day we write down everything we spend in a hard-cover blank book. At the end of each month we—that is Barbara—add up our expenses.

Of course, it is impossible to know with any accuracy what your new life will cost until you try it out. Obviously, if your dream is to live in a million-dollar house in Puerto Vallarta with 10 servants and a heated Olympic-size pool, life can get a little pricey (it will still cost you less than it would in the States, however). But the majority of retirees from the United States, living on pensions or savings, will be amazed at how much further their money goes and how much higher the quality of their lives is in Mexico.

A word about lifestyle: Ask yourself how important it is to maintain your current lifestyle. You must be seriously considering changing it or you wouldn't be reading this book. Not being locked into your former lifestyle can allow you the freedom to move to Mexico. It can also increase your options greatly and give you maximum flexibility and liberation. Much about your new lifestyle will depend on your attitude, as well as a realistic assessment of what

Ken Luboff

A Mexican friend in front of Lloyd Asociados, the most popular bank among foreign residents

you can afford each month. Maybe you will live in a cozy house with a peaceful little garden and a small painting studio instead of your current 5,000-square-foot showplace. You may have to drive your car for a few extra years or take fewer vacations. But, so what—your entire new life is a vacation! Or you may be able to afford a much nicer house in Mexico than you could in the States.

Buy or Rent?

When you first arrive in Mexico, renting makes perfect sense. You can get a feel for the culture, town, and neighborhood without making a long-term obligation. You can chat-it-up with longtime retirees and get the inside scoop without tying up a lot of money in real estate. If you have just sold your home in the States and are feeling flush for the first time in years, you can invest in stocks or bonds and rent a place on the interest. It is easy to find reasonable rents, and Mexican laws favor the renter, giving you protection against weird and unscrupulous landlords. If you want to try another part of the country, you can just pick yourself up like a turtle and move on. There are a few downsides to renting, of course. You may have to deal with steady increases in rent or wait forever to have a leak fixed.

If you feel more comfortable owning a home or enjoy investing in real estate, this may be the perfect time to buy. Real estate is appreciating rapidly in many parts of Mexico, including coastal areas around Puerto Vallarta, Zehuatanejo, and Manzanillo; Quintana Roo; parts of Baja; and inland towns like San Miguel de Allende and Chapala. There are still many deals to be had. If you dream of owning a home near a palm-shaded beach, an elegant colonial, or a small B&B, you may be able to afford it, even if you don't have the cash. Several U.S. mortgage companies have started lending money on Mexican real estate. Ownership laws were changed during the recent Salinas administration, making it as easy and safe to buy a home in Mexico as in the States (see Chapter 10: "A Roof over Your Head").

Taxes

The IRS expects you to pay taxes on "earned" income anywhere on earth and probably from outer space as well. If you live and run a business in a foreign country, the IRS assumes that you are paying taxes in that country and exempts the first $70,000 of profit (net after expenses). This amount began rising by $2,000 a year, starting in 1998, and will continue until it reaches $80,000. The $80,000 exclusion will be indexed for inflation starting in 2008. You are required to pay a self-employment tax of 15.3 percent, and you are required to file a return if you earn more than $6,000 a year anywhere.

The capital-gains tax laws in Mexico are more complex than those in the United States. The tax you pay on the sale of a house can differ in different locations and under different circumstances. Discuss this issue with your Mexican lawyer. You are expected to include the sale of your Mexican home on your U.S. tax return. Any Mexican tax you pay is considered by the IRS to be an expense, and it reduces your U.S. capital gain. Filing as a foreign resident exempts you from paying state income tax and allows you to put off filing your federal return until June 15, although tax owed is due from April 15.

Mordita—The Bite

Hector Ulloa, editor of Atencion San Miguel *(the weekly "gringo rag"), offers his observations about* mordita, *a national custom:*

Perhaps the most extended (and accepted) form of corruption in Mexico is bribery—although most Mexicans do not see it as bribery but as a "tip" or "gift." The name itself suggests a share of something—*una mordida*, a bite. Would you like a bite of my apple? Although this kind of bribery is practiced all over the world, it has become both an art and a nuisance in Mexico. It is a fact of life—and as difficult to get rid of as cockroaches.

The line between bribery and tipping is a thin one. If you drive into a gas station, the attendant will smile, fill your tank, clean your windshield, and check your oil—alas, not for free. Along with the cost of the gas, he will expect a small tip. If the tip is not to his liking, he will frown and you may see him in the rearview mirror grumbling to another attendant. Tips have always been common in restaurants; now they're common everywhere. Smiles can be bought, and people expect you to buy them.

One morning you show up at a government office, ask to see the topmost official, and smile. The person behind the desk, most often a young woman, will smile back and say, "He's not here yet." Then, nothing else matters. It doesn't matter if you see the official walk in. The clerk will bluntly deny that he's in or will say he's busy, even if you can peek through the partially open door and see the official looking out the window. It doesn't matter if you say you are the official's best friend. It doesn't matter if you say the building is on fire. The clerk will smile and continue filing her fingernails, saying "Can't you see he's not here?"

Next comes the magic. You smile and, with apparent naiveté, say, "Is there some way I could see him right away?" and flash a 20-peso note that you immediately hide inside a folded newspaper. Then she will definitely smile back and say, "I'll see what can be done," as she grabs the newspaper and pretends to be interested in the latest news about Pakistan. Is this a tip? Is it bribery? Or is it simply "buying" your way around?

There are more obvious situations, like skipping a red light and paying off the traffic cop. The officer will never say the payment is bribery, of course. It is a "gift" or a "fee" for his time. The longer it takes you to understand that you must pay, the higher the fee. First the officer will give a long explanation about how you broke the law and how he wants to help save your valuable time. Second, he will offer a simple arithmetic problem: "If the fine is 100 pesos and half the fine is 50 pesos, how much money do you have with you?" Third, he leaves the penalty "up to you" and abides by whatever "your will is." Fourth attempt—if nothing has worked so far—he will threaten to impound your car and put you in jail.

Any advice, you ask me? It is probably easiest to play the game. Smile and tell the officer that you understand you broke the law and ask him for your ticket. Then take mental note of his badge number and squad car or motorcycle number. As soon as you are on safe ground, report him.

To this, Barbara and I add some practical advice from a foreigner's point of view: If the mordita seems reasonable, or if you live in a small town where you and the cop will be seeing each other again, pay the mordita and forget the whole matter. Reporting the bribe is not worth the potential bureaucratic hassle. We would report the incident only if there was no infraction and the whole thing was just highway robbery.

Banking

You will be amazed at the high interest rates being paid to depositors by Mexican banks. For instance, Lloyd Asociados, both a Mexican bank and an investment house, is now paying between 16 and 26 percent interest, depending on the type of account. The interest rate changes daily, depending on the strength or weakness of the peso, the state of the Bolsa (Mexican stock market), foreign exchange, and other factors. On some rare occasions, the change is dramatic. After the devaluation of the peso in 1995, interest rates shot up to over 100 percent for borrowers. Depositors were paid over 90 percent interest. Those who had money in a peso account at that time lost about 50 percent of its value, but regained ground as interest rates on deposits climbed to over 90 percent. These astronomical rates dropped as the economy strengthened, and by now many depositors have more than recovered their losses.

Foreign residents debate whether it is better to keep dollars in the States and bring them to Mexico as needed, thereby taking advantage of a steadily devaluing peso, or to keep one's savings in a peso account in Mexico, achieving interest rates as high as 40 percent but with the risk of another major devaluation. Barbara and I keep our savings in the States and transfer to Mexico enough to meet our expenses here. Dollar accounts are not permitted, ostensibly to stop drug-money laundering.

Handling common money transactions in Mexico is relatively easy. Most foreigners have a peso account in a Mexican bank into which they deposit funds from home when they need more money. They can write checks on the account, just as in the United States, and all major banks have branches throughout the country.

Less common transactions can be a nightmare. Large checks to buy a house or land can sometimes take as long as six weeks to clear. It helps to have a good personal connection with the banker.

While Mexican banks provide the usual services, Lloyd Asociados, S.A. goes further. This is the most popular bank among American and Canadian residents in towns where it has branches. Don't ask them to insure your good looks, though. This is not the

Lloyd's of London that insured Betty Grable's legs and Jimmy Durante's nose! Lloyd is a Mexican-owned organization, and, though it has many Mexican customers, it caters to the needs of foreign residents, offering high interest, investment accounts, and other services. Unlike the major Mexican banks, Lloyd allows transactions by fax, phone, e-mail, or regular mail. It will pay household bills when you are out of town, including employees' salaries, and Lloyd's insurance division will cover your home and car. Lloyd has eight branches in Mexico, all in areas with high concentrations of foreigners.

Banamex, Mexico's largest bank, has an interesting program—Programa Amistad (friendship)—aimed at foreign residents. Our friends have found it convenient. They have a checking account at Banamex's U.S. branch, California Commercial Bank, and their U.S. Social Security, pension, and other checks are deposited directly into it. Banamex issues a checkbook and a debit card, which can be used to withdraw up to $200 at any Banamex ATM in Mexico. Banamex claims the account can be opened only in person at their Los Angeles, San Francisco, or Guadalajara offices, but a friend opened an Amistad account in the San Miguel de Allende branch. Banamex's main office in Los Angeles is located at 2029 Century Park E., 42nd Floor, Los Angeles, CA 90067.

We also have friends who never bring money into Mexico. They make arrangements with a *casa de cambio* (money changer) to cash personal checks drawn on their U.S. accounts. Almost all U.S. credit and debit cards can be used at ATMs throughout Mexico—an easy way to get quick cash at the best exchange rate. However, these machines have been known to run out of money occasionally, especially on weekends in heavy tourist areas.

Federal Benefits

If you receive a monthly federal benefit check, it will be sent from the Department of the Treasury in the United States to the U.S. embassy or consulate in Mexico. You might look into the possibility of having your check deposited directly into a bank account in the States or even Mexico.

Bargains Galore

To get an idea how much you will save by living in Mexico, note the price in Mexico of the items listed below (prices as of January 1, 1999, in U.S. dollars):

premium unleaded gas:	$1.83/gallon
regular unleaded gas:	$1.64/gallon
one-bedroom condo: (long-term rental)	$350/month
two-bedroom house :	$350–$600/month
fancy three-bedroom house:	$600–$1,500/month
utilities and basic phone service:	$50/month
basic cable TV service:	$20/month
maid (two days a week):	$50/month
gardener (two days a week):	$40/month
bottled water (for two):	$10/month
milk:	$.93/liter
oranges:	$.15/pound
bananas:	$.23/pound
mangos:	$.50/pound
head of lettuce:	$.28
tomatoes:	$.25/pound
broccoli:	$.30/pound
eggs:	$.83/dozen
onions:	$.19/pound
pork chops:	$2.24/pound
T-bone steak:	$2.71/pound
ground beef:	$1.86/pound
whole chicken:	$.70–$1.20
butter:	$.85/pound
long-stemmed roses:	$2/dozen (for heaven's sake)
haircut:	$6–$7.50
movie ticket:	$2.50

Wills

If you own property or have a substantial number of other assets in Mexico, you should look into drawing up a separate Mexican will. An American friend, a lawyer practicing international law in Mexico, tells us that a properly drawn U.S. will can cover assets in Mexico, but to avoid confusion and tax problems later, it is wise to have a Mexican will drawn up as well. Our friend handles such matters, and she recommends finding someone who is familiar with the laws of both countries to do the job.

Funny Money

There can be some comical aspects to money matters here. For example, Barbara was buying some handmade trinkets as gifts. The price of each was 10 pesos. Assuming there would be a discount, she said, "If I take 10, then what will the price be?" The vendor looked at her for a few seconds and replied, "For 10 it will cost 150 pesos."

"But why?" she incredulously asked, "can't I have a discount or at least pay 100 pesos for 10?"

"Because if you like them so much," replied the vendor with his own brand of logic, "you will pay more."

Another friend once had a plant vendor come to her door with petunias. He quoted a reasonable price, and our friend said she'd buy the lot, all 20 of them. The man looked stricken. "But if you buy them all, what will I do for the rest of the day?" he asked. From then on, whenever he came to her door, he brought just a few plants and hid the rest in a doorway around the corner. He wasn't having his day ruined by this woman again.

Often foreigners find they are charged more for certain things than Mexicans are, especially services such as plumbing and electrical work. Even dentists and veterinarians sometimes charge us more than they do Mexicans. At the market, you may see a local Mexican buying fruit and vegetables for a few less pesos than you're paying. It's really up to you if you want to make an issue of this practice. Having lived here many years, we find we are no longer overcharged as much. If we are, we ask about it jokingly. Usually the vendor (or electrician) will grin and lower the price a fraction. Keep in mind that it is not just foreigners who are charged more than the locals. Mexican tourists or weekenders from Mexico City, with their shiny cars and expensive clothes, also pay higher prices. It's a question of what the market will bear. And, after all, most locals have many relatives and old family friends who automatically get a reduction. The system is fair enough.

Tourists visiting Mexico invariably feel that the peso is not real money. It is not unusual to hear a tourist ask a shopkeeper or spouse, "How much is that in real money?" This feeling is understandable because prices are low, and Mexican money does look a little like play money, with the different denominations in different colors and some with gold sparkles. We have seen tourists throw Mexican bills around like they were playing Monopoly, happily overpaying and over-tipping waiters, vendors, and even taxi drivers (usually not tipped in Mexico). Such behavior tends to widen the gap between local and foreign-resident economies. It tends to increase prices in general for foreigners, whether or not they are tourists. Most foreigners are aware that they live in far more comfortable conditions than local Mexicans, and some feel uncomfortable about the difference. Nevertheless, no one likes being gouged.

Locals generally expect foreigners to have more money and are not at all upset about it. Their attitude for the most part is, "Such is life." I once heard a Mexican maid say, *Dios les da el dinero a los ricos, porque si no lo tuvieran, se moririan de hambre*—"God gives money to the wealthy because without it they would starve to death."

However, foreigners flaunting their money is offensive to every Mexican. But, then, it's offensive everywhere, so use common sense. If you run around spending as if pesos were play money, feeling like a millionaire, your budget will soon fall flat. Used wisely, your money will take you far and definitely give you a good life here. But don't be niggardly. Being closefisted is not politic in

Mexico—in fact it's downright alien to Mexicans. Wealthy Mexicans tend to spend readily and usually with generosity, and even poorer Mexicans are generous. Money is not hoarded, even by rich Mexicans. If they have it, they spend it. Mañana will somehow bring more.

Should you give money to beggars? That is entirely up to you. Many foreigners have a favorite beggar whom they support. Our own rule is that if the beggar appears genuinely in need or ill, and we have some coins in our pockets and are in the mood, we give. If he or she is clearly a drunk or a fraud, we ignore the person and walk past. The larger the city, the larger the scam. So be astute in deciding who is in genuine need.

Children from poor families may see you on the street and screech "Money! Money!," holding out their small hands. Again, it's up to you whether or not to give, but we have often offered children food instead of money. Sometimes they take it greedily; other times they give us a dirty look and turn away.

Many retirees can afford household help.

Ken Luboff

Hiring Help

One of the pleasures of life in Mexico for most retirees is being able to afford household help. You can easily find a gardener and a housekeeper to help clean, do laundry, baby-sit, and maybe even cook. Most servants speak only Spanish, so you will also have a great opportunity to practice the language. Our housekeeper, Gisela, is a wonderful cook. She makes breathtaking chicken mole, and a spaghetti sauce that would make your Italian grandmother salivate, and her green chicken enchiladas are to die for. Gisela's secret ingredient is oil. We have asked her to use less oil many times, and she has cut back a little, but seems constitutionally unable to go any further. Finally, we just switched to olive oil and gave in. Nowadays, she cooks for us a few times a week, especially when we are in the mood for a great old-fashioned, stick-to-your-ribs meal. Gisela is also a wonderful housekeeper and has a great sense of humor.

The average weekly pay for a full-time housekeeper/cook is about 300 to 400 pesos, depending on where you live, how much you expect done, and length of service. We highly recommend that you pay someone you like the high end of the salary range. Having a servant here is very different than having one in the United States. After your housekeeper or gardener has been with you for a while, you become the patron and have an unspoken responsibility not only to the servant but also to his or her entire family. If one of a servant's kids gets sick and the family can't afford medicine, you will offer to buy it for them. When a servant's daughter gets married, you may be asked to pay for the ring or even the entire wedding. A friend of ours recently did just that for her maid, who had become a friend and confidante after five years of service.

The amount of time, energy, and money you give to a servant is entirely up to you. But strict laws protect the basic rights of domestic workers. For instance, when an employee leaves after many years, he or she is legally entitled to severance pay equal to one month's salary for every year of service.

Even if you pay your employees a great deal more than others might, if for any reason you insult them or cause them to lose face, you cannot count on them staying with you. To your employees, respect is far more important than money.

Shifting Perspectives

Basically, we and many other expatriates in Mexico have come to realize that less is more. For one thing, we have so much more than the average Mexican. For another, we find that things that were important to us in our "past lives" just don't matter as much anymore. Who cares if you're wearing last year's (or even last decade's) fashions? How often will you need a necktie or three-piece suit? Who cares if the placemats don't match or that one of your wine glasses broke and you have to use a glass jar instead?

Staying Healthy

O ne of the primary concerns for people moving to Mexico is the quality of health care. "Are the doctors and hospitals any good?" was one of our first questions. We were surprised to find that the health-care system is generally quite good. Every mid- to large-sized city has at least one first-rate hospital, many of them associated with hospitals in the States. In Mazatlán, for example, it is the Sharp Hospital, a sister of the Sharp Hospital in San Diego. In Queretaro, the new Hospital San Jose is associated with the Herman Hospital at the University of Texas Medical Center. The most renowned hospitals in Mexico are said to be in Mexico City and Guadalajara, the two largest cities in the country. A friend who went to the ABC (American-British-Cowdry) Hospital in Mexico City for surgery on her neck raved about the care she received, especially from the nursing staff: "Can you believe it, when it came time for my first shower after surgery, two nurses actually slipped off their clothes and climbed into the shower to get me good and clean?"

Since moving to Mexico we have had a few minor health problems—mostly stomach and flu-type stuff—that have been easily solved by local doctors and clinics. Our favorite doctor is Dra. Juliana Taylor at the Dispensario de Nuestra Señora de Fatima. A Mexican, she was trained in the United States, speaks perfect English, and is very caring and sharp. She knows when to refer patients to a specialist, the local hospital, or a much larger hospital in another city. She is typical of the GPs who can be found in every part of the country, especially in large cities and those with sizable foreign populations. Where we live there is a large number of older retirees and, as you would expect, a large number of heart specialists and plastic surgeons.

Hospitals are a different matter. Some are very good and some are pretty poor. If one of us had a really serious illness and enough time, we would go to one of the better-known hospitals in Mexico City for a consultation, then make a trip to the States for a second opinion. The good quality of care in Mexico and high medical costs in the States might bring us back to Mexico for treatment.

The low cost of health care in Mexico is one of its great attractions. On average, an office visit with a doctor—specialist or otherwise—costs 250 pesos ($25). A visit to the dentist for a cleaning costs less than $20. An overnight stay in a private hospital room costs about 320 pesos ($32). Recently, a friend who needed a CAT scan went to a local hospital in the morning, had the scan done, and returned after lunch to pick up the films and a written interpretation. The entire experience was hassle-free and inexpensive. It cost about $215—about 25 percent of what it would have cost in the United States. On average, the price tag of most medical services in Mexico is about one-half or less of the U.S. cost. Prescription drugs made in Mexico on average cost about 50 percent less than the same drugs in the States. On the other hand, drugs not manufactured in Mexico but imported from the States can cost up to 50 percent more.

The Mexican Red Cross (Cruz Roja) operates ambulances and medical clinics throughout the country. It provides transport in the event of an accident or emergency and is a revered institution in Mexico. In large cities, private ambulance services can also get you to a hospital fairly quickly. If you are in the middle of nowhere and have an accident, you may be forced to ride to a nearby clinic in the back of a pickup or strapped to the back of a burro. If your injuries are severe, you may have to be flown out. Many Mexican and U.S. health insurance companies include emergency helicopter evacuation services in their policies. Some pay to fly patients back to the United States for treatment. As anywhere, those who have allergies, reactions to certain medicines, or other unique medical problems should wear medical alert bracelets or carry similar warnings at all times.

Traveling Healthy

When Norteamericanos think of Mexico and health, they think mostly of the dreaded Montezuma's revenge. When "la turista" hits, it's an understatement to say that this kind of diarrhea can really ruin your day. Fortunately, it hits residents far less often than it does short-term visitors. Most foreign residents know how to take precautions against stomach problems, and their systems adapt somewhat to the local bacteria, although a bout of amoebas every now and then is not uncommon. We've actually gotten diarrhea when we've visited the States!

Before cooking, residents know to wash and soak all veggies and fruits in a solution of one quart water to one drop of Clorox, or

Mexican Red Cross

Ken Luboff

another purification product that can be found in any Mexican market. Visitors, who are generally eating all their meals out, are at the mercy of the restaurant or food stand. Residents soon learn which restaurants and stands to avoid.

The basic rules of thumb for good stomach health are: (1) always drink bottled water, (2) wash your hands many times during the day as though you are possessed, and (3) hope for the best. Even though most tourist restaurants are attentive to good hygiene and serve both purified water and purified ice cubes in drinks, people get sick. Our guess is that one of the main ways that turista is passed is by handling money. For years during our travels in Mexico, Barbara and I would eat the same foods in the same places at the same time, and I

Retiring in Mexico brings immediate relief from one of the most debilitating health problems—stress.

was the one who got sick. We realized that I was the one who handled the money most of the time. I soon got serious about washing my hands—four, sometimes five, times a day, like a crazy man. To this day, I rarely have stomach problems. New antiseptic hand lotions are now on the market; we keep one in the glove compartment of our car for quick food stops.

Other than stomach-related illnesses, there are few especially dangerous health problems endemic to Mexico—nothing that will require you to get shots before crossing the border. However, there are occasional outbreaks of hepatitis in one part of the country or another. As in every country, you should take precautions against AIDS and other sexually transmitted diseases. AIDS in Mexico seems to be completely hidden. No good statistics are available as to the number of cases, and no public information is being disseminated. The country appears to be in total denial about AIDS, called SIDA in Mexico.

In parts of the country, especially the more tropical areas, you'll see some scary-looking bugs. The stings and bites of scorpions and black widow spiders can be dangerous and painful, but are rarely deadly. When we travel to places where these crawly creatures live, we stock an antihistamine. If you wind up living in the tropics, you will probably assemble a special tropical medicine cabinet containing such items as anti-scorpion venom. You will also learn a few preservation tricks like this one: If you are stung by a stingray or jellyfish (both strings can hurt like hell), the best immediate antidote is for you—or someone close to you—to pee on the sting! If you are not in the mood for such a remedy, don't worry. No matter where you are in Mexico there are health clinics nearby—in even the remotest areas.

Medicine

Mexican campesinos have traditionally gone to the local pharmacist for medical advice. This is especially true in small villages, where often the only people in town with any medical information are the *curanderas* (healers) and the druggist. Many Mexicans can hardly afford to put food on the table, let alone the luxury of seeing a doctor. So Mexicans get medical advice, diagnoses, and drugs from their trusted pharmacists. The same is true for many foreigners with minor health problems, who don't want to go through the hassle or expense (although it is pretty cheap) of seeing a doctor.

Many drugs that are restricted in the United States are available in Mexico without a prescription. The exceptions are narcotics, sleeping pills, and the like. Note that some drugs prescribed in Mexico, either by doctors or pharmacists, are not approved by the FDA. Some can be extremely strong. Barbara once took an antibiotic that was strong enough for an elephant. Within 15 minutes of taking it, she felt like she had been hit by a truck.

Prescription drugs are quite inexpensive in Mexico. The average price to fill a prescription is $3.90, compared to $12 in the United States. Mexicans on average spend $34 per person on medicines annually—that figure in the United States is $334.

Health Insurance

Your U.S. health insurance will most likely not cover you in Mexico. Some companies do provide a rider covering certain medical prob-

Ken Luboff

Medical clinics like this one treat health problems.

lems, for which they will reimburse you at a later time. If you retire in
Mexico, we suggest that you buy an insurance policy that provides
international coverage. Several companies in Mexico sell just such
policies, including Sanborn's, 800-222-0158, the American Society in
Guadalajara (3) 121-2395, and Club Mex (3) 52-2992. Lloyd's bank
is also a good bet for insurance. In the United States, Worldwide
Health (602/857-2597) offers comprehensive international coverage.
You can be sure that cities with large numbers of retirees have
attracted an army of independent insurance agents. One knowledge-
able agent is John Williams in Mexico City. His telephone numbers
are (5) 514-9828 and (5) 511-6963. He can also give you information
about the many HMOs in the country.

Medicare does not cover hospital or medical services outside the
United States. The Department of Veterans Affairs will pay for hospital and medical service outside the United States only if you are a
veteran with a service-related disability. Anyone living legally in the
country can sign up for IMSS, the Mexican Social Security health
program, but only during January, part of February, July, and August.

IMSS health insurance costs about $250 per year and must be paid in one lump sum. The cost covers lab work, X rays, and other procedures. Once you sign on, undergo a medical examination, and pay, it takes about six months for coverage to become effective. Then, if you need medical care, you must go to an assigned clinic for evaluation. If you need a specialist or a more complicated procedure than that clinic can handle, you'll be referred to a larger clinic or hospital. The downside is that all this takes time. More importantly, not all the clinics and hospitals are of equal quality. It is a good idea to check out in advance the hospitals that you will be referred to in an emergency or for a difficult procedure.

Health-care Alternatives

Medicine men and women (*brujos* or *curanderos*) and other alternative healers hold a place of honor in Mexico, probably because of the country's deep Indian and spiritual roots. In every Mexican town, healers offer everything from treatments like chiropractic to herbal remedies, homeopathy, Reiki (energy work), and massage. It is not unusual to find an Indian shaman, well known in the area for his or her healing power, taking on foreign clients.

Mexico is a land of natural hot springs. Throughout the country, a wide variety of beautiful spas and healing clinics offer nutritional, relaxation, and body cleansing programs, usually including thermal waters, mud baths, and vegetarian cuisine. We have visited several of these. One, located next to a very hot river, channels the river's water (first filtered) into hot tubs in each guest room. What a treat for about $50 a night for two! Another spa, located in a semitropical area, offers rigorous weeklong packages with special vegetarian meals, daily massages, hot herbal wraps, and high colonics—all for a fraction of the cost of a health spa in the United States.

Smoking

Unlike in the United States, smoking is completely accepted everywhere in Mexico. Restricting smoking in public places is unheard of;

we have rarely seen a smoking section in a restaurant. When you live in Mexico, you get used to the fact that someone may sit at the table next to you in a restaurant and light up. That is just (cough, cough) the way it is.

AA

We have not yet been in a town of any size that does not have AA meetings. Towns with a large number of foreign residents hold meetings in English as well as Spanish. We have heard of a women's meeting in San Miguel and a gay meeting in Puerto Vallarta. Even if you don't speak Spanish, don't be intimidated by a Spanish meeting. People will be very welcoming and friendly, and may even encourage you to talk. Just look for the AA symbol inside a triangle and a circle, usually on a blue background, or in the local paper or phonebook. The people you encounter at the meeting can usually direct you to the local Al-Anon, if there is one.

Staying Healthy in Life

Retiring in Mexico may bring immediate relief from one of the great and most debilitating health problems of our time—stress. Living in a laid-back culture will improve your mental health. And once you eliminate the commute to work, the high cost of everything, and the crazy, competitive, fast pace of life in the North, improvement in your physical health will miraculously follow.

Communications

When we first visited about thirty years ago, Mexico was in the Dark Ages of communications. Even in large cities, private phones were rare. Local and long-distance calls were made at centrally located booths, often with long waiting lines. Believe it or not, this situation still exists in many small towns—in sharp contrast to the rapid modernization of communications in Mexico's cities and more sophisticated towns.

Telephone Service

The Mexican telephone system—Telmex, a government monopoly—is undergoing a major change. In 1998 the system saw its first competition with the introduction of Alestra (AT&T) and Avantel (MCI) into some areas of the country. Now individual users will finally have a choice of phone companies, and costs may subsequently fall. This change is especially important to retirees, most of whom have telephones in their homes and run up large phone bills calling family and friends in the States.

Home phone service usually includes a limited number of free local calls each month (about 100), after which there is a small additional charge per call. For international calling, you can either dial directly, use a call-back service (least expensive), or place calls through an operator (most expensive). When you sign up with a call-back service, you receive a phone number in the States. Calling that number connects you to a computer (usually), which automatically calls you back with a dial tone. You then dial your stateside number. The per-minute charge is fixed (currently 26.5 cents), regardless of time of day, and includes calls to 800 numbers. You can also call the States through AT&T by dialing 95-800-462-4240 or 95-800-674-4000, but such calls are astronomically expensive—costing many times more than direct calls. Telmex has just introduced a four-peso-per-minute deal for all direct calls to the States. That translates to about 45 cents per minute.

> *Your modem might not go faster than 28.8. But, hey, what's the rush!*

Telmex has placed phone booths (look for a booth with a Ladatel sign) on street corners in most towns, at airports, and in gas, bus, and train stations. You can call locally or internationally from

Ken Luboff

An Internet café in San Miguel de Allende

these phones with a Ladatel card—sold everywhere and well worth having. You can buy it at a store with a sign that says "Vende Ladatel Aqui." Cards come in 20-, 30-, 50-, and 100-peso denominations. During your call, the value of the card is reduced until it reaches zero. You then buy a new card. We often use our cards around town and sometimes to call the States from the road. We have great fun calling our daughter at work in Washington, D.C., from small villages in the middle of nowhere.

A surprisingly large number of towns still have no private phones in homes. In these towns, people use *larga-distancia* (long-distance) phone booths, generally located in shops or ice cream parlors, for calling in or out of town. Usually, phones operate from 8 a.m. to 8 p.m. only. We often use these booths to plug in our computer and collect our e-mail.

Cellular phones have become very popular among Mexican yuppies, businesspeople, and retirees who live in areas without phone service. The phones are also handy in the car in case of emergencies. The costs are about the same as cellular phone costs in the United States.

Internet

Just three years ago, San Miguel had no local Internet service provider. To pick up e-mail, we had to make a long-distance call to

MEXICO ON-LINE?

In terms of communications technology, Mexico lags behind its neighbors. The country has only 9.2 phone lines per 100 inhabitants, compared to Chile with 14.7 lines, Argentina with 15.6, and the United States with 64.2.

Only about 1 percent of Mexicans are connected to the Internet. In the United States, 50 percent of the population under age 35 is connected.

AOL in Mexico City. Not only was this costly (forget surfin' the Net) but half the time we couldn't connect for one reason or another. We always considered it a miracle to hear, "Welcome, you've got mail!"

But e-mail and the Internet are now catching on all over Mexico. All major retirement cities have at least one local provider and an Internet café or two. San Miguel has two Internet providers.

For foreign residents, e-mail is the easiest and least expensive way to stay in touch with kids, family, and friends. All you need is a computer and a modem. The manual that came with our computer proudly proclaims that our modem can run at up to 56 Kbps. Maybe so—but not in Mexico. Mexico still has copper, not fiber optic, phone lines, with a capacity of only 33.6 Kbps. Indeed, our Internet speed is always 33.6 Kbps. In other parts of Mexico, your modem might not go faster than 28.8. But, hey, what's the rush! If you don't have a computer, you can still access e-mail or the Internet at the local Internet server or a cybercafé.

Mail services offer a reliable alternative to the Mexican postal system.

Mail

The Mexican postal service is not always safe or reliable. Reportedly, many millions of dollars' worth of checks sent from the North disappear from the postal system each year. Packages also have a way of disappearing.

We used to have a Mexican post office box (*apartado*), until we got fed up waiting for weeks to get our mail. We then switched to one of the more reliable private mail services, Mail Boxes, Etc., which operate in most large and medium-sized towns. These services provide patrons with a U.S. mailing address, from which mail is shipped daily via UPS to a private box in Mexico. We now receive letters from the States and Canada in as little as five or six days. The companies safely send mail out of Mexico and offer overnight and second-day service. Many have fax and copy machines for customer use (people who do mucho faxing have machines at home). When you receive packages through these services, however, the customs duty can be astronomically high (whereas the Mexican post office is free—if the package arrives at all). Some services also charge dearly for weight, which can eliminate mail-order goodies, especially books.

Our mail service costs $144 per year. Most services also charge five pesos per letter (about 55 cents) to mail them in the United States. Instead, most people who live in Mexico give mail to friends who are heading back to the States. Remember to bring a supply of U.S. stamps with you when you move to Mexico.

Making the Move

Foreigners entering Mexico either to travel or live need one of the following visas: FMT, FM3, or FM2. An FMT is the official tourist visa most people receive when entering Mexico. You can get one at any Mexican consulate, at the border, or on a flight into the country. When you fly in, your visa will be good for 90 days, after which you can have it renewed for an additional 90 days. If you drive in, you'll usually receive a 180-day visa at the border. If border officials give you less, ask for the full 180 days. If you enter in your own car, that will be noted on your visa, and you must leave with the same car. To get an FMT when driving into Mexico, you need only fill out a simple form, have a credit card, and show your passport and car registration (see Chapter 9, "Travel and Transportation," for more details). When you leave the country, you will have to turn in your visa.

An FMT visa costs $15 at the border. This new fee is automatically added to the cost of an airline ticket. Foreign residents with FM2 or FM3 visas should give notice that they are exempt from the fee, or they will be charged. On an FMT visa, you are not allowed to work. It is typically given to tourists on short trips, but we know people from the States who have been living in Mexico for more than 20 years on tourist visas. They never got around to switching and just

Waiting in line for immigration papers

keep renewing their visas every six months. The number of personal and household items that you can bring into the country is supposedly limited on this visa—although the amount isn't really specified. We have occasionally asked friends, driving down from the States and entering on tourist visas, to fill their cars with goodies for us. None have ever been hassled—as long as they unwrapped the stuff first so it looked used.

FM3

If you are going to be living in Mexico, in our opinion an FM3 visa is the way to go. An FM3 is a non-immigrant residency visa that is renewed only once a year. With a valid FM3, you can leave and re-enter the country as often as you like and in any way that you like. If you drove into Mexico with an FM3, and you want to fly back to the States for your high school reunion, no sweat! Just leave the car in Mexico and go. (See Chapter 9 for more details.)

   With certain FM3s (there are 13 types in all), you can work in

Mexico. If you know in advance that you want to work, go to an immigration office (or consulate) and find out what documents you will need to apply for working papers (see Chapter 11, "Working in Mexico").

Getting an FM3 is more complicated than getting an FMT. We suggest that you apply the first time at a Mexican consulate in the States—generally faster and less complicated than applying in Mexico. However, we have recently heard that some consulates won't take FM3 applications—so call first.

In either country, you will need certain documents to apply. These include proof, in the form of bank or investment company statements, that you have an income equal to at least 250 times the minimum wage in Mexico City, which means about $1,000 per month if you are single, plus half that for each dependent. This amount is reduced by 50 percent if you own real estate (in which you claim to live) in Mexico. Along with proof of income, you will need to write a letter to the immigration office giving your name, address, and reason for wanting an FM3—something like, "I want an FM3 because I am retired and plan to live in Mexico for the foreseeable future." You will also need a passport, tourist visa if you have one, and marriage certificate (if your spouse also wants an FM3). You then fill out a form, provide photos of yourself and your spouse, make copies of all the documents, and pay a fee of about $70.

Sound easy? Could be, but we know people who have had to return to an immigration office in Mexico five times before getting their FM3s. Because of the frustrations some foreigners feel, private immigration services have begun cropping up to guide people through the process. By the way, if you get your FM3 in the States, you must register it at the nearest immigration office within 30 days of entering Mexico.

Several FM3 business visa designations have been created since the passage of NAFTA. These do not affect most retirees moving to Mexico. They include a 30-day business visitor visa, a one-year professional visa (in certain fields), and visas for intra-company transferees in managerial or executive capacities or investor/traders.

FM2

FM2 immigration status is for those who know they want to reside permanently in Mexico. Years ago, FM2s were the only visas available to foreigners who wanted to work in the country. These days, the FM3 replaces the FM2 as a working visa.

The FM2 must be renewed every year for five years, after which you can apply for immigrant status and need not renew again. During those first five years you cannot leave the country for more than 18 months or you will lose your status and need to start over again. Once you achieve *imigrante* status, you will have all of the rights of a Mexican citizen, although you cannot join the army, vote, or run for office.

The application process for an FM2 is about the same as that for an FM3, but you have to show a higher monthly income—about $1,500 if you are single and half that for each dependent. Applying also costs a bit more—about $100. As with an FM3, the monthly income requirement is reduced by 50 percent if you own Mexican real estate in which you claim to live. Neither an FM3 nor an FM2 changes your U.S. citizenship, only your country of residence.

There are downsides to an FM2. A friend of ours, Tom Horn, has lived in Mexico for many years with FM2 imigrante status. Earlier this year, Tom decided it was time for his first new car in years and headed up to Texas, very excited to buy a model he liked that was not sold in Mexico. When he returned to the border with his shiny new acquisition, he was turned away. He was an imigrante and therefore not permitted to import a foreign-bought vehicle into Mexico. Finally, after all his powers of persuasion (and he has many) failed to move the immigration officials, he sadly returned the car to the dealer, got his money back, and bought a car in Mexico.

Shipping Household Items

One of the advantages to FM3 status is the one-time opportunity to import a large amount of personal household items duty-free. Before

Expatriate Perspective

Unless you know the country well, speak Spanish, or are Albert Schweitzer, you will most likely live in a city with an established foreign population. A friend, Maureen Earl, describes the relationship between the local and foreign people in her town:

My town has a large foreign population—and sometimes an uneasy mix between the foreigners and Mexicans. We foreigners have certainly improved the economy of the town, but we have also bought up some of the best real estate and inflated prices. As a result, poorer Mexicans find themselves pushed farther and farther out of the center of town.

Still, it remains solidly a Mexican town, and gringos are very much the minority. Most of us moved here for one reason: We love Mexico and its people. While most expatriates make efforts to learn Spanish and fit in with the mores and precepts of the country, others do not. They enjoy servants, bridge games, and cocktail parties and continue to live what is essentially an American lifestyle.

Whether we fit in with the locals or not, for the most part we foreigners are much like a ship at sea. We are tight knit and are often obliged to tolerate people with whom we wouldn't be bothered under other circumstances. It's very much like living on an island—and actually makes for an interesting life.

we shipped our furniture and other household goods to Mexico, the Mexican consulate in Albuquerque told us that the total value of items shipped could not exceed $5,000. Since everything we owned was used, we simply placed a low value on the whole lot, which included a piano, and easily stayed under the five-grand limit. Unlike some people we know, we had a hassle-free shipping experience.

As required, we made a list of everything we were shipping, including serial numbers for electrical appliances. We numbered each box, listed the contents of each, left three copies of the list with the consulate, and paid the required $100 fee. Then, after getting heart-stopping and outrageous quotes from giant moving companies like Mayflower and United Van Lines, we located a Mexican shipper out of San Diego with references and a good reputation. He charged about 50 percent less than the others. He came to our home, carefully loaded our furniture, took care of all the border-crossing hassles, and delivered everything in tip-top condition to our new home in Mexico.

Some say that it's wise to register with the nearest embassy or consulate when you arrive at your permanent residence in Mexico. They say that registration will make your presence and whereabouts known in case of an emergency. We have been considering registering for about five years now and will probably get around to it someday.

Moving with Children

A child entering (or leaving) Mexico with only one parent must have notarized consent from the absent parent. Similar consent is required if the child is traveling alone or with a non-parent. A U.S. court order authorizing the travel will work if one parent refuses consent or cannot be located.

Many years ago, when our daughter Liza was about five, the three of us spent some time on the beach near Manzanillo on the Pacific coast. I needed to go inland to do some business, and we decided that Barbara would fly back to the States with Liza. I left first on a flight to Mexico City, never thinking that I needed to write a letter authorizing Barbara to take Liza out of the country.

Barbara found herself in the immigration office at the airport with a ticket, a young child, and nowhere to go because she couldn't prove that I had agreed to let our daughter leave the country. She was boiling! Finally, after some serious hassling and haggling, Barbara paid a *mordita* (a bribe) of $20 to an official—big bucks in those days—and was able to leave Mexico with Liza. It is unlikely that this method would still work, as rules have been tightened. It would now be a lot easier to write the letter.

Moving with Pets

There is no quarantine and absolutely no problem crossing the border in either direction with a cat or a dog. Theoretically, whether driving into Mexico or the States, you need an international health certificate for your pet (vets charge an arm and a leg for these), but we have never been asked for one for Jane, our Rhodesian Ridgeback. Instead, we always carry Jane's latest shot records.

If anything, it is easier to travel with a dog than without one.

Ken Luboff

You will encounter few problems crossing the border with a pet.

Jane is big and expressionless, so when we pass through checkpoints or customs in Mexico, officials usually take one look at her and ask if she bites. We kind of shrug noncommittally, and they wave us on. If our car is loaded down with valuables, which it usually is, especially coming back from the States, we know we don't have to worry about break-ins while Jane is in the car. At the few hotels or motels where she isn't welcome, she simply sleeps in the car all night.

Senior Citizen Card

An agency of the Mexican government, Instituto National Senectitud (old age), issues INSEN cards, which can be used by people over 60 to get discounts. Most retirees don't know about the card. To get one, you have to first find an INSEN office—not an easy task, but someone at the local city hall can usually point you in the right direction.

You will need proof of age and residency (an FM3 will do) and two or three photos of yourself. There is no fee, but there may be resistance on the part of officials who are not aware that all residents of Mexico, whether nationals or foreigners, are entitled to the card. Just persist if officials balk, and you should eventually get one. With the card, you'll get free admission to museums and exhibits, discounts on buses and national flights, and discounts at movie theaters and some hotel chains.

Travel and Transportation

It is not surprising that most foreigners living in Mexico love to travel. After all, they live in one of the most beautiful and culturally exciting countries on earth. But travel in Mexico can take some getting used to. Sometimes it takes a while for new arrivals to become brave enough to begin exploring the country. But, once they do, it's hard to keep them at home.

Barbara and I sometimes take a bus ride to the big city for a weekend of museums, shopping, and opera. On other occasions, we ride our bikes on country roads or simply walk along a quiet river. And we have been known to jump in the car for a vacation at the beach or mountains, or to explore an exotic river or jungle town. Traveling in Mexico is safe and easy, as long as you take some simple precautions and plan ahead.

Driving in Mexico

Driving in Mexico used to be quite a hair-raising experience. Every road was a narrow two-lane blacktop with a surface like a potato grater. These days, we have the pleasure of driving on modern four-lane toll roads called Autopistas or Maxipistas. Though the tolls are very high, Autopistas are the best way to travel long distances.

At points where an Autopista has not been completed, you will be directed back to an old highway. Be cautious here. Even when straight, the old roads are dangerous. They are frequently used by slow-moving, overloaded trucks and buses and the occasional pedestrian guiding livestock. When these roads curve over hills and mountains, they are even more hair-raising. Many Mexican drivers put their lives into God's hands and think nothing of passing just before the crest of a hill. Corkscrew mountain roads are rarely banked well and have few guard rails. Whether curvy or straight, none of the older roads have shoulders, and many have steep drops on both sides. Fortunately, these days you can drive between most cities in Mexico, at least part of the way, on a four-lane highway.

We love driving on back roads and exploring lovely out-of-the-way villages and hidden natural wonders. We can hop in the car spontaneously and take off for the weekend, a week, or even a month (Hey, we're retired!). We recommend having a car here unless you hate driving and the hassles and cost of occasional auto repairs, parking problems, traffic tickets, and so on. (If so, don't worry. You will do perfectly well in Mexico without a car.)

Driving across the Border

Bringing a car into Mexico the first time is less time consuming if you prepare all your papers in advance. You will need your driver's license, a tourist card (available at the border or beforehand at AAA or the Mexican consulate), a credit card, and your car's registration papers. Having a passport is a good idea, but not absolutely necessary for a U.S. citizen. If the car is borrowed, a company car, leased, or owned by the bank, you will need a notarized letter from the owner giving permission for the car to enter Mexico.

With your papers in hand, at the immigration building on the Mexican side of the border, you'll get the permits to import yourself and your car into Mexico. You can use your credit card to pay the permit fee of $11.

We suggest stopping at AAA near the border. They have the

Driving in Mexico presents a whole new set of hazards.

Ken Luboff

necessary visa forms and can give you border-crossing advice. At some border towns (Nuevo Laredo, for instance), AAA even has special windows in Mexican customs offices (*aduana*) where members can get help.

One word of caution: Before crossing the border, make sure that the numbers on your car and your car registration match. A friend had two numbers on his registration certificate reversed and was forced to return to the States to get the mix-up straightened out.

You should also stop at a bank or money-exchange booth on either side of the border and get at least enough pesos to get you to your destination. From El Paso to Mexico City, for instance, you'll need a minimum of $200 in pesos for just gas and tolls. Exchange rates at all points of entry into Mexico, including airports, are generally better than those in the interior. In addition, exchange booths near the border are open long hours, seven days a week. Farther into the country, booths may be closed on weekends and at night. In a bind, you can always pay for gas and tolls in dollars, but you will get ripped off on the exchange rate. And very few toll booths and gas stations take plastic. Paying in pesos will make your trip far less complicated. Remember that all large towns have ATMs.

Auto Insurance

Your U.S. auto insurance policy will not cover you in Mexico. We advise buying Mexican insurance before you arrive at the border. AAA sells it, as does our insurance agent, John Williams, at (5) 514-9828 in Mexico City, and many other reputable companies. Here are a few choices; check the Internet for others:
• ASD Insurance, 800/909-4457
• Oscar Padilla Insurance Agency, 800/258-8600
• Sanborn's, 800/222-0158
• Lewis and Lewis, 800/966-6830 or 310/657-1112
• Discover Baja Travel Club, 800/727-BAJA, fax 619/275-183, e-mail: discovbaja@aol.com
• Palms Mexican Insurance, 915/533-0062, fax 915/532-5353

All have good reputations for paying claims promptly. Some insurance companies also have travel clubs, which you automatically join when you buy their policies. Club membership usually costs extra, but you may find the services useful.

The typical policy covering liability costs only $160 per year, although we have heard of liability policies selling for as little as $60 per year. For full coverage (no club membership), cost depends on the value of your car. For a vehicle valued at $10,000 to $15,000, expect to pay about $180 per year. For a vehicle valued at $15,001 to $20,000, expect to pay about $200 per year. These prices change often.

As you approach the border, you will be barraged by signs offering insurance deals. If you haven't already bought insurance, buy enough to get you to your destination and a bit more—say six days' worth if you are traveling from Nogales to Puerto Vallarta. This will give you coverage until you find an agent in PV. Once you arrive in PV or another large city, or one with a large foreign population, insurance agents there can advise you about a longer-term policy. If you are traveling around and exploring the country, buy enough insurance for the whole trip.

Aduana (Customs)

You could be one of the lucky ones who are waved through at the border, but you are just as likely to be pulled over by a customs official. The agent will most likely check your papers, look in your car, and send you on your way. He may ask to see pet papers and could decide to search your car. Be courteous and do as the agent says. Usually, the inspection is only cursory. After you leave the aduana, resist the urge to get out of town quickly. Border towns are notorious speed traps.

About 15 miles south of the border you will come to another aduana checkpoint. It is here that your entry documents will be checked. You may be asked to step out of your car so it can be searched for weapons or anything that looks suspicious. Again, be polite and patient, show your papers, and let the agents look. You will usually be back on the road quickly.

At some point farther down the road you will probably arrive at yet another checkpoint. This one—with evil-looking men in black T-shirts pointing automatic weapons—may be intimidating. Do not fear. These are federal police looking for guns and drugs. They will probably wave you through, although they have the authority to pull you over and search your car.

At any checkpoint, there is the small chance that you will be hassled and delayed until you offer to pay a bribe. This type of harassment is more common along the west coast, south of Nogales, where customs agents and federal police may threaten to search cars in the hot desert sun. Be polite and try to understand the situation. Once it is clear that you are better off paying, do it and be gone.

Auto Import Laws

When you bring a car into Mexico on a tourist visa, you will get a temporary vehicle importation permit, which allows your car to remain in the country for up to six months. When the permit expires, the car must leave—and you with it. The policy is intended to stop people from selling cars in Mexico. It is possible to have your vehicle permit and visa extended, but it can be a real bureaucratic hassle.

If you intend to live in Mexico with a car, it is best to have FM3 immigration status (see Chapter 8, "Making the Move"). Then, theoretically, your car can remain in the country indefinitely. A new law states that as long as your FM3 is current (renewed annually), your car can legally stay in Mexico, even if its immigration papers have expired.

The problem with the new law is that no one has bothered to explain it to all the various kinds of cops in the country. Friends of ours, Richard and Gail, were pulled over by a policeman to have their papers checked. Their FM3s were current, but the policeman made a great fuss when he noticed that their auto import document was out of date. Richard and Gail calmly explained that the car was legal because their FM3s were up to date. They even showed the cop a copy of the Mexican law, in Spanish, which a U.S. consular agent had given out for just such occurrences. The cop looked at the paper, looked at them, then put one hand on his gun and said, "Right here, I am the law." Richard and Gail grudgingly paid a $100 mordita to get away.

To avoid this sort of "misunderstanding," we renew our auto import documents annually at a nearby aduana, right after we renew our FM3s. To us, the $15 cost is well worth not being hassled. Both FM3 and car papers are renewable at many locations throughout Mexico.

Road Safety

The number-one auto safety rule in Mexico is *never drive at night*—especially not on the old roads. Who knows what you might encounter on the road at night. We've seen slow-moving and stopped vehicles of all kinds, many without back-up lights. At dusk, when it is especially hard to see, people walk home from the fields along narrow roadsides. Later in the night, livestock may wander into the road. In a few cases, "police cars" with lights flashing have pulled people over at night and robbed them. In the daytime, it would have been clear that these cars were not police.

Toll roads are the safest and fastest roads in the country. Since the tolls are expensive ($30 from Laredo, Texas, to San Miguel de Allende; $22 from Puerto Vallarta to Guadalajara), the roads are used almost exclusively by foreign travelers and wealthy Mexicans. Thus, driving these roads is like having your own private highway.

> *Driving on the toll roads is like having your own private highway.*

Most of the toll roads are in excellent condition, are well lit, and have emergency phones every few kilometers. Near the toll booths you'll find shiny new gas stations with clean bathrooms (sinks and toilets work automatically, no less!) and nearby snack bars. Be aware that some macho Mexicans drive on toll roads like they are trying to break the sound barrier. Cars have sped by us so fast that we felt like we were driving in reverse! Nevertheless, we highly recommend that you use these roads when you travel long distances.

Most other major Mexican highways are two- or four-lane blacktops. The four-lane roads are usually not too bad, but in some places truck and bus use is heavy, and you'll feel like you're driving in a monster Roller Derby. Major cross-country, two-lane highways may be the most dangerous roads of all. Buses and trucks clog these roads and play chicken as drivers try passing one another. These roads are very narrow, without shoulders. Many have potholes, washboard surfaces, and no center line. There is not nearly the margin for error here as there is on a two-lane highway in the United States. Driving these roads, you'll need both caution and the protection of the gods of the Mexican highway.

To explore Mexico's back country you'll need to take the two-lane country roads. On these roads, you'll pass through villages that haven't changed much in a hundred years. You'll see incredible natural beauty and, if you are lucky, small village processions and celebrations.

Even though they have less traffic, country roads still offer their share of hazards. One of the most frightening is the infamous

Mexican left-turn signal. Often, the left-turn signal is a courteous driver's way of telling you that the road ahead is clear and that it is safe to pass (which may or may not be the case). Other times, drivers give a left-turn signal, then pull off to the right, waiting to turn left when the road is clear. On rare occasions, a driver will actually turn left after giving a left-turn signal. Caramba!!

On our first trip to Mexico, I innocently gave a left-turn signal well in advance of my turn, looked back to see that the car behind me was slowing, and began turning left. Only then did I realize that the car behind had speeded up and was trying to pass me. Amazingly, we somehow missed each other by a hair, but my heartbeat hit 185. Looking back, I realize my simple but potentially deadly error. The driver mistook my turn signal for a friendly signal to pass.

Speed limits on all Mexican roads are clearly marked but rarely enforced. Only in cities, where there are speed traps, are you likely to be pulled over for speeding. Recently, we have seen more police cars on the roads, so maybe officers are starting to give out tickets.

Look out for *topes* (toh-pays)—speed bumps—on two-lane country roads. These suckers often appear before you have time to react. Eventually, you will come to expect them before and after small towns, but not always. When you are lucky, you'll see a warning sign about 500 meters in advance of a tope so you can slow down and take the bump with finesse. But some topes are not marked. If you hit them at full speed they can shake your teeth loose, blow a tire, or do serious damage to your car.

Ron Mader

Solar-powered emergency phone on a Mexican toll road

Gas

The gas stations in Mexico are all part of the huge government gasoline monopoly called Pemex. As little as 10 years ago, Pemex stations were few and far between and rarely sold unleaded gas. Now the stations are popping up all over the country, so your chances of running out of gas are low. Nevertheless, if we are out in the boonies and see a Pemex station, we fill up even if we still have half a tank left.

These days, almost all of the filthy gas stations of old have been destroyed, cleaned up, or renovated. If you need to pull into an older station, especially if you have to use the bathroom, hold your breath! Note that all the newer stations have spanking-clean bathrooms and small snack shops.

When you pull up for gas, get ready for a flurry of activity around your car. While you are telling the attendant how much gas you want, some young kid may already be cleaning your windshield and a vendor or two may be trying to sell you a car-seat cover or a bag of fruit. After a few fill-ups, you will get used to activity and take it all very calmly.

Filling up will not be as cheap as it is in the States, and gas prices are steadily increasing. *Magna sin* (regular unleaded gas) now costs more than $1.60 a gallon. *Premium* (super unleaded gas) costs about $1.80 a gallon. Diesel fuel costs about $1.20 a gallon.

Self service has not yet hit Mexico. It is the custom to tip the attendant a peso or two, especially if he or she has checked your tires or oil. Give whoever cleaned your windshield a few pesos as well. Note that a few stations will try and squeeze a few more pesos out of you by not resetting the pump to zero or by over-filling your tank. Make sure the gauge has been reset before the attendant starts pumping (newer pumps are reset automatically), and when the nozzle clicks when your tank is full, tell the attendant that you have enough gas.

Repairs and Maintenance

Maintenance is one of the best aspects of owning a car in Mexico— it is much less expensive here than in the States. A complete tune-up can cost as little as $25, and a brake job about $30. We have been lucky to find good and fairly fast Mexican mechanics.

Not long ago, we limped into Guadalajara with almost no brakes and a group of thirsty friends in the back seat of the van. A Pemex station attendant pointed the way to a small, funky repair shop a few blocks away. The shop had a cool dark room where our friends sagged uncomfortably into ridged aluminum chairs to escape the heat. When the problem was explained, the mechanic went to work, but not before bringing each of us a cold Coke. An hour later, with much thanks, we were on the road again, our brakes working like new. Total cost—cokes and all—$8, plus a nice trip.

Mexican mechanics are wizards at cannibalizing other cars and pieces of machinery to get repairs accomplished. Several have had their creativity put to the test when parts were not available and they were forced to jury-rig devices to get us back on the road. Don't be scared off by mechanics whose shops look like they came straight out of a Dickens novel. But shops are rapidly modernizing as more new cars are sold in Mexico. All major car manufacturers with show-rooms in Mexico have repair shops.

Road Signs

Generally, Mexican highways are pretty well marked. There are those occasional confusing intersections that drive you crazy—three or four roads with the same number all heading to different locations. Sometimes, there are no signs at all. Worse, signs might unexpectedly stop—especially in Mexican cities, the easiest mazes on earth in which to get lost. We have often followed signs through a complicated jumble of streets just to have them disappear completely and leave us totally confused and stranded. Asking directions often doesn't help because many Mexicans don't drive and don't know how to get from place to place in a car. But that *never* stops them from giving you detailed directions anyway!

Before arriving in a city, look for signs that say *Libramiento* and *Centro*. Following the first sign will take you around the city, and following the second will take you into its heart. Other important highway signs are *Libre* (free road) and *Cuota* (toll road). Always take the cuota, unless you are exploring back roads, heading for an out-of-the-way place, or broke.

Mexico seems to have no consistent rules for highway repair crews. They each have their own style—or lack of it. We have run across flagmen on the highway, waving wildly some mysterious signal. Usually, after a moment of panic, we drive slowly around the guy, hoping that there is actually a road up ahead.

Maps

We are on a perpetual search for a great road map of Mexico. Most Mexican maps are not updated as regularly as U.S. maps and fail to show new extensions of toll roads. Many maps are downright wrong. We have followed maps deep into the back country, eventually finding ourselves on roads that don't exist on the map.

Once, on a trip through the Sierra Gorda region in the state of Queretaro, we ended up on a road that was three times removed from the last road marked on the map. Not surprisingly, this thrice-removed road went through lovely towns and forests and even passed a beautiful ex-hacienda hotel, where we stayed overnight. However, if we hadn't been with friends who knew the area well, we may never have found our way home.

The best guide we have found is the *Guia Roja*, a book of area maps in color. The AAA map is not bad. It will get you from big city to big city, but can be confusing and useless in the back country.

Green Angels

The Mexican Department of Tourism runs a fleet of about 925 distinctive green pickup trucks that patrol all the major highways in Mexico from 8 a.m. to 8 p.m. Known as the Green Angels, the fleet provides aid for motorists in need. Drivers carry gas, water, and oil and can make minor repairs—or tow you to the nearest mechanic. If you need a Green Angel, pull off the road, lift the hood, and get comfortable with a good book. You may have a long wait, but a Green Angel will eventually arrive. If you are near a phone, call 01-800-90392 or

01-5-250-0123. Drivers are supposed to speak English. Luckily, we have never had to use their services. Nevertheless, it is reassuring when a Green Angel passes us on the road. In an emergency, you can also call the Mexican Highway Patrol at 01-5-684-2142 or 01-5-684-9512.

Driving in Mexico City

We highly recommend against driving into Mexico City. If you must, be aware that the city has instituted a no-drive-day plan to reduce air pollution. The day you cannot drive in the city is determined by the last number on your license plate. If your plate ends with the number 1 or 2, no driving on Thursday; if it ends with 3 or 4, no driving on Wednesday; if it ends with 5 or 6, no driving on Monday; if it ends with 7 or 8, no driving on Tuesday; if it ends with 9 or 0, no driving on Friday. All cars may drive on Saturday and Sunday and during the week between the hours of 11 p.m. and 5 a.m. If your plate ends in a letter, call 01-800-90392 or 01-5-250-0151 to find out which day is off limits to you.

People with out-of-country (or even out-of-state) license plates are notoriously hassled on the freeways encircling Mexico City. The police here will do anything in their power to extort money from you. Some friends were pulled over twice in a 10-minute period! We have often added hours to our driving trips just to make a broad sweep around Mexico City.

Car Rentals

Retirees without cars rarely use rental cars. Often, they take the bus to visit friends in the countryside or the next town. If retirees get the urge to cruise country roads by car, rentals are easily available most of the time (see Chapter 12: "Planning Your First Trip," for rental-car company phone numbers). Sometimes it is easier, cheaper, and more fun to hire a taxi (or private car) and a driver for the day. The driver may even take you to his Aunt Rosa's house for comida.

Traveling by Air

An abundance of direct flights head from the United States to every major city and most major tourist areas in Mexico. To enter Mexico by plane, you will need only a picture ID, preferably a passport. During the flight, you will be asked to fill out an immigration/customs card. Check with your travel agent or directly with the airline for flight costs and schedules.

Within the country, more than 60 local airports are served by regional and national airlines such as Aero California, Aero Carib, Aero Cozumel, Aviacsa, Aero Guadalajara, Aeromexico, Mexicana Airlines, Taesa, and Aeromar. Even with all these airports and regional airlines, flying from point to point within the country often requires changing planes in Mexico City.

Traveling by Bus

Buses travel to every city and into every little corner of the country in Mexico. In most cases, more than one bus line will cover the same route, giving you a choice of schedules, prices, and quality. Other than walking, riding the bus is the most common form of transportation in Mexico.

Long-distance buses in the United States seem shoddy in comparison to first-class Mexican buses. Surprised? Mexican *Lujo* ("luxury"—the best) and *Primera Clase* (first-class—next best) buses are no longer the overcrowded, broken-down contraptions—with chickens in cages precariously tied to the roofs—that you have seen in old Hollywood flicks. The new top class of buses are ultra-modern, with reserved, plush seats, plenty of leg room, no smoking, air-conditioning,

AIR CARRIERS SERVING MEXICO

Aero California, 800/237-6225
Aeromexico, 800/237-6639
American, 800/433-7300
Continental, 800/231-0856
Delta, 800/241-4141
Mexicana, 800/531-7921
United, 800/241-6522

clean bathrooms, movies, refreshments, and even stewardesses. The movies are not always Oscar caliber, however. More often than not they are shoot-em-ups starring Sylvester Stallone or Steven Seagal. We usually bring a Discman with a few good CDs for entertainment.

Any of the top-class buses is a hassle-free and inexpensive way to travel between distant cities—costing much less than a rental car. Of course, buses travel much more slowly than rental cars. They usually leave and arrive on time. If you want, you can usually talk with a Mexican en route and practice your Spanish. It is best to call ahead for reservations. If you can't do that, arrive at the station at least a half-hour early to buy a ticket. A travel agent might be able to help.

Second- and third-class buses operating between small towns—usually old school buses or mini-vans—are less comfortable than first-class buses. They generally run on time but can be very slow, making not only many scheduled stops but also picking up anyone who flags them down. Two friends of ours regularly take a third-class bus four or five miles out of town, disembark when they spot an appealing dirt path, and hike off into the country for a day with a picnic lunch. They return to the highway in the afternoon to catch a bus back to town. Such buses are dirt cheap but are not recommended for long-distance travel—they can be back breakers!

Large cities have centralized bus terminals used by many bus lines. Mexico City has four terminals: North, South, East, and West. Your destination will determine which terminal you'll use. You may have to take a taxi from one terminal to another to switch bus lines and complete your trip. In smaller cities, each bus line has its own easy-to-find storefront terminal.

Train Travel

Train travel in Mexico is a questionable affair. When trains run, they can be frustratingly slow. The exceptions are the El Regiomontano, which travels from Nuevo Laredo to Mexico City, and the west coast Pacifico line, starting in Mexicali on the U.S. border and traveling through Nogales, Mazatlán, Tepic, and eventually Guadalajara.

If you decide to take a train, buy a first-class ticket if you can afford it. In our opinion, the faster and far-more-comfortable buses are the way to go, unless you are a train buff or hate buses.

Taxis

Forget about paying 10 bucks for a 10-block cab ride as you might in the States. In all but the biggest cities in Mexico fares are cheap. Though fares are set in most small towns (there are no meters), it is still a good idea to ask the price of a trip before getting into a cab. Short trips should cost no more than two or three dollars. Taxi drivers are never tipped, but usually charge extra for handling luggage.

A Roof over Your Head

We are in awe of people who arrive in San Miguel, Chapala, Puerto Vallarta, or another Mexican city and become so charmed with the place that within days they buy a house. We can't imagine having the confidence, money, and impulsiveness necessary to do such a thing. Surprisingly, many of these people are still very happily living in Mexico with no regrets. Those who returned to the States for one reason or another have generally done well financially by buying in retirement areas with quickly appreciating real estate values.

Nevertheless, no matter how much you love a town, we highly recommend that you "cool your jets" and rent a place, especially if this is your first foray into the expatriate lifestyle. Renting allows you time to explore the town both physically and spiritually and to ferret out the best deals when you are ready to buy.

Buying

Some newcomers to Mexico arrive with the expectation that they can buy a hacienda in this Third World country for a few thousand dollars. Forget it—unless you want to live in the middle of nowhere. Real estate in Mexico works the same way it does in the United

States: The most desirable areas are the most expensive. Once you move out of the highly sought-after areas, the cost of real estate plummets. But you can still find deals almost anywhere if you are willing to take the time.

Finding the property you want is relatively easy in tourist areas, large cities, and retirement communities. In all these places, real estate agents advertise heavily in local newspapers and through brochures. Quite a few even have Web pages. And they are easy to find, with well-marked offices, usually in high-profile locations. In the Ajijic area, if you are not paying attention, you could easily bang your head on a Realtor's sign.

Most of the Realtors we run across are American or Canadian expatriates who are riding the Mexican real estate wave. Some came to Mexico to make their fortunes, but many others retired here, got bored, and went into real estate to entertain themselves. Mexican Realtors seem to keep a lower profile, but they are worth talking to. Many speak English and list properties owned by Mexicans that would not make it onto the lists of American Realtors. As in the States, Realtors in Mexico generally work for a commission of 6 percent of the sale price, paid by the seller.

If you don't like dealing with real estate agents or you just want to try finding a house on your own, go to a part of town you like and ask people if they know of places for sale. The corner grocer or a woman sweeping the stoop may have a cousin who has a friend who knows a guy who wants to sell his house. This is exactly what happened to us in San Miguel de Allende.

Barbara and I were walking through the narrow streets of a Mexican barrio (neighborhood), just sort of looking around, when a very nice man came out of a *tienda* (shop) and asked if we would be interested in buying a house. We gave each other a quick look and simultaneously shook our heads yes. Why not look? The man's name was Carmelo, and he explained that the house belonged to a cousin who had gotten work in a beach resort town and was not planning to return to San Miguel. We liked the house and extracted a promise from Carmelo not to tell anyone else about it until we made up our minds. For the next two weeks we almost

Ken Luboff

A lot for sale in Puerto Vallarta

lived in that house, redesigning it at least 100 times. Then, after some haggling with Carmelo, we bought it. The price was $25,000!

Another good do-it-yourself method is to look for signs that say *Trato Directo* (direct deal)—the equivalent of For Sale by Owner. And keep in mind that many houses in Mexico are sold completely furnished.

Once you decide on a property, hire a *notario publico* (like a lawyer) to research the deed and help you get a clear title. Your Realtor will be happy to help with this process. The title gives you essentially the same rights as it would in the United States. The only difference between a Mexican and a U.S. real estate purchase is that in most cases you will pay cash in Mexico. Good-bye mortgage payments—hello clear home. The entire process usually takes from three to six weeks.

If you don't have the cash to make the buy, take heart. In the last few years at least two U.S. and Canadian mortgage companies have begun offering mortgages on Mexican real estate. No doubt, in coming years the number of such companies will grow. Typically, mortgages are offered for up to 70 percent of the appraised value of the property, at about 2 percent above comparable U.S. rates. For the latest mortgage rate information, contact lenders directly.

Fideicomiso

Buying property on the coasts and along the borders of Mexico is done differently. The Mexican constitution of 1917 essentially gave common ownership of all beaches and borders to the Mexican people. Foreigners cannot hold direct title to any lands within 30 miles of the coast or within 60 miles of the border (the restricted zone). In 1994, amendments to the constitution allowed foreigners to buy land for commercial purposes, but residential ownership is still restricted.

To create tourist development and encourage private ownership in the restricted zone, while not violating the constitution, the government has created a trust arrangement known as a *fideicomiso*. Under this system, the coastal or border home you want will be placed in a trust, in a Mexican trustee's name. The Mexican trustee, the trust department of a Mexican bank, is the owner of record of the property. But ownership rights belong to you, the purchaser of the property and the beneficiary of the trust. The trustee is prohibited by contract and Mexican law from transferring the property or beneficiary rights without written permission of the beneficiary. For all practical purposes, a fideicomiso is the same as private property ownership in the United States. You can develop the property, sell it, rent it, and pass it on to your heirs when you die.

A 1993 law allows foreigners to obtain direct ownership rights by forming a Mexican corporation. A minimum of $50,000 pesos (now $5,000) is required. The two required partners may be foreigners, even though the corporation is a Mexican entity and as such can own land. The law limits ownership to commercial property but is unclear as to what constitutes commercial property. For instance, a property in which one room is used as an office might qualify. Creating a Mexican corporation may be ideal for commercial real estate deals, but a fideicomiso is simpler and easier for private homes.

The Mexican government has also started to grant title to

owners of private property in some areas along the coast, a process known as regularization. You will definitely hear more about this process when you are looking for coastal property.

Ejidos

In most areas of the country, some property may be owned in common by an *ejido*. Ejidos were Indian land collectives that disintegrated after La Reforma, a war to eject Emperor Maximilian from Mexico, ending in 1861. It was not until after the revolution of 1910–20 that ejidos were reformed, as a way of redistributing land to the *campesinos*, or country people. Until the law was changed in 1994, these lands could not be sold.

Under the new law, the ejido can meet and evenly divide the land among its members. With the ejido's approval, an individual member can sell his or her parcel. A potential problem for the buyer is that though the sale has been approved by the ejido it may not be approved by the government, especially along the coast. It is wise to see a notario to determine if you can get clear title to the property.

Some foreigners who buy from an ejido simply place the title to the property in the name of a Mexican citizen, called a *prestanombre* (borrowed name), usually a trusted friend. The prestanombre is generally paid a fee for this service. Be aware that this arrangement can turn into a disaster. A friend of ours who made such an arrangement is now in court, trying to keep her land.

Building

If you decide to build a house, you will be very pleasantly surprised by the low cost of contruction. Your greatest savings will be in labor costs: The average Mexican laborer earns about $42 a week; a first-class foreman about $200 or more a week. Plumbers and electricians earn more because they charge by the piece. Material costs will be fairly low as long as the dollar remains strong against the peso. These factors help keep building costs in the range of $40 to $60 per square foot in most parts of the country.

Expats who build in Mexico seem to fall into four categories. First are those who have lived in Mexico for some time, speak Spanish, and know the ropes. Often, they hire a crew and run the job themselves, achieving very low costs—as low as $20 to $30 a square foot. Then there are the newcomers who hire a reliable architect and builder to do the work for them. These people pay more, but usually have a relatively hassle-free experience. Next are the newcomers who design a house, hire a *maestro* (foreman) and crew, and begin building. They must use serious oversight and a watchful eye to be certain that materials don't walk away. If the owner has previous building experience and some good luck, this scenario can be satisfying. It is also a great way to learn Spanish and begin to understand the Mexican culture. Finally, there are the newcomers who get ripped off. They find either an unreliable architect who charges big bucks for poor work or a maestro who siphons off materials for his next job or just doesn't do the work.

We hired a Mexican architect/builder to help us renovate our

This couple lives aboard their boat in a Mazatlán marina.

house. She charged us 18 percent over the cost of materials for both designing and building the house. She also passed on discounts from suppliers (we were able to verify this by accompanying her to plumbing and electrical supply houses and lumber yards). The house was completed in record time with relatively few problems. Friends were amazed that we had such a smooth building experience.

Of course, it wasn't always painless. Almost every day, something would cause us to look at each other and say, "unbelievable." It became our daily mantra. Usually, "unbelievable" referred to the total lack of coordination among workers—like when one group putting in the patio was followed by another group digging up the patio to run electrical conduit. Our architect often forgot to order supplies until the last minute. She might call early in the morning, frantic to have us run to the plumbing store to choose a bathtub because the plumber had unexpectedly decided to finish the bathroom that day. Of course, the tub we wanted would be sold out, and ordering one might take two months.

One of the biggest frustrations foreigners have when building is the Mexican sense of time. Carpenters, plumbers, electricians, and others will make appointments for a specific time the next day and often won't show up until hours, sometimes days, later. However, workers who are used to dealing with foreigners are more likely to be on time.

Renting

You can find a house to rent in Mexico much like you would in the States. Check with Realtors, many of whom also manage rental properties. Look through ads in the local newspaper. Look around town for bulletin boards, usually loaded with posters advertising everything from bicycles to boxer shorts. You are sure to find a few houses for rent.

Expect to pay more if you want to live in the most desirable parts of the most popular cities. As you move away from these areas, rental prices drop radically, especially in Mexican neighborhoods.

Unless the house you are renting is out in the sticks, you will have city water and electricity. Trash will most likely be collected daily at a fixed time, and the propane gas truck will come by to fill your tank when needed. The water truck will regularly deliver five-gallon bottles of drinking water. If you want a telephone, make sure the house already has one. In some cities, it can take months to have a phone installed.

The water pressure in your house will be "compliments of gravity," unless you happen to rent one of the few new and very "uptown" houses with a water-pressure tank. These same houses might even have a water purification system. Most amazing of all would be to find a house with central heating.

The Mexican housing scene is changing rapidly. Planned and gated developments are being built all over the country. Some of these developments are surprisingly well designed and constructed. Others are built quickly for the fast buck, with shoddy materials. Beware of the too-good deal.

Working in Mexico

Carol, a 47-year-old friend of ours, moved to San Miguel de Allende four years ago, looking for a new lifestyle. After a year in Mexico she started what has turned out to be a profitable export business. Here is how it happened:

Carol operated a successful graphic-design business in San Francisco for 13 years. Burned out from the stress of deadlines and the demands of corporate clients, she decided she needed a change. Around the same time, she met some people from San Miguel de Allende. She remembered hearing years before that it was an artist community. After trying unsuccessfully to sell her business, she eventually walked away and relocated to San Miguel for a chance to reevaluate her life and have an adventure at the same time.

When she arrived in Mexico, Carol had enough money to relax for a while, but always in her mind was the gnawing realization that she needed to figure out her next money-making move. When friends from San Francisco offered Carol space in an indigenous arts exposition, she saw an opportunity. She began traveling around Mexico, buying antique masks, candlesticks, and *santos* (carvings of saints), which she shipped to San Francisco for the show. Although she sold everything she sent, Carol felt that antiques were difficult to market. She had seen many other items in her travels that she thought would sell better in the United States.

When she returned to San Miguel, Carol decided to begin designing original pieces that could be made locally, in the traditional manner, out of brass, tin, and wood. She began contacting craftspeople, most of whom worked in small backyard shops, to determine which ones would be reliable manufacturers and how much they could produce. She finished a business plan and began talking to friends about investing in her company. She then signed up for booth space in several gift shows in the United States.

Carol nervously attended her first gift show in San Francisco and was delighted to walk away four days later with over $30,000 in orders. She felt like she was levitating. The next two shows were even more successful and netted large orders from stores like Nieman Marcus and Saks Fifth Avenue. She returned to Mexico and began overseeing the manufacture, packing, and shipping of orders. The secret, Carol said, was to stand constant watch over each manufacturer to maintain schedules and quality control. She rented warehouse space and hired a staff to pack and ship orders back to the States.

Carol's business has doubled in sales each year since that first show. She has had to overcome many frustrating problems doing business in Mexico: shipping across the border, language difficulties, finding sharp people to help manage, and trying to keep craftspeople working on schedule. Luckily, she had little if any hindrance from government officials.

Carol is just one of many people we know from the United States who have successfully started small businesses in Mexico. These include restaurants, a natural foods market, Internet service

The U.S. government breaks down the Mexican workforce by industry:

services:	31.7%
agriculture, forestry, hunting, and fishing:	28.0%
commerce:	14.6%
manufacturing:	11.1%
construction:	8.4%
transportation:	4.7%
mining and quarrying:	1.5%

providers and cybercafés, a dress manufacturing company and retail shop, many real estate and development companies, bed-and-breakfasts, insurance businesses, and adventure touring companies.

Working Papers

If you are interested in starting a business or working in Mexico, you can apply for working papers at the same time you apply for an *imigrante* visa. If you become inspired to work after living here a while, you can apply at that time.

To get working papers, you must have an FM3 or FM2 visa. You must submit a letter detailing the type of work you want to do and any licenses or certificates from the United States that may be relevant. These documents will increase your credibility. You will then fill out forms and pay a fee. If you are granted permission to work, the papers will indicate the exact activities permitted. The initial authorization runs for one year.

It is relatively easy to get working papers if your endeavor is unique or if you will be creating employment for Mexicans. But you cannot do a job that will take work away from locals. (We've heard a Mexican joke that the two jobs foreign women can't apply for are waitressing and prostitution!) Recently, foreigners have complained, it is getting more difficult to obtain permission to work. Nevertheless, if the work you want to do meets the criteria, be persistent and you will probably succeed.

After living in Mexico for about 18 months, Barbara decided to begin teaching yoga regularly. For more than 30 years she had been practicing yoga, especially a form called Ashtanga. She could have begun teaching without official working papers—many foreign residents do. But Barbara wanted to advertise and teach in a high-profile downtown location. She risked being exposed to the authorities if she didn't have the proper documents. The result could be a fine and, in rare cases, expulsion from the country.

Barbara assured the authorities that she was the only qualified Ashtanga teacher in town. They asked to see her certification. She explained that certification was not a requirement for teaching yoga

Ken Luboff

A bed-and-breadfast in Cuernavaca—you could open one, too!

in the United States and that many highly qualified teachers were not certified. The immigration authorities asked her to return the next day. She did—with an offering of cookies and letters from several students. The immigration people kindly issued the papers.

Business Taxes

Many foreign residents operate low-profile businesses to earn extra money or fill time. Many who own homes rent out rooms. Others give massages, take tourists on walking tours of town, teach aerobics, or run small export operations. For the most part, these foreigners do not register to pay Mexican taxes. They become part of the "informal economy," along with huge numbers of Mexicans who also work and run businesses illegally.

The numbers are high because starting a business legally in Mexico usually requires hiring an expensive accountant to take you through the complicated process. This process can include over 500 administrative steps, 70 percent of which are requirements of the

Secretaria de Hacienda (Treasury Department). Business owners also remain in the "informal economy" because of high tax rates.

If you're opening a high-profile operation, like a hotel or fancy restaurant, you must obtain a tax number and hire an accountant. He or she will prepare the necessary documents (in at least triplicate—using carbon paper, no less!) and take them to Hacienda to get you a *cedula* number, the equivalent of a tax I.D. number in the United States. The accountant will also tell you whether you'll be reporting your taxes quarterly, semi-annually, or annually, depending on the type of business you're in. Accountants also help organize businesses and create partnerships and corporations. If a particular business situation becomes too complicated, the accountant will refer you to a *notario publico* (like a lawyer), and they will work together to solve your problem.

There are two types of business taxes in Mexico. IVA is a value-added tax that is equivalent to 15 percent of gross receipts. (This is the tax that is added to your hotel tab when you come to Mexico as a tourist.) You can offset IVA by showing that you incurred it while paying a business expense, but only with a special receipt called a *factura*. A normal business receipt is not sufficient, even though it shows that you have paid IVA. Facturas can be obtained only by showing a cedula number, proving that you are a registered business.

The other type of tax is income tax. It is very rarely paid in full by small businesspeople, Mexicans or foreigners, because it rises very quickly from just a few percent to over 50 percent. Most small businesspeople claim only a very small portion of their sales on their income-tax returns. Tax collection in Mexico is a fairly hit-and-miss affair.

Maquiladoras

Small-business owners are not typical of the foreigners doing business in Mexico. Most foreigners run larger operations inspired by the maquiladora program, in place for the last 30 years along the border between Mexico and the United States.

The program started in a relatively small way, allowing the temporary duty-free import of materials into Mexico for production, with the proviso that almost all the products would be exported. Provisions allowed for the importation into Mexico of a small percentage of the production.

Since its inception, the program has grown at a rate of about 20 percent per year and has been modified from time to time. With the passage of NAFTA, the maquiladora law was changed to allow a larger percentage of the production to be sold in Mexico each year; in 2001, the figure will be 100 percent. At the same time, import tariffs are being reduced, making the Mexican market more accessible to U.S. companies. Some companies have moved plants from Asia to Mexico to take advantage of such changes.

If you are hired by a maquiladora to work in Mexico, you will need an FM3 working visa and temporary residency visas for your family. Visa applications are generally filed by the company and are easily obtained.

A bustling street in Puerto Vallarta filled with delivery trucks and businesses

Labor Force

Many Americans hang onto the stereotype of the Mexican who sits by the side of the road all day wearing a four-foot sombrero. They think of Mexicans as lazy, willing to put anything off until *manana*. This stereotype is not true today—and may never have been true.

Mexicans are hard workers. Many have large families and must work for low wages at a time of high inflation. It is difficult for many to make ends meet, and often the whole family works. It is not unusual to see a room of a family home turned into a shop for selling shoes, clothing, or food. Nor is it unusual to see kids running the store while their parents are out working. Small family enterprises are forever opening, some of them very strange. Stores might sell weird combinations, such as stuffed animals and liquor, Tupperware and jewelry, and shoes along with groceries. As you can imagine, many don't last very long.

Mexico's labor force was estimated by the U.S. government to total 36.3 million in November 1996. About two-thirds are unskilled workers. At least another 6 to 8 million work in the underground economy at low-skill jobs. Many are kids or older people. Foreigners considering starting a business in Mexico will find an abundance of young workers (nearly 30 percent of the population is between the

INDUSTRIES TO WATCH

- In 1997 Mexico produced 114 million liters of tequila, more than half of which was shipped to the United States.
- In 1997 Mexico exported more than 21 million pairs of shoes to the United States, with another 5 million going to South America and Europe. Mexicans bought about 80 million pairs.
- According to the Gold Institute in Washington, D.C., Mexico is a leader in a new Latin American gold rush. It produced 10,194 metric tons in 1987 and 29,488 metric tons in 1997 and is predicted to produce more than 41,375 metric tons in 2001.

ages of 15 and 29) available for low wages. They are adaptable, skillful, and energetic.

Depending on the job, salaries can range from $35 per week for a full-time maid or laborer to $250 or more per week for a construction *maestro* (foreman)—much more for a skilled plant worker. The average minimum wage in Mexico is 32 pesos per day—about $3.20.

It is important to realize that if you legally hire a worker for the long run, you will have obligations to that worker. By law, you will pay him or her for 14 vacation days at Christmas and at least seven other national holidays. After the first year, the worker will receive paid vacation time. You will pay social security (IMSS) benefits and high severance pay if the worker is fired without cause. You may also have some unexpected social obligations, like paying for, or at least taking part in, the worker's wedding and other family events. You might even be asked to give the bride away!

Volunteer Work

Every "retired" person we have met in Mexico is completely involved in a variety of activities. They might be learning to paint, speak Spanish, or play the piano. They might be off playing golf, fishing, or writing their memoirs.

Many people take great pleasure in doing community service. Mexico is in need of all the help it can get on so many levels. Volunteer organizations throughout the country do everything from feeding and clothing the poor to solving environmental problems. Volunteering is an easy way to get involved in a worthwhile project, meet new people, and feel good about yourself.

Planning Your First Trip

If you are intrigued by the idea of retiring in Mexico and have never been here, it is time to plan your first trip. Visiting any one area of the country is a breeze, but if you want to see it all, you face a great challenge. Mexico is a large country with a culturally diverse population and geographical extremes. Although all Mexicans speak the same language, people in different parts of the country have different accents, customs, and cuisines. Rather than trying to experience the entire country on the first trip, it is better to sample the representative parts where most expatriates have settled.

If your fantasy is to live on a palm-studded, semitropical beach, you can fly into Puerto Vallarta, rent a car, and drive up the coast to Mazatlán or down to Manzanillo. You can fly into Cancún and explore what is now being called the Mayan Riviera or visit any one of the other fabulous beaches in the country. Somewhere along the way you might just unpack your bags and set up housekeeping. If you are attracted to a more European ambiance, you can fly directly into the Leon, Guanajuato, airport, rent a car or get on a bus, and begin exploring San Miguel de Allende, Guanajuato, Morelia, Zacatecas, and the entire area of colonial Mexico.

Spend as much time as you can in the cities that make you feel most at home. Amble through the streets to get an idea of what it would be like to live there. Most importantly, be open to talking with local people, both foreign and Mexican, anywhere you can. Many Mexicans speak some English and will graciously answer any politely asked questions. Ask foreign residents what attracts them to the town, where they shop, what kinds of foods and supplies are available, what they do for entertainment, and how much they spend each month. Most people enjoy talking about the town they live in. A good way to make contact with foreigners is to stop by the local Internet provider. Almost every expatriate we know has e-mail service to stay in touch with kids and friends back home.

When you arrive in town, buy a copy of the local English-language newspaper. It will offer insights into the character (and characters) of the town. A scan of the activity, social, and real estate sections should give you a pretty good idea of the cost of living there. If you have time, hire a car and driver (or rent a car) and explore the nearby villages.

The following is an eight-day, seven-night whirlwind itinerary that will introduce you to some of the most beautiful areas of Mexico. These also happen to be some of the main retirement areas of the country. This itinerary does not give you enough time to get to know each place in any depth, however. If you can double or even triple the length of your trip, we strongly recommend that you do so. Or you can adjust the itinerary to give yourself more time in one location (say, the coast) than in another. Stay flexible.

TOURIST MECCA

An estimated 25 million tourists vacationed in Mexico in 1998, 90 percent of them from the United States. This was a 14 percent increase over 1996 and represented $8.5 billion in revenue (surpassing revenue from the export of oil). At the same time, Mexicans spend about $4 billion a year traveling abroad.

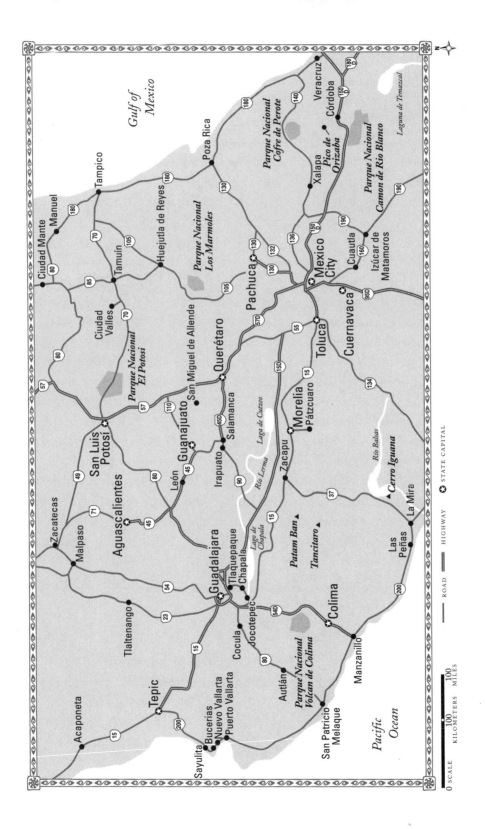

Do not plan everything down to the minute. Don't worry, you will always find a hotel, spa, or B&B for the night.

Before leaving, read as many books about traveling and living in Mexico as you can (see the recommended reading list in the appendix) and read the chapters in this book devoted to each of the cities on the itinerary.

Suggested Itinerary

Day 1: Fly into Puerto Vallarta as early in the day as possible. Explore the city that evening.

Day 2: Explore Puerto Vallarta, then head north and visit the nearby towns of Nueva Vallarta, Bucerias, Punta de Mita, and Sayulita.

Day 3: Drive (four hours) or take a bus (six hours) to Ajijic on Lake Chapala. Those in a hurry can fly from Puerto Vallarta to Guadalajara in about 45 minutes and be in Ajijic 45 minutes later.

Day 4: Explore Ajijic, Chapala, and as many of the other lakeside villages as possible.

Day 5: Drive (four hours) or bus (six hours) to San Miguel de Allende. Or fly from Guadalajara to Leon, Guanajuato, in 45 minutes. A taxi from the airport to San Miguel takes an hour and a half and costs about $50. Explore San Miguel that evening.

Day 6: Explore San Miguel and, if there is time, Guanajuato.

Day 7: Return to Guadalajara by car, bus, or plane. Spend the rest of the day seeing sights in Guadalajara and Tlaquepaque.

Day 8: Fly home from Guadalajara.

Optional

Day 7: Take the bus from San Miguel to Mexico City (three and a half hours). You will arrive at the Terminal de Autobuses Norte. From there take a taxi (buy your taxi ticket in the station) to the Terminal de Autobuses Sur. From there, take a bus to Cuernavaca, one hour away. Several bus lines have service to Cuernavaca.

Day 8:   Explore Cuernavaca.

Day 9:   Return to Mexico City by bus, van, or taxi and fly home.

If this itinerary makes your head spin a little, you're not alone. We got dizzy just writing it. But don't worry. The distances are not that great, and you will have time to do it all. The schedule gives you a chance to see a coastal city, Puerto Vallarta; an inland village and former artist colony, Ajijic; a colonial town, San Miguel de Allende; and Mexico's second largest city, Guadalajara. Add Cuernavaca to see an elegant and beautiful garden city. Adjust the itinerary to fit your pocketbook and travel schedule. You can save money by flying both in and out of Puerto Vallarta. Renting a car to drive from city to city will give you the most flexibility and the best view of the countryside. Traveling by first-class bus is very comfortable and relatively inexpensive, and you can meet and talk with more people along the way.

Ken Luboff

Your first trip to Mexico should include a variety of locations, including beaches such as this one in Puerto Vallarta.

If you have unlimited time and enjoy driving, driving to Mexico from the States will give you an interesting cultural experience. You will be challenged to deal with everyday activities like buying gas, ordering meals in Spanish, changing money, and navigating the Mexican highway system.

Speaking of which: Avoid driving in or around Mexico City. Mexico City is one of the most beautiful and sophisticated cities in the world. It is blessed with fantastic museums, restaurants, musical events, architecture, and areas of natural beauty. Unfortunately, it is also plagued by crime, traffic jams, and very poor air quality. Unscrupulous Mexican traffic cops (known as sharks) lie in wait to pounce on drivers, both Mexican and foreign, and hit them up for *mordita* (see Chapter 5: "Money Matters"). Once you move to Mexico, you will learn a few tricks from old hands that will help you enjoy visiting the city. For instance, during Christmas and Easter, when many Mexicans are on vacation at the beaches, the city is quieter and less polluted. Conversely, these are times to avoid crowded tourist towns.

Tour Groups

If you prefer to travel with a group, look into one of the many organized tours to Mexico. A good source of information is the *People's Guide Travel Newsletter*, P.O. Box 179, Acme, WA 98220-0179, e-mail: mexico@peoplesguide.com. You'll find tours to colonial towns, beach resorts. Real estate tours can help you scout out housing options.

South of the Border Tour & Travel, 40 Fourth St. Suite 203, Petaluma, CA 94592, 707/765-4573, publishes the quarterly newsletter *Retire in Mexico*. Moore Diversified Services, 3001 Halloran St. Suite C, Fort Worth, TX 76107, 817/731-4266, is another source of information.

The Internet is another place to look. Here are a few choices:
• Mexico Travel Link, 604/454-9044; info@mexicotravel.net
• Majestic Mexico Tours, 888/949-9399; www.infosma.com
• Tour By Mexico, tourbymx@netgate.net; www.tourbymexico.com

Clothing and Supplies

Pack lightly for your first trip to investigate Mexico, especially if you are flying or plan to take buses. Except for a night at the opera or a fancy dinner party, Mexicans and foreigners living in Mexico normally dress very casually. The only exceptions are Mexican businessmen and executives in the larger cities. You can easily have clothes washed. Most hotels have laundry service or can point you in the direction of a nearby Laundromat.

Be aware of Mexican sensibilities. Women should avoid going braless and wearing see-through tops. Wear short-shorts only at beach resorts. These days, some Mexican men have taken to wearing short pants in hot climates, but they are still very much in the minority. Most Mexicans are poor and dress in whatever clothes are available, although middle-class Mexican kids often dress like they are about to shoot an Armani commercial.

For travel to Puerto Vallarta or any of the other coastal towns, pack lightweight clothing. When we go to the coast, I always bring my favorite Hawaiian shirt, cotton slacks, shorts, a swimsuit, lots of T-shirts, and a cool hat. Barbara brings a light cotton dress or two, cotton slacks, and her own version of a Hawaiian shirt. We both pack sandals and bring light sweaters or jackets for cooler evenings, especially in winter.

Inland, even in summer, it can be cool at night almost anywhere in the country, so a light sweater is a necessity. If you are traveling to San Miguel de Allende or another a high-elevation town in winter, be prepared for warm days in the low 70s and very cool nights with temperatures sometimes dropping into the mid-30s. In April and May, temperatures in these towns can reach into the 90s during the day. Wherever you are going, you will need good walking shoes and a hat (you might want to wait and buy a good-looking Mexican sombrero).

Name-brand toiletries are sold almost everywhere. Revlon and other well-known brands of cosmetics are available in larger cities and tourist areas. If you run out, don't worry. Mexican-made cosmetics are sold everywhere; many are high quality and very inexpensive.

People who need special medications will want to pack enough for the entire trip. Many medications available in the United States are not sold in Mexico, but substitutions can usually be found. "Officially," prescriptions are required for narcotic painkillers, sleeping pills, and the like, though some pharmacies sell restricted medications without a prescription. Antibiotics and stomach remedies can easily be bought without a prescription. Pharmacists can also recommend a nearby doctor who speaks some English.

To stay healthy on this trip, take the same precautions you would while traveling in the States. If you are walking around on a hot sunny day, wear a hat and use sun block. While Mexican food, drink, and ice cubes, especially in tourist areas, are entirely safe, we recommend that you wash your hands at every opportunity. It helps to pack a bottle of antibacterial hand cream.

When Barbara and I travel, we always pack a light pair of binoculars to view distant sights and Mexico's exceptionally diverse bird population (Mexico is a birder's paradise). We also throw in our swimming goggles and diving masks. Flippers, which we love to use, are just too heavy, unless we are driving. We usually rent them instead.

If you don't speak Spanish, bring along a small dictionary. If you are planning to shop (which is almost impossible to resist), pack a lightweight empty luggage bag, which you can fill to the brim.

Money

We recommend that you bring a modest supply of traveler's checks and some U.S. dollars for emergency situations, but you should get most of your traveling money from ATMs, which take most U.S. credit and debit cards. They give a better exchange rate than banks or money changers and save you from having to carry too much cash. From time to time, these machines run out of money, thus you should have some back-up cash. Note that once you are out in the sticks, finding an ATM is as easy as finding a rabbi.

When traveling around Mexico, I carry enough pesos in my pocket for just one day. I hide extra cash somewhere else on my body or in my car. That way, if I get my pocket picked, it won't hurt too much (by the way, this has never happened to me). Most travel writers recommend using money belts to hide cash, traveler's checks, and passports. But I have the feeling these writers never got a chapped chest or waist from wearing a money belt on a hot day, to say nothing of the hassle of reaching into one without looking a little like a pervert. When you stay at hotels, make use of the hotel safe deposit box.

Most Mexicans are very honest people who will call you back or chase after you to return change that you forgot in their shop. But take normal precautions against thieves. Leave valuables in a safe place when you go out walking or carry them in a fanny pack or a tightly held handbag. Be aware that pickpockets, as in all countries, love operating in large crowds, at parades, and at other public events. Don't leave baggage lying in full view in a parked car on a street overnight, and don't flaunt large rolls of cash. These days, theft seems to be prevalent in Mexico City, but cities like San Miguel de Allende, Ajijic, and Puerto Vallarta, as well as the countryside, are still fairly crime free.

You'll do some of your best bargaining from the comfort of a beach chair, margarita in hand.

By now you surely know that the currency in Mexico is the peso. Bills come in denominations of 20, 50, 100, 200, and 500 pesos. Coins range from 10 centavos to 10 pesos. They are all different sizes, although the one- and two-peso coins are close in size and often confused, even by Mexicans. Occasionally, you may see N$ written before a price. This is an archaic symbol referring to the "new peso," which came into existence several devaluations ago. These days, pesos are written with a single-bar dollar sign before the number. For the exchange rate, check your nearest big-city newspaper or call a large bank.

Bargaining

In most shops in Mexico, prices are fixed and bargaining is a thing of the past. But look for an outdoor arts and crafts market, called a *tianguis*, where bargaining is still accepted and expected. Almost all Mexican towns have a market day, on which farmers and craftspeople from surrounding towns come together to sell their wares. On this day, you can hone your haggling skills and walk away with all sorts of bargins.

You'll do some of your best bargaining from the comfort of a beach chair, with a margarita in hand. A constant flow of beach peddlers move from tourist to tourist all day long, hustling jewelry, wood carvings, rugs, T-shirts, and clothing. Bargaining is so expected that if you said yes to the first price given, the salesperson would probably faint from shock. We have gotten some wonderful items at great prices on the beach. Bargaining can be a lot of fun, but also quite time-consuming. But, who cares!

Rental Cars

One-way rental cars are very expensive, so fly in and out of the same airport if you can. If you have the time and money, driving, in our opinion, is far and away the best way to see Mexico (it may actually be less expensive than flying around the country).

Most U.S. rental car companies operate in Mexico. It is a good idea to reserve a car in advance, especially if you will be traveling during a holiday (including Mexican holidays). Here are a few numbers to call to reserve a car:

Avis, 800/331-1084
Budget, 800/472-3325
Dollar, 800/800-4000
National, 800/227-3876

A Few Hotels

Every city in Mexico has a vast number and variety of hotels from expensive and elegant, to inexpensive and nice, right on down to bare-bones dumps. The following is a short list of hotels. For more extensive listings check with AAA, the Internet, or one of the many Mexico guidebooks.

Real estate agents are a great source of information about Mexican towns. Of course, their opinions will be at least a little sugar coated. Here is a list of a few real estate agents in each of the retirement towns covered in Chapters 13 through 18.

Ajijic

Laguna Axixic Realty, tel. (376) 6-1174 or (376) 6-1186, fax (376) 6-1188, e-mail laguna@laguna.com.mx, Web site http://southmex.com/laguna/realestate.html

Ajijic Realty, tel. (376) 6-2077, fax (376) 6-23-31, e-mail ajijic@infosel.net.mx, Web site www.ajijic.com

Eager & Associates, tel. (376) 6-1917 or (376) 6-1918

Chapala Realty, tel. (376) 5-2877, fax (376) 5-3528, e-mail chapala@infosel.net.mx, Web site www.chapala.com

Cabo San Lucas

Land's End Properties, tel. (114) 3-3748 or (114) 3-4168

Paradise Development, tel. (114) 3-0552

Cuernavaca

Century 21 CuernaMax, tel. (73) 22-5252 or (73) 22-4981

Esquerro & Associates, tel. (73) 26-0128 or (73) 24-1003

Guadalajara

Continental Century 21, tel. (3) 122-4580

Lloyd Investments and Real Estate, tel. (3) 647-5047 or (3) 647-5056

Guanajuato

Carlos Ordaz Chico, tel. (473) 2-1222

Manzanillo

Real Estate Lomelin, tel. (333) 4-0340

Mazatlán

Pacific Properties, tel. (69) 13-0117 or (69) 13-4411

Riviera Pacifico, tel. (69) 14-5323 or (69) 14-4001, fax (69) 14-5328, e-mail realtytour@acnet.net, Web site www.realtymex.com.mx

Dulce Vida Real Estate, tel. (69) 13-9804, e-mail
dinom@red2000.com.mx

Oaxaca

Century 21 Grupo, tel. (951) 6-0323, (951) 6-0347, or
(951) 6-0367

Bienes Raices Arlette Escobar Olie, tel. (951) 5-4737

Inmobiliaria Propiedades Productivas, tel. (951) 3-0180

Pátzcuaro

Century 21 Rodriguez Voirol, tel. (43) 14-9800 or (43) 14-2381

Puerto Vallarta

Puerto Vallarta Real Estate, tel. (322) 2-4288, fax (322) 2-4287,
e-mail pvrealty@tag.acnet.net

Brock Squire and Associates, tel. (322) 3-0005, e-mail
bsa@brock-squire.com, Web site www.brock-squire.com

Applegate Realtors, tel. (322) 1-5434, e-mail applegate@
applerealtors.com, Web site www.applerealtors.com

Bill Taylor Real Estate, tel. (322) 4-6900, fax (322) 4-8203

San Carlos Bay

Snowbird Realty, tel. (622) 6-0551

Star Realty, tel. (622) 6-0000, e-mail starreal@tetakawi.net.mx

Sunshine Realty, tel. (622) 6-0980

San Miguel de Allende

Real Estate San Miguel, tel. (415) 2-2284, (415) 2-6510, fax
(415) 2-7377, e-mail resmig@unisono.net.mx, Web site
www.unisono.net.mx/realestatesm

Zavala Garay, tel. (415) 2-5389, e-mail
zavalag@unisono.net.mx, Web site www.unisono.net.mx/
zavgar/zavgar.html

Dotty Vidargas Real Estate, tel. (415) 2-0286 or (415) 2-6382,
fax (415) 2-2347, e-mail Vidargas@unisono.net.mx

Re/Max, tel. (415) 2-7363 or (415) 2-7365, e-mail
mail@realestate-sma.com

Cabo San Lucas

Cabo San Lucas, tel. (114) 3-0123, is a huge resort that includes five pools, wonderful snorkling beaches, a marina, restaurants—the works! **Hacienda**, tel. (114) 3-0666, is a beautiful mission-style hotel. **Finisterra**, (114) 3-0590, is set on a hill with great views of both the Pacific Ocean and the gulf.

Cuernavaca

Suites Paraiso, tel. (73) 13-3665, is an inexpensive hotel with clean, adequate rooms set in a lovely garden. **Las Mananitas**, tel. (73) 14-1466, is one of the most desired and beautiful small hotels in Cuernavaca. Book early for this one. **Las Campanas de San Jeronimo**, tel. (73) 13-9494, is an unusual bed-and-breakfast set in gorgeous grounds. The staff can connect guests with art, writing, music, and cooking classes.

Guadalajara

Hotel San Francisco Plaza, tel. (3) 613-8954 or (3) 613-3256, fax (3) 613-3257, is a pretty colonial hotel in downtown. **Camino Real**, tel. (3) 121-8000, fax (3) 121-8070, is more a fancy country-club resort than a hotel. It has four pools, a putting green, gym, tennis courts—you get the picture. **Hotel de Mendoza**, tel. (3) 613-4646, is a former convent with very nice rooms.

Guanajuato

La Casa de Espiritus Alegres (House of the Happy Spirits), tel. (473) 3-1013, is a small bed-and-breakfast. Each room is colorfully decorated with a different motif. **Posada Santa Fe**, tel. (473) 2-0084, is a colonial building located on a romantic square with outdoor restaurants and strolling musicians. **Real de Minas**, tel. (473) 2-1460, is the largest hotel in town, with a pool, restaurant, tennis courts, a nightclub, and all the trimmings.

Lake Chapala

La Nueva Posada, tel./fax. (376) 6-1444, has Old World charm, even though it is a fairly new. The rooms are large and comfortable.

It has a very nice restaurant with outside seating in a garden over-looking the lake.

Ajijic B&B, tel. (376) 6-2377, fax (376) 6-2331, is located half a block from the plaza. It is fairly new and attractive. **Real de Chapala,** tel. 800/522-0457 in the United States, (376) 6-0007 in Mexico, fax (376) 6-0025, has large rooms and beautiful grounds. Located right on the lake, this is a very comfortable place to stay in Ajijic.

Inn of the Plumed Serpent, tel. (376) 5-3653, fax (376) 5-3444, e-mail qq_rlh@hotmail.com, is a unique bed-and-breakfast in Chapala. It is expensive, but worth visiting. Each suite is a completely a different work of art, and the gardens are breathtaking. D. H. Lawrence lived and wrote his novel *The Plumed Serpent* here.

Laguna Bed & Brunch, tel. (376) 6-1174, fax (376) 6-1188, e-mail 104164.2603@compuserve.com, is located about a block and a half from the plaza. It is reasonably priced, has offstreet parking, and serves a good breakfast.

Ken Luboff

Walking down the streets of any town you visit (such as Cuernavaca) will give you a feeling for the life of the place.

Manzanillo

Las Hadas, tel. (333) 4-000, is a spectacular Moorish style "city." Whether or not you stay there, it is worth the trip just to see it. **Club Santiago**, tel. 303/841-7099 in the United States, (333) 3-0413 in Mexico, is part of a large complex including private homes, tennis courts, restaurants, pools, and a great beach. **Hotel Villas La Audiencia**, tel. (333) 3-0861, has nice rooms overlooking a beautiful small beach, and check out **Hotel Miramar**, tel (333) 2-1008, if you prefer to stay in town.

Mazatlán

Fiesta Inn, tel. (69) 89-0100, offers nice rooms overlooking the beach at reasonable prices. **Pueblo Bonito**, tel. (69) 456-8008 or (69) 14-3700, offers large rooms and suites on the beach. **Camino Real**, tel. (69) 13-1111, is a deluxe hotel with all the trimmings.

Oaxaca

Hotel Victoria, tel. (951) 5-2633, is located on a hill overlooking the city. It has nice gardens, a pool, and tennis courts. **Camino Real**, tel. (951) 6-0611, is a luxury hotel with all the frills, located in a former convent. **Hostal de La Noria**, tel. (951) 4-7844, is located in a colorfully and beautifully decorated colonial building.

Puerto Vallarta

Camino Real, tel. (322) 1-5000, is a beautiful high-end, high-rise resort hotel. **Hotel Molino de Agua**, tel. (322) 2-1907 or (322) 2-1957, is a nice downtown hotel. **Krystal Vallarta**, tel. (322) 4-0202, is a deluxe low-rise hotel. It offers individual rooms in a garden setting. **Hotel Rosita**, tel. (333) 2-0941, was one of the first hotels in Vallarta and is still popular.

San Carlos

San Carlos Plaza, tel. (622) 7-0077, is a clean, mid-range hotel with a pool and cable TV. **Howard Johnson Plaza Hotel & Resort**, tel. (622) 6-0777, overlooks the sea and offers all the amenities. **Posada**

de San Carlos, tel. (622) 6-0015, is not far from the San Carlos country club.

San Miguel de Allende

Pasada de Las Monjas, tel. (415) 2-0171, is probably the nicest inexpensive hotel in San Miguel. Casa Carmen, tel. (415) 2-0844, is more a pension than a hotel. It is small and charming. La Puertacita Boutique Hotel, tel. (800) 336-6776, (415) 2-5011, or (415) 2-2250, is small and very pretty, with beautiful grounds. Casa Luna B&B, tel. (415) 2-1117, is a small bed-and-breakfast with wonderfully and uniquely decorated rooms.

Lake Chapala Area

In this chapter and the five that follow, we profile the principal retirement locations in Mexico; U.S. escapees retiring to Mexico are most likely to land in one of these areas. Although each city has a relatively large group of foreign residents, proportionally they make up a small minority of the total population. Have no doubt that each city is very Mexican in its nature.

We begin with Lake Chapala, Mexico's largest lake and the center of one of the most strikingly beautiful areas in the country. The lake is over 75 miles long and averages 18 miles in width. It is surrounded by mountains, giving the villages along its shores a sense of remoteness that belies their proximity to Guadalajara, Mexico's second largest city. Looking at the lake's rugged coastline from one of the surrounding hills, Barbara and I felt like we had somehow been beamed up to the northern California coast.

With the exception of Chapala, the villages on the north side of the lake (where the majority of foreign residents live) are quaint and tranquil, with the mellow feeling of old, well-established European mountain resort towns. Each has its own unique character, especially Ajijic (Ah-hee-heek) and smaller villages like El Chante, San Juan

Cosala, La Floresta, and Chula Vista. Chapala is larger and more commercial, but it has sections that retain an Old World charm.

Along the narrow streets of the older parts of these villages, you'll see a remarkable variety of colorful flowers and trees. Multicolored bougainvilleas, the laden limbs of giant mango trees, and flowering vines accent old stone walls. Behind them are homes with lush gardens and pools. Inside the modest front gate of an area B&B, typical of many private homes, we entered a huge garden with trees and flower-lined paths meandering through a verdant lawn. The garden rivaled city parks in some towns in the States. As you can imagine, the house was also spectacular. On the hills overlooking the lakeside towns are newer homes, many in gated developments. Most of these homes offer views across the lake to the layered mountains in the distance.

Lakeside residents are also blessed by the area's nearly perfect climate, with a year-round high temperature averaging 77.4 degrees Fahrenheit, lows averaging 58.3 degrees, and average rainfall of 31.9 inches. The coldest months are December and January; the hottest and driest are April and May—before the start of the rainy season. There is little humidity, probably due to the lake's relatively high altitude of 5,200 feet. But there's enough so that when we visit Ajijic, Barbara does not have to slather on copious amounts of body lotion the way she does in most other high-dry locales.

Another obvious attraction is the lake's proximity to Guadalajara, a city of 5 million people. Just 45 minutes away, Guadalajara offers big-city energy and sophistication in direct contrast to the laid-back life in towns along the lake. Villagers head into Guadalajara when they need a big-city hit, for first-class medical care, or to do some serious shopping. But Guadalajara's proximity is also a disadvantage on weekends, when thousands of Guadalajarans crowd lakeside villages and create traffic jams on the lakeside's only highway.

On the road south of Guadalajara, about halfway to the lake, is the Miguel Hidalgo International Airport, providing dozens of flights each day to airports in the States and elsewhere. With the completion of an *autopisto* to the west of the lake, drivers can reach Puerto Vallarta and other Pacific beaches in only three and a half hours (it used to take six to eight).

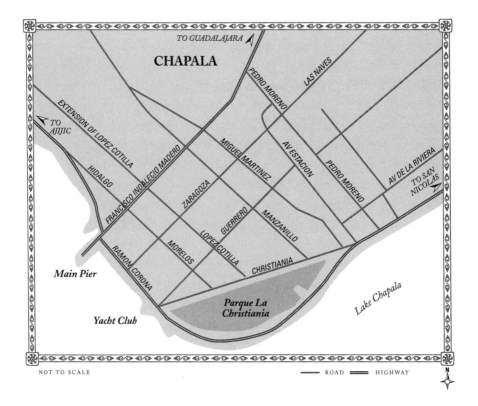

NOT TO SCALE   ▬▬ ROAD ▭▭ HIGHWAY

The villages along the lake are fairly calm, with few activities (a movie theater is planned), which may turn some people off. The sense of tranquillity is created in part by the dearth of young people. There are no universities or language or art schools to attract youth. The majority of expatriate residents are in their sixties or older. We asked about crime and were told that burglaries in homes and cars have increased over the last few years, with an occasional mugging.

History

Historians argue that Chapala may have been a pre-Hispanic village, settled by Nahuatl Indians sometime before the 12th century A.D. What is known is that a tribe called the Cocas settled for a while near the site of the town of San Juan Cosala.

In 1524, five years after Hernan Cortés landed in Mexico,

Spanish soldiers and priests entered the area. The town of Chapala was officially founded in 1538. For the next three centuries the area was inhabited mainly by Indians and Franciscan missionaries.

In the years of Mexico's fight for independence from Spain, Mezcala Island, one of two islands in the lake, served as the base for a band of insurgents, who held out against repeated attacks from the royalist army. Several structures built by the insurgents stand today and can be visited by taking a boat to the island.

It was not until the end of the nineteenth century that Mexicans began living near the lake. At the turn of the century, a parish priest described Chapala as a small fisherman's village with neoclassical Mediterranean-style summer residences. Nineteenth-century buildings remaining include the Arzapalo Hotel, the Casa Braniff (now the Cazadores Restaurant), the old Hotel Palmera, and Hotel Niza, now the Hotel Nido. The Town Hall (Palacio Municipal) and the old railroad station were built between 1913 and 1930.

The railroad connecting Chapala with Guadalajara and then Mexico City enabled Guadalajara's high society to spend weekends and the Easter and Christmas holidays at the lake. The trip from Guadalajara by rail took only three hours, as opposed to 12 hours by stagecoach.

Foreigners have been coming to the lake for a hundred years; some of the most famous include D. H. Lawrence and W. Somerset Maugham. The first large wave of expatriates from the United States arrived in the 1950s and early 1960s, in the form of young artistic men and women. The area soon developed a reputation as an art colony. During the 1970s, there was a large influx of retired military people to the area, especially to the town of Chapala.

How to Get There

We hear that the best connections into the Guadalajara's Miguel Hidalgo International Airport are with Continental and American Airlines, though it is probably worthwhile checking with Mexicana, Aeromexico, Taesa, and Delta. The airport is located roughly

Ken Luboff

Art galleries line this Ajijic street.

halfway between downtown Guadalajara and Lake Chapala. The trip to Lake Chapala takes only 25 minutes on a four-lane highway. The taxi fare is about 120 pesos ($13).

The drive to Lake Chapala from the States can be very beautiful, depending on the route you choose and the time of year. From the east Texas border towns of Eagle Pass, Laredo, and Brownsville, the trip is about 700 miles and takes two days (with an early start). The first night you can usually make it to Zacatecas, a friendly and pretty colonial town with silver jewelry and other crafts for sale.

From the El Paso area, you'll drive about 1,000 miles, on a route that also takes you through Zacatecas, but you won't make it there the first night. From Nogales, south of Tucson, it's about 1,050 miles to Lake Chapala. From Mexicali, south of San Diego, it's about 1,300 miles. From both of these starting points, it is a straight shot down Mexico's west coast Highway 15. We do not recommend the road from the coast to Durango. It is known as the Devil's Spine, and unless you have time and enjoy driving on twisting mountain roads, it can be tedious. If you do have the time, it is a very beautiful drive.

If you decide to travel by bus, be sure to take a *lujo*, or luxury-class bus, or at least first class (*primera clase*). At the Guadalajara bus station, you'll switch to a Chapala or Ajijic bus—about an hour's ride.

By train, the two best options are the El Regiomontano, which travels from Nuevo Laredo to Mexico City, where you then switch for Guadalajara, and the Pacifico Line on the west coast. Starting in Mexicali on the U.S. border, it travels through Nogales, Mazatlán, Tepic, and eventually on to Guadalajara. For these long and somewhat grueling trips, you'd better have a love affair with trains. If you decide to travel this way, check first that the trains are still running and buy a first-class ticket.

The Foreign Community

About 100,000 people live along the shores of Lake Chapala. Included among them are about 3,000 to 6,000 permanent foreign residents. Most are from the United States, with a growing number of Canadians and a few Europeans. The numbers more or less double during winter with the influx of snowbirds escaping cold weather to the north.

Many of the area's early expatriates—those who arrived in the 1960s and 70s—still live in the lakeside communities, bringing the average age of foreign residents to about 65. But this average is beginning to drop, with a new and younger generation of retirees who have discovered the area. These days, an equal number of people from the United States and Canada are moving in—many in their fifties and some younger with small children.

Foreigners have been visiting and moving to the lake for so many years that they have become an integral part of the community. Foreign residents feel a sense of acceptance, and interaction with the local population is friendly and polite.

Some foreign residents choose to keep themselves apart, however. They do not learn the language and separate themselves from the richness of the Mexican culture. This sad trend will probably increase as more foreign newcomers move into gated developments.

Real Estate

Almost all of the foreigners live on Lake Chapala's north shore, between the towns of Chapala and Jocotepec, 15 miles to the west. The largest concentrations are in Ajijic and Chapala. Located about halfway between Chapala and Jocotepec, Ajijic is the most expensive town in which to buy a house. Surrounding towns, many of which are just as beautiful, can cost as much as 50 percent less. In general, a house on the lake—if you can find one—will cost more than one in town. Houses on the hills are also expensive, but not as high as a lakeside property.

For the last few years, gated real estate developments have been springing up like weeds here. So far, they have not greatly damaged the "Old Mexico" look and feel of the area, but parts of the north shore villages could soon start looking like a U.S. suburb.

An enjoyable way to see the variety of homes in the area is to sign up for the weekly home tour, which operates every Thursday from November through April. You can buy tickets at the Nueva Posada Hotel in Ajijic.

Ajijic

Because of its beauty and history as an art colony, Ajijic is the most popular town among foreign residents. Its name derives from a spring called Eye of the Water, found at the foot of the mountains that slope gently uphill from the lake.

The town itself is divided in two by the highway from Jocotepec to Chapala. The part of town above the road is called, appropriately, Upper Ajijic. Below is the Village of Ajijic. The distance from the lakefront to the road is about five long blocks (at some points four), an easy uphill walk. The upper part of town climbs more steeply into the hills for another four or five blocks. The town itself is about one mile long from end to end.

Many newcomers want to live within walking distance of Ajijic plaza. This desire is understandable because of the quaint atmosphere of downtown. But keep in mind that this part of town is also the noisiest, with frequent festivals, church bells, rooster calls, and the clop of horses' hooves along the narrow streets (not to mention cars and trucks).

Houses in this area, when they can be found, can be expensive in comparison to those in other towns along the lake. For instance, a three-bedroom house with a nice big garden can sell for $200,000 to $300,000. For houses directly on the lake, be prepared to spend much more.

One recently advertised house on the lake was described as an "architectural masterpiece with an oasis garden, two terraces, a Jacuzzi, multimedia room, four bedrooms, skylights throughout, a guest house, and a six-car garage on a large lot." The asking price was $449,000. This type of house comes on the market only rarely.

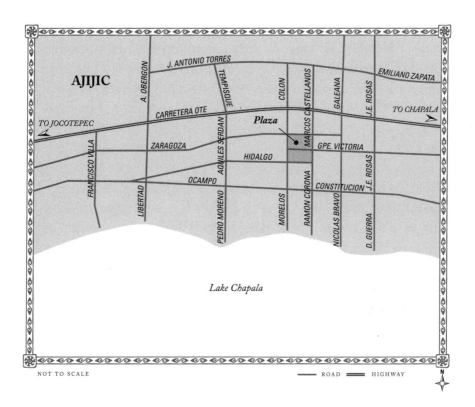

Fairly large two- and three-bedroom houses in upper Ajijic, with great views and wonderful gardens, come onto the market between $85,000 and $180,000. One new two-bedroom, two-bathroom house, completely furnished with cable TV, a two-car garage, and a garden was recently advertised for $165,000.

Chapala

Though it is home to a large number of foreigners, many of them retired military people, Chapala is very much a Mexican town. It is particularly attractive because it mixes the qualities of a small, quiet village with those of an old-fashioned, seaside resort. As the closest town on the lake to Guadalajara, it receives more weekend visitors and offers more diverse activities than the other lakeside villages.

Housing is inexpensive here, making the town attractive to retirees on small pensions. Recently, a fixer-upper—three bedrooms, two bathrooms with carport—was selling for $37,500. A three-bedroom, two-bathroom apartment with off-street parking listed at $39,000. A house with mountain/lake views, two miles outside Chapala, was recently advertised for $35,000. A large three-bedroom, two-bathroom house on a hill was selling for $129,000. This is not to say that all homes in Chapala are inexpensive. The range of prices goes from $35,000 all the way up to $500,000.

Other Lakeside Villages

San Antonio, San Juan Cosala, Jocotepec, and other lakeside villages all have a unique look and feel. While some consider Ajijic the most picturesque, the other villages have appealing characteristics of their own. La Floresta, for instance, has wide tree-lined streets, with large houses set back behind old stone walls. Parts of it feel like some of the better residential areas of Houston. San Antonio has narrow, active streets, with houses set close together behind walls and gates. It has a small, very pretty plaza. Jocotepec, at the end of the lake, is a busy crossroads with a large, active downtown. Artists have settled in the hills above town, which offer wonderful views of the lake and mountains. El Chante, on the lake before Jocotepec, is an old Mexican village, quiet and a little funky. Along the lakefront are large houses set among grand trees, giving the village a sense of old-fashioned elegance.

Prices in these villages can be much less than in Ajijic, and all are just a few miles away. A nice three-bedroom house on a large lot in San Antonio recently sold for $75,000, close to the asking price of $78,500. A two-bedroom, one-bathroom furnished condo in La Floresta, with a satellite dish and parking, is listed for $29,500. In Jocotepec, farther from Ajijic, we ran across a great buy: a six-bedroom, three-bathroom house with Jacuzzi, terrace, and gardens for $65,000. Throughout the area developers are pushing sales in small gated communities.

The South Shore

At Jocotepec you will encounter the road that heads to the south side of the lake. The road passes lush rolling farmland that climbs gently from the lake up into the hills. From Ajijic, it takes about 45 minutes to get to San Pedro Tesistan, one of a number of small villages that dot the south shore.

The villages themselves are rural, primitive, and pretty in an Old World but somewhat rundown way. So far, they have been more or less undisturbed by development. Until recently, only a few foreigners had purchased land on the south shore. We have been told that more people are now looking at property on that side.

Renting

A friend rents a nice two-bedroom, two-bathroom house in the village of Ajijic, not far from the main square, for $250 per month. Furnished houses in gated developments in Ajijic, with two bedrooms and two bathrooms, rent for $500 to $800 per month. In Jocotepec, a furnished house with three bedrooms, a garden, and a two-car garage rents for about $300 per month. In Las Fuentes, an upscale gated community near Jocotepec, a luxurious furnished home with pool, satellite dish, and views rents long-term for $1,100 per month. And a two-bedroom, three-bathroom furnished house with a garden in Chapala rents for $500 a month (probably a very nice place because it is possible to find rentals in Chapala for much less).

Publications

The *Guadalajara Reporter,* tel. (3) 615-2177, fax (3) 616-9432, is the primary source of local news for non-Spanish readers in the Guadalajara area. It is a weekly newspaper with sections on the metro area, sports, crime, and tourism. An extensive section covers the lakeside communities in some detail. There are also a large number of local display advertisements and an extensive classified section. The paper will help you understand the character of this area before you visit. You will get the skinny on real estate prices, and you can read the gossip column to see who's doing what with whom.

The *Bargain Hunter* is a free monthly bilingual classified-ad newspaper covering all the towns along the lake. It not only prints hundreds of classified ads but also a large number of display ads. It lists everything from houses for sale and rent to auto and garage sales. Most useful may be its column listing ongoing activities and coming events. Its business and services directories are also handy.

El Ojo Del Lago is a monthly newspaper containing general information about lakeside entertainment and events and articles of interest to area residents. It is published by David Tingen, tel. (376) 5-2877 or (376) 5-3676.

The News Stand, on the main highway in Ajijic, sells daily editions of *USA Today* and the *L.A. Times,* as does a store two doors down from Lloyd Bank in Chapala.

Volunteer Organizations

The Lake Chapala Society in Ajijic, a nonprofit charitable organization, has been a gathering place for expatriates for almost 50 years. The society runs an English-language library and a video rental service, offers language classes, and provides a meeting space for various local groups. It acts as an information clearinghouse, with regular visits from the U.S. consulate and Social Security personnel, who help U.S. citizens solve passport and other problems.

Volunteers also assist the Mexican Red Cross in raising funds for people who have been injured or have serious health problems. Other volunteers put their time and money into the School for the Deaf, the local orphanage, programs for disabled children, and Casa Ancianos, which helps poor older people. The American Legion Post 7 in Chapala raises money for needy kids, runs an English-language library, and provides space for various classes and activities. The Humane Society takes in stray animals, finds them homes, and provides a neutering service free to needy families.

Arts and Recreation

Ajijic has long been known as an art colony, and art is still a large part of the life of the community. Several good galleries show the work of local artists. Many artists also welcome visitors into their

Ken Luboff

Lake Chapala shoreline

studios. Outdoor art shows and exhibitions are held occasionally near the plaza and sometimes in the Nueva Posada Hotel.

The 465-seat Lake Chapala Municipal Auditorium in Ajijic is the site of a variety of activities, including chamber groups and other musical performances, the Ballet Folklorica, an annual chili cookout in February, and a number of charitable events. The Lakeside Little Theater in Chula Vista presents productions throughout the tourist season.

When residents and tourists feel like "taking the waters," they go to one of the pools at the San Juan Cosala Spa thermal springs, about 10 minutes west of Ajijic, or to the Villa Montecarlo Hotel. Both offer an inexpensive way to chill out from all the stress of being retired in such a tranquil part of the world.

The Rio Caliente Hot Springs Spa, about an hour from Chapala on the road out of Guadalajara toward Tepic, is a hidden jewel. It is a 50-room retreat nestled in a hot river valley. It is relatively inexpensive—about $100 per night including vegetarian meals—and is a great place to relax and detoxify. The spa's e-mail address is RioCal@aol.com.

The Chapala Country Club is about 15 minutes east of Chapala near the town of San Nicolas. It is a well-maintained, 36-par, nine-hole course with a clubhouse offering drinks and light lunches. The Chula Vista Country Club, about 10 minutes west of Chapala, is a nine-hole course with manicured fairways and two tennis courts nearby.

The list of 18-hole courses in Guadalajara is long. Most are available to the general public for a greens fee. Perhaps the best and most challenging 18-hole course is the Atlas Golf and Country Club, only 30 minutes from Chapala. A few others in Guadalajara are the Club de Golf Santa Anita, Las Canadas, and the new Palomar Country Club.

The general public can use the tennis courts in Christiana Park in Chapala. For about $2, you can spend the day playing tennis or lounging by the pool at the Ajijic Racquet Club. A few hotels that have tennis courts are the Real de Chapala, the Danza del Sol, and the Montecarlo, but they are restricted to guest use only.

Market Basket

All the villages along the lake, even Chapala, have managed to retain a small-town feeling—in spite of the lake's proximity to Guadalajara. So far, the lakeside villages have not been modernized with large boulevards, traffic lights, museums, movie theaters, nightclubs, and bowling alleys. Like most big cities, Guadalajara has it all, both the beautiful and the ugly, taking commercial development pressure off the lakeside communities.

We are happy to report that there are no lakeside shopping malls. Shopping in the area usually means walking along the quaint streets of Chapala or Ajijic and exploring the many small shops and boutiques selling shoes, clothing, jewelry, and arts and crafts. In Chapala, the outdoor arts and crafts market along the waterfront is open every day, and nearby is the *mercado*, a group of open-air stalls under one roof. In and around the Chapala plaza you'll find numerous shops selling meats and poultry, fruits and veggies. The number of outdoor sellers explodes on market days—Monday in Chapala and Wednesday in Ajijic.

Ajijic has shops near the square, around the Lake Chapala Society office, on streets in between the two, and on the main road through town. Billy Moon's place is a well-known shopping attraction, carrying handmade household items and Mexican arts and crafts, as well as a fine restaurant.

Foreign residents shop for groceries mostly at the Super Lake and El Torrito supermarkets. These are not like the giant supermarkets you find in the States but more like old-fashioned grocery stores. Both Super Lake and El Torrito are on the highway outside Ajijic, heading toward Chapala.

Both have good selections of Mexican and imported items. El Torrito even has an Asian food section that includes sweet and sour sauce, fish and soy sauces, and oyster sauce for about $2 a bottle. A five-pound bag of California brown rice costs about $4.50. We have also found Kellogg's Nutra Grain ($5.50), Wheaties ($4.70), Purina Dog Chow ($12.34 for 16.5 pounds), Danon Yogurt ($2.13 for 2.2 pounds), and Nescafé Diplomat coffee ($4.75 for one half pound).

Local residents enjoy the convenience of a weekly bus that takes shoppers into Guadalajara for day trips. It stops at all the villages on the lake, then heads into the city, stopping at malls and many large stores, including Price Club, Sam's Club, and Sears. The bus will also drop people off at a movie theater, then pick them up when the film is over. On the trip home, the hosts serve margaritas!

Of course, you can easily go into Guadalajara any day of the week by bus or car. A trip to the huge and exciting Mercado Libertad is as much a cultural experience as it is a shopping experience. But after a few trips you may not want to fight the crowds and traffic. Residents also shop at many of the large Mexican department stores and upscale malls.

The towns of Tlaquepaque and Tonala make a particularly good day trip when friends from the States visit. The towns, which have now been engulfed by Guadalajara, are two of the oldest and most important arts and crafts centers in Mexico. Tlaquepaque, five miles from Guadalajara's center, still retains its old character. It has cobblestone streets, quaint plazas, outdoor cafés, and hundreds of shops selling beautiful handmade pottery, glass, jewelry, leather goods, wrought-iron and wooden furniture, and artwork. Tonala, not quite so picturesque, has similar items at lower prices.

Social Life

Social life in the lakeside villages is mainly determined by people's interests. There are groups and clubs for just about everyone: writers, investors, gardeners, readers, bridge players, computer hackers, and ham radio enthusiasts. There is even a yacht club, though there isn't a yacht in sight (all we saw on the lake were small fishing boats). Residents meet and befriend others at Spanish, exercise, and art classes, at theater group rehearsals, at AA and Humane Society meetings, at Gurdjief discussion groups, at the Ajijic Society of the Arts, and at Save the Lake meetings. Of course, there are those who just enjoy meeting their friends for a drink.

Locals get together for dinner with friends and celebrate holidays as a community. But local society is stratified. It is normal for retirees to befriend people from similar backgrounds—enlisted men with enlisted men, officers with officers, artists with artists, and ex-CEOs with ex-CEOs.

Traditional churches in the area include Catholic, Evangelical, Lutheran, Baptist, Unitarian, Presbyterian, Anglican, and a couple of Christian nondenominational congregations. A small meditation centers offers weekly yoga classes. Many different AA groups meet in the area. Ask for information at the Little Chapel in Chula Vista.

Dining and Nightlife

When you feel the urge to move your body, you can line dance on Tuesday night in Ajijic and on Thursday night in Chapala. In San Antonio near Ajijic, Banana's offers lively music and dancing. People in the mood to hear a little jazz can do so at La Tasca, across the street from the Nueva Posada Hotel in Ajijic.

EXPATRIATE PERSPECTIVE

Ajijic resident Carroll Williams talks about her town:

In Ajijic I enjoy the convenience of walking to whatever service or accommodation I need. Banks, the post office, grocery stores, a bakery, and restaurants are just blocks away. The residents of this village are very kind and considerate to the gringos. They are extremely hard workers, honest and fair for the most part. The prices here, compared to those in North America and Canada, are very reasonable. We are fortunate to have several stores that cater to tastes other than Mexican. And don't forget that the sun shines daily, unless a storm from the coast sends a few tailwinds. Our reliable public bus system makes the need for an automobile a personal decision.

Though there are no movie theaters in any of the towns along the lake, there are plenty of video rental shops. Many homeowners have satellite TV setups, because local cable channels are fairly limited.

A few good restaurants offer opportunities for a nice night out. At the high end are the Ajijic Grill, offering Japanese beef, chicken specialties, and sushi, and La Luz de la Luna. Both serve good food in pretty settings. The garden at the Nueva Posada Hotel in Ajijic, with good Mexican food, is a beautiful place to eat and see the lake.

Other restaurants offer steak, ribs, and good Italian food. One even serves good Chinese food. You'll also find a waffle house, Dona's Donuts, and good Mexican restaurants, many with very reasonable prices.

For a sunset drink and a great view of the lake, one of the oldest and best-known places is the Beer Gardens, which is over 65 years old. Another is the Villa Montecarlo, with its beautiful grounds. Both are located in Chapala. Other pleasant places for lake viewing are the Club Nautico in Ajijic and the Chapala Yacht Club.

Medical Services

No matter where you live around Lake Chapala, you will never be far from a health clinic, dental clinic, or hospital. There are at least 10 local clinics, each offering a complete operating room, emergency services, and a doctor who most likely speaks English. Most clinics are associated with hospitals in Guadalajara and will provide quick ambulance service directly into the city if necessary. The Clinica Ajijic and the Clinica San Jose de la Ribera are just two of the better ones. The Red Cross also has an ambulance on 24-hour alert.

Guadalajara's many first-rate hospitals and two university medical schools have modern equipment and high-quality medical personnel. The American Hospital is considered one of the best. The city also has about every type of alternative practitioner you can imagine. In every case, the cost of care is half, or less, what it is in the United States.

Money

Most banks in the area are located in Chapala, at the street corner with the only traffic light on the lake. There you'll find branches of three of Mexico's largest banks and an office of Lloyd, an investment house and a favorite of foreign residents. Lloyd is currently planning to open a new branch in Ajijic, where there is already one bank.

Residents generally have an account at one of the local banks, which helps expedite changing money and paying bills. They also change money at the Nido Hotel in Chapala and at the El Mexicano gift shop next to the plaza in Ajijic.

Communications

Many small towns in Mexico suffer from a shortage of telephone numbers and lines, causing delays in installation. Take this into consideration when buying a house; try to find one that already has a phone. Telmex claims it will soon be remedying this situation. *A ver*—we'll see.

The only local Internet provider is southmex@southmex.com, serving the towns of Chapala, Ajijic, San Antonio, and Vista del Lago with local calls. From the San Juan Cosala and Jocotepec areas, calls to southmex @southmex.com are long distance.

For "snail mail," you'll find post offices in both Ajijic and Chapala. But, as anyone who lives in Mexico will tell you, the Mexican postal system is "hit and miss." It is preferable to sign up with Mail Boxes, Etc. They will give you an address in the States where you can receive mail, which will then be sent to Mexico the next day via UPS. In general, it takes a week to receive mail from the States.

Environmental Concerns

Lake Chapala has some serious environmental problems. The lake, which used to be crystal clear, has lost much of its transparency. It contains high levels of toxins from agricultural fertilizers, heavy metals from industry, and human wastes from inadequately treated sewage. Continued development in Guadalajara and the entire area will only exacerbate the problems.

Because of dry conditions in recent years, more water has been diverted from the Rio Lerma for irrigation, reducing the water level of the lake. Heavy rains in the summers of 1998 and 1999 helped alleviate this problem, at least temporarily.

On the positive side, the Mexican government recognizes the importance of keeping Lake Chapala healthy. Individuals within the government have begun working with scientists from Mexico, Canada, and the United States to save the lake and the entire Rio Lerma ecosystem. Who knows what the outcome will be? In Mexico things tend to move very slowly.

Puerto Vallarta

Though Mexico has many thousands of miles of spectacular coastline, the region around Puerto Vallarta offers a mix of characteristics that make it one of the top coastal retirement choices. It has great natural beauty, a wonderful climate, diversity of housing and lifestyle, availability of consumer goods and services, and easy access to the States. The local people are friendly, and the foreign community is varied enough to make it interesting.

Puerto Vallarta is located on one of the most beautiful bays in the world. The Bahia de Banderas is horseshoe shaped, with almost 100 miles of magnificent coastline rimmed with rugged mountains, jungles, farmland, small picturesque villages, almost-virgin beaches, and several major tourist developments. It is also said to be one of the cleanest bays in Mexico—cleaner than required by international standards (though friends of ours in Vallarta dispute this claim).

Over the past forty years, Puerto Vallarta (or Vallarta, as it is known locally, or occasionally PV) has grown from a small fishing village into a city whose official population is 250,000. This level of growth becomes obvious as you drive into town from the north, past the Puerto Vallarta International Airport, and begin passing a long line of huge hotels and resorts along the beach.

Still, Puerto Vallarta is much more than just beachfront hotels

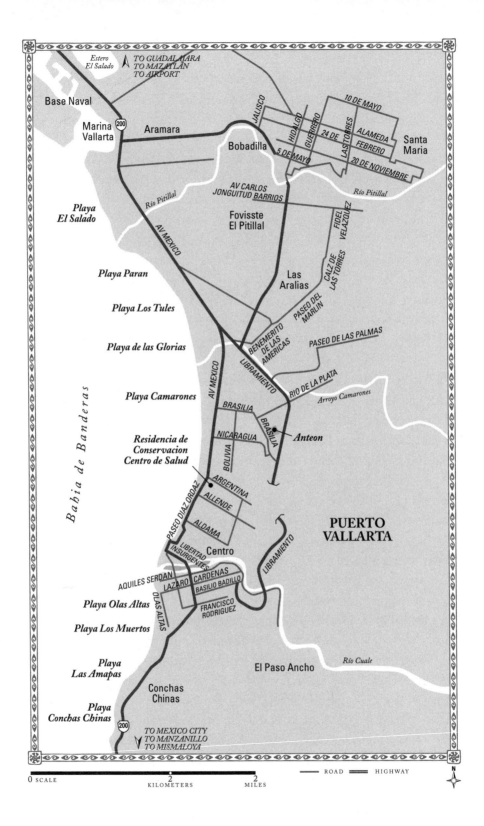

and condos. When you enter downtown (called Viejo Vallarta, or Old Town), you get a sense of the quaint village that Vallarta once was. The cobblestone streets and tile-roofed houses give downtown an Old World romantic charm, especially if you are able to see beyond the large crowds of tourists and traffic jams.

Most of the year, the Vallarta climate is wonderful. From November to June there is virtually no rain, and the sun shines almost every day. During that time, temperatures average 85 to 90 during the day and 75 to 85 at night. The rainy season starts in mid-June and lasts until mid-October. During this time, many foreign residents escape to the mountains or cooler inland towns or head to the States to see family and friends.

During the rainy season, the heat and humidity can be oppressive, although year-round residents say that jumping in a pool and staying off the streets during the afternoon can make it bearable. We've been in Puerto Vallarta in August, in a casita on the beach without air conditioning, and the spectacular lightning shows over the bay helped compensate for the heat. And the rainy season probably never gets as uncomfortable as a summer day in Washington, D.C.

Puerto Vallarta stretches along the bay to the north and south of downtown. To the south of town is the Conchas Chinas area of hillside homes and Italianesque villas—some extremely grand—perched on rocky cliffs overlooking the ocean. Farther south are the outlying beaches of Mismaloya and Boca de Tomatlan.

To the north of downtown is the Hotel Zone and the Marina Vallarta, which has more than 500 boat slips, hundreds of condos, and an 18-hole, private golf course. A few minutes north of the international airport is the Ameca River, the dividing line between the states of Jalisco to the south and Nayarit to the north. The river also divides the Central and Mountain time zones, a circumstance new residents and even old-timers find very confusing. North of the river is Nuevo Vallarta, Mexico's largest seaside residential development. Farther around the bay are the villages of Bucerias, Cruz de Huanacaxtle, and finally Punta de Mita, future site of another large development (including a Four Seasons Hotel, wildlife sanctuary, and 18-hole golf course).

It is obvious that Puerto Vallarta's economy depends on tourism, which may be a turnoff to some. During winter, the town is swamped by plane-, boat-, and busloads of short-time fun seekers. The effect on the city is profound. Tourists crowd the hotels, bars, and restaurants. They help create traffic jams, noise, and rowdiness and swarm downtown sidewalks and beaches.

Retirees living away from downtown are affected less. But anyone who lives in a seasonal tourist town has to learn how to deal with the onslaught. There are certain times when locals venture out, and others when they stay home and batten down the hatches. Some long-term residents, feeling that Puerto Vallarta has lost much of its charm, have moved to smaller outlying towns like Bucerias and Cruz de Huancaxtle, claiming that they are what Vallarta was 20 years ago.

If your dream is a quiet little beachfront pueblo, away from it all, Puerto Vallarta will not be for you. But in spite of its problems, it is one of the best all-around retirement areas on the Pacific coast.

History

Legend has it that farmer Guadalupe Sanchez first settled the valley around Puerto Vallarta in 1851, on land near the Rio Cuale, which runs through present-day Old Town. Other farmers soon began migrating to the fertile river valley, and by the late 1800s more than two thousand people lived in the town, then called Las Penas. Corn and other crops were shipped out on boats that regularly used the bay as a safe harbor. The name of the town was changed in 1918, to honor a popular former governor of Jalisco, Ignacio Luis Vallarta.

Nothing much happened in the area for the next 35 years until Mexicana Airlines, prohibited from landing in Acapulco, decided that Puerto Vallarta could be the beach resort for Guadalajarans that Acapulco was for residents of Mexico City. Mexicana Airlines began regularly scheduled flights onto a dirt runway in Puerto Vallarta in 1954.

Once Puerto Vallarta was relatively easy to reach, outsiders began filtering in, and some stuck around. A few pioneering foreigners began living along the Rio Cuale, in an area that later became known as

Gringo Gulch. Even then, Puerto Vallarta remained quiet and relatively unknown until John Huston filmed *Night of the Iguana* there in 1963. It wasn't the film but the hot romance between Richard Burton and Elizabeth Taylor that drew Hollywood reporters and paparazzi to Vallarta like flies on banana peels. The reporters and everyone connected with the film fell in love with the village. It was suddenly on the map. Soon, every Mexicana Airlines flight was booked by fans flocking to see the town where Taylor and Burton had their famous tryst.

How to Get There

The drive from Guadalajara to Puerto Vallarta, about 250 miles, passes through green fertile hills and valleys and takes about three and a half hours by toll road. The toll is about $20. From Tepic in the north to Vallarta, you'll drive 98 miles on a beautiful, but often frustratingly slow, heavily trafficked two-lane highway. The road from Barra de Navidad, 132 miles to the south, is a straight, traffic-free, two-lane highway for about two-thirds the distance, and then it winds through some pretty mountains for the other third.

Buses depart many times each day from Guadalajara for the six-hour trip to the coast. From Mexico City the trip takes 15 hours and from Manzanillo about five hours. Buses leave Tepic every half hour for the four-hour trip. You can fly directly to the Puerto Vallarta International Airport from Phoenix, Dallas, L.A., and other cities in the States and Mexico. We do not recommend taking the train, because even after you get to Guadalajara or Tepic, you still have to take a bus to Puerto Vallarta.

The Foreign Community

No one knows exactly how many permanent and part-time foreign residents live in the Vallarta area, but numbers run as high as 15,000 to 20,000. This estimate includes snowbirds who come for the winter. The majority of expatriates are from the United States and Canada, but there is also a small European community.

As far as we can tell, everyone living in Vallarta gets along well.

Ken Luboff

Downtown Puerto Vallarta

Full-time foreign residents share the expatriate experience together.
Mexicans and Americans relate very well, especially in the middle to
upper classes. It is not unusual to see a group of foreigners and
Mexicans out on the town together. But it is most common for foreign residents to socialize at private homes.

Most expatriates do some type of work, either charitable or for
profit. This work may involve a professional skill, like nursing,
teaching English, or selling real estate. Charitable organizations are
always looking for volunteers. A solid core of artists also work in
the community.

The U.S. and Canadian consulates are located at Zaragoza 160.
You can reach the U.S. consulate by telephone at (322) 3-0074 or
(322) 2-0068, and the Canadian consulate at (322) 2-5398.

Real Estate

Foreign residents are concentrated in Gringo Gulch, Conchas
Chinas, the south shore, Marina Vallarta, the Las Gaviotas area,

and the north shore. Residents who want less-expensive housing tend to live in the nearby villages of Las Gaviotas and Versalles, east of the Marina.

You may be the "last" lucky person to find that deal on the perfect fixer-upper that everyone dreams about. You may even find a condo or house with a breathtaking view. There are so many hills, overlooking so much coastline in Puerto Vallarta, that your chances are pretty good.

You will have more difficulty finding a good building lot. If you do, you will find that the cost of building in Puerto Vallarta is higher than in many other parts of Mexico—in part because of strong labor unions in the Vallarta area.

Building costs depend on materials, location, and the availability of workers. Generally, it will cost $60 to $70 per square foot to build a high-quality home. A pool will cost a minimum of $10,000. If you use exotic or imported materials, the price can increase substantially. These estimates assume that an architect/ builder will oversee the job. You can reduce costs by getting drawings and building permits from an architect and finding a *maestro* (contractor) to do the work that you oversee. (Choosing this route is fraught with risks and is only for the brave at heart with construction experience.)

Downtown

Downtown reaches from the ocean up into the hills along the Rio Cuale. Gringo Gulch is on El Cerro (the hill), which overlooks the river. The first foreigners settled here to take advantage of the cool breezes in summer, and the area has some fancy homes of early foreign residents, including Elizabeth Taylor. The hills offer wonderful views of the Church of Guadalupe and the red-tiled roofs and whitewashed walls of Old Town. Downtown is fairly expensive, but it is still possible to find deals.

A large three-bedroom older home with an ocean view and pool will cost $250,000 or more. A smaller two-bedroom house without a view will cost $90,000 or more. A one-bedroom condo can cost as little as $35,000. Occasionally, you can still find a house for $25,000 or $30,000, but that is getting very rare. With an older house, inquire about restoration costs.

Conchas Chinas and South

South of the Rio Cuale, past the restaurants and nightlife of Los Muertos Beach and Colonia Emiliano Zapata, are the hills of Conchas Chinas. Here you will find grand homes and condos overlooking the bay. The lush hills and large homes continue south of Conchas Chinas, all the way to Mismaloya, where *Night of the Iguana* was filmed.

A large three-bedroom hillside home with ocean views costs $300,000 or more. Many beachfront villas sell for millions of dollars, and prices remain high along the coast down to Mismaloya, about seven miles south of Puerto Vallarta. Smaller condos south of the city begin at around $70,000.

Marina Vallarta

Marina Vallarta is a huge, first-class development on 220 hectares (550 acres) of land. It includes an 18-hole golf course, a 353-berth marina, private boat slips, and a wide variety of real estate choices.

A large three-bedroom house on the golf course starts at $280,000. Larger, fancier homes with pools cost $500,000 and up, and a small number of guarded beachfront villas are selling for close to a million dollars.

Most of the properties for sale in the Marina are condos. A furnished two-bedroom, two-bathroom Marina-front condo sells for between $120,000 and $140,000. Condos set back from the Marina start at $70,000, while luxurious, large beachfront condos start at $300,000. Many other townhouses and condos are available in a wide range of prices. If you like beautifully tended and clipped surroundings, as well as golf, tennis, sailing, and a boardwalk with some very nice restaurants, it's worth checking out the Marina.

Las Gaviotas/Versalles

Las Gaviotas and Versalles are a few miles inland, to the east and south of the Marina. These are pretty, middle-class areas, with wide cobblestone streets. Each has a mix of homes—some modest, some grand.

In Las Gaviotas, a four- or five-bedroom home with pool starts at about $120,000. Versalles is less expensive, with homes starting as low as $90,000. Both areas have public and private schools and shopping centers nearby. Las Gaviotas has a clubhouse with tennis courts, a pool, and a playground. Though not on the water, these areas are quite beautiful.

North of Town
Apart from Nuevo Vallarta, which is a mega-resort, the other towns along the bay to the north remind old-timers of Vallarta years ago. Punta de Mita, a small village at the northernmost end of the bay, is now being inundated by its own mega-development, however. So far, the village itself is still tranquil.

Nuevo Vallarta is the largest development outside of Puerto Vallarta on Banderas Bay. Resort hotels take up most of the beach-front property, but there are pretty residential areas with tree-lined streets near the beach. This is a new and decidedly upscale neighborhood. Farther from the beach, you'll find an area of newer homes surrounding a beautiful large lagoon. Most of these homes have boat docks and start at $200,000. There is also a 175-slip marina area where two- and three-bedroom condos start at $125,000.

North of Nuevo Vallarta, the beach town of Bucerias has some fancy homes, but it still has the funky feel of an old Mexican village. From Bucerias you can walk for miles along a mostly deserted beach in either direction. Past Bucerias, along the bay, the next town is Cruz de Huanacaxtle (where one of our favorite seafood restaurants serves fish prepared in the *sarandeado* style, which we have found mainly in the State of Nayarit). "Cruz" is fairly small, built on hills, and pretty. Finally, at the northern point of the bay, is the village of Punta de Mita.

Renting

If you are lucky, a real estate agent in Vallarta will help you find a nice two- or three-bedroom apartment or condo in a good location, possibly with a view, for as little as $500 per month. You may find an even-better deal through ads in the paper, local bulletin boards, or word of mouth. We have heard of people finding apartments for as little as $300 per month, though the bulk of rentals are in the $500 to $900 range. People have complained about the difficulty of finding good long-term rentals. Many property owners hold properties off the long-term rental market in order to get higher rents from short-term tourists.

Publications

The best sources of information about what is going on in town are *Vallarta Today*, tel. (322) 4-2829, Vallarta's daily English-language newspaper, and a section of the *Guadalajara Colony Reporter* called "The Vallarta Reporter" (e-mail: reporter@informador.com.mx). Both have calendars of events and display ads. "The Reporter" has a better classified section, but the daily *Vallarta Today* is more up to date. Both have good and interesting editorial sections and are available at most newsstands throughout the city.

Puerto Vallarta Lifestyles (tel. 322-1-0106, fax 322-1-2255, e-mail: jgyserpr@zonavirtual.com.mx) is a slick, four-color, English-language quarterly filled with restaurant and real estate advertising and stories about local personalities and happenings around town. Tours and other activities are also listed.

Through donations from the community, the new *biblioteca* (public library), which opened in October 1996, is building its collection of both English and Spanish books. It now has more than 12,000 volumes.

Arts and Recreation

Puerto Vallarta offers retirees a variety of ways to entertain themselves. Once you land at the airport, you can be home in 20 minutes and an hour later be hiking in a remote mountain village, fishing on the deck of a luxury sailboat, playing a round of golf or tennis, or snorkeling off a deserted beach.

Puerto Vallarta's art galleries (more than 20) are a major focus of the foreign community's cultural and social life. Gallery parties and openings attract hundreds of people. Even greater numbers come to art walks organized by galleries in different parts of town.

The luxurious Camino Real Hotel has been bringing in entertainment for the past 25 years, on the first Thursday of every month. The hotel has presented the Guadalajara Philharmonic Orchestra, jazz and Latin trios, solo acts, and small groups. Friday night often brings entertainment to the Los Arcos Amphitheatre or at times to the Presidencia in the center of town. Puerto Vallarta presented its first Jazz Festival in May 1997 and plans to make that an annual event. Dozens of bars and restaurants throughout town offer live music, sometimes for dancing, sometimes just for atmosphere.

EXPATRIATE PERSPECTIVE

Longtime resident Gary Thompson, owner of Galeria Pacifico, has this to say about Puerto Vallarta:

Puerto Vallarta has certainly gotten bigger. When I moved here in the 1970s there were 35,000 residents. In those days, if anyone was here for more than two weeks you knew their name, you knew their former jobs, even their blood type—everything about them. Now I meet people all the time who have lived here 10 years already, and I don't remember ever having seen them, let alone met them.

I started spending winters here in 1974. I would stay about five months. By 1980 I was a full-time resident, but I didn't really move down to become a full-time resident. I came down as a winter resident and just didn't go home—spring came and I never left. I was here partly because I like to swim and I like the ocean, but I didn't spend much time on the beach. I wasn't like a Californian who migrated here for the good surf—I liked the people and the culture.

I still think Puerto Vallarta is a great place to live—better than ever! I've been to a few new places in Mexico, but I don't know of any place that I think I'd like better.

Most of the time, you can find at least one or two recent releases at the movie theaters. When we were last in Vallarta, we were pleased to find a first-run film, released only a few days earlier in the States. If you can't find a film you want to see at a theater, you can just rent a movie and hunker down in front of the tube. There are plenty of video rental stores in town.

As for TV, most cable channels in Vallarta are in Spanish, so those addicted to *Seinfeld* reruns will have to purchase a satellite setup. These offer hundreds of channels in English.

The 18-hole Flamingos Golf Club, open to the public, is a quick and easy 20-minute drive north of town. The Marina Vallarta 18-hole course is private and can be used only by residents of the Marina, their guests, and guests of one of the Marina hotels.

Tennis is available all over town, as many hotels have courts open to the public. The premier courts are at the John Newcombe Tennis Center in the Continental Plaza hotel.

Market Basket

Apart from sitting on the beach and eating and drinking, the main Vallarta tourist preoccupation is shopping. Boutiques sell fashionable resort clothing and fancy jewelry. Some sell exotic items from India, Africa, Cuba, and other parts of Mexico. There are even a few well-known designer and brand-name shops like Ralph Lauren, Aca Joe, and Benetton. At the other end of the spectrum are the ubiquitous T-shirt and trinket stores.

Residents are more likely to shop in one of Vallarta's department stores, modern malls, large supermarkets, or mega-stores, which carry most everything you could find in a small town in the United States. The outdoor market, down by the river, is a great place for those who enjoy the energy of crowds and like bargaining at stalls.

Traditional Mexican foods and spices, like fresh cilantro, chiles, and fresh tortillas, are available everywhere. Markets and delis also have a wide assortment of U.S. and international goods. Rizo's Super-market, located near the Rio Cuale in Old Town, carries everything from Grey Poupon mustard and soy milk to Smucker's jelly and Newman's Own salad dressing. (The store also has one of the best bulletin boards in town—a good place to find a house or apartment for rent or a car for sale.) Like most supermarkets, it has a selection of wines and liquors.

Community Organizations

We found a depth of volunteer and cultural activities in Vallarta that connects residents to one another and to the community. For instance, the International Friendship Club of Puerto Vallarta was started in 1987 by a group of expatriates from the United States and Canada. The club's mission is to "provide services and collect and distribute funds in response to humanitarian and educational needs of the community." It is one of the most active clubs in the area, raising funds to assist local schools, hospitals, day care centers, and playgrounds. One of its projects collects money to repair cleft palates, another supports an HIV testing lab. Volunteers from both the foreign and Mexican communities organize various fund-raising events, including weekly home tours.

The American-Mexican Foundation provides scholarships for financially stressed Mexican schoolchildren. It holds fund-raising events and seeks private donations and volunteer help. Over 200 children are involved in the program.

A wide variety of congregations are represented, including Baptist, Jewish, Jehovah's Witnesses, Mormon, Seventh Day Adventist, and, of course, Catholic. All year, individuals and groups offer spiritual retreats, classes, and workshops. Recent offerings have included past-lives workshops, sensitivity training, and the Course in Miracles. AA, OA, NA, and Al-Anon all meet at the Alano Club in Vallarta.

Schools

Art and language schools attract tourists who are interested in something other than just drinking and hanging out. Schools add an intellectual and artistic energy to the city, and they are a convenience for retirees who want to improve their Spanish or take an art class or two.

Ken Luboff

The *malecón* (boardwalk) along the beach in Puerto Vallarta

The Vallarta branch of the Instituto Allende de San Miguel de Allende is highly recommended. The main campus in San Miguel is one of the oldest and best-known language and art schools in Mexico. Aside from language classes, it offers classes and workshops in drawing, painting, jewelry making, ceramics, and textiles. All classes can be taken for credit that will transfer to most schools in the States.

The University of Guadalajara's Centro International offers classes in Spanish and Mexican culture at its downtown campus. Other schools offer classes in dance, ballet, judo, and karate. A call to a local gym will get you exercise-class schedules. Experts from the States, Canada, and Mexico present workshops throughout the year, on topics as varied as self-improvement, dance, drawing and painting, meditation, and sculpting.

Dining and Nightlife

For a night out on the town, restaurants and bars run the gamut from cozy, expensive, and romantic to sleazy and cheap. You'll find restaurants serving American, Argentine, Chinese, Szechwan, European, French, German, Japanese, Indonesian, Italian, Thai, natural, California, and Swiss cuisines.

One day, on the way to a greatly anticipated deli meal, Barbara and I passed a café serving bagels, crepes, and pancakes. We also found several first-class, high-end Mexican restaurants with great atmosphere. At the other end of the spectrum are the ever-present fast-food chains like McDonald's and Domino's Pizza. For a totally unique eating experience, try a street-corner taco stand—but first talk to a local who knows which ones are clean and safe.

These days, there is more music in Vallarta than ever before. At night, you can hear mariachi, marimba, salsa, and jazz bands and young bands playing old-time rock and roll. There are discos, night-clubs, and sports bars. If all this noise is not your thing, find a quiet café or cyber-café for a cup of coffee and an e-letter to a friend.

Getting Around in the City

Buses and VW *combis* (passenger vans) stop at corners marked with bus-stop signs and run until midnight. They charge only two pesos a ride and provide a convenient way to get around the city. Taxis cost from 15 to 25 pesos, but can cost more if you do not work out the price beforehand. When you live in Vallarta, you learn a few tricks, like buying your ticket from a taxi sitting outside the airport for maybe 20 pesos, rather than from the booth inside the airport for 60 pesos.

Medical Services

Foreign residents tell us that the quality of health care in Puerto Vallarta is very good. The Puerto Vallarta phonebook includes more than 20 pages of doctors and alternative health care specialists. Everything from cardiologists, gynecologists, and dentists to homeopaths and naturopaths are listed.

Hospitals and 24-hour clinics handle normal medical problems and emergencies. Facilities include Ameri-Med, a diagnostic medical center at the entrance to Marina Vallarta, the Hospital Medasist Vallarta, at the south end of town, and—also south of the Rio Cuale—the Hospital CMQ. Each hospital has some bilingual staff. The Critamovil Ambulance service is on duty 24 hours a day.

Money

Most major Mexican banks have branches in Puerto Vallarta. They provide basic banking services that you would expect from banks in the States. The most popular bank and investment house among American and Canadian residents is Lloyd Asociados, S.A. It caters to foreigners and will help with financial investments. Lloyd accounts offer high interest rates. Lloyd also provides insurance services and will pay household bills.

Internet Service

Internet access is a snap, with three local service providers and two cybercafés. For about 25 pesos ($2.50), you can download your e-mail while drinking a cup of coffee. The service providers are ICANET Vallarta, tel. (322) 4-1050, e-mail info@pvallarta.icanet.net.mx; PVNet, www.pvnet.com.mx; and AcNet, www.vallarta-online.com.

San Miguel de Allende

It takes energy and a strong heart to walk the narrow, cobbled, and hilly streets of San Miguel, but it's worth every breathless moment. A colonial town, over 400 years old, San Miguel has the feel of an old European town transported to Mexico. In fact, with its antique doors set in sixteenth-century buildings, colorfully painted bougainvillea-draped walls, ornate churches, clear skies, and steep surrounding hillsides, it could easily be mistaken for an Italian hill town. Six thousand feet above sea level, in Mexico's central mountain plain, San Miguel is home to about 80,000 Mexicans and 4,000 to 6,000 foreigners. At the center of town, on one side of its main square, stands a majestic, fantastical, pink stone gothic cathedral (the Parroquia). To us, it looks a little like the castle in Disney's Magic Kingdom. The builder reputedly designed and built it after seeing a postcard of an Italian church.

As you can imagine, San Miguel's beauty attracts a continual flow of tourists throughout the year. During winter, when snowbirds and large numbers of students are in residence, it can seem like San Miguel has been completely invaded by foreigners. The truth is, the large majority of tourists visiting San Miguel are Mexicans. Certainly, gringos are conspicuous, but San Miguel remains a solidly Mexican town.

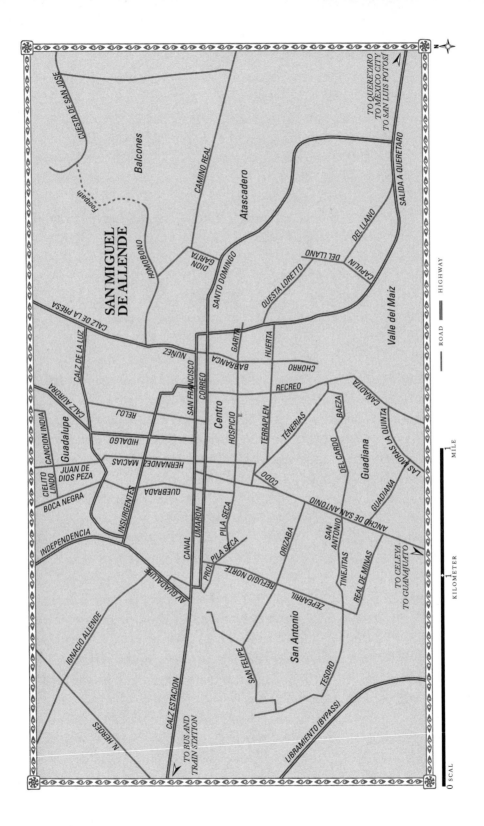

SAN MIGUEL DE ALLENDE

Balcones

Atascadero

Homobono

DION GARITA

CUESTA DE SAN JOSE

Footpath

CAMINO REAL

SANTO DOMINGO

Valle del Maiz

DEL LLANO

CAPULIN DEL LLANO

QUESTA LORETTO

SALIDA A QUERETARO

TO QUERETARO
TO MÉXICO CITY
TO SAN LUIS POTOSÍ

CALZ DE LA PRESA

CALZ DE LA LUZ

NUÑEZ

GARITA

HUERTA

CHORRO

RECREO

CAÑADITA

CALZ AURORA

RELOJ

SAN FRANCISCO

CORREO

Centro

BARRANCA

TERRAPLEN

TÉNERIAS

BAEZA

CANCION INDIA

Guadalupe

HIDALGO

HOSPICIO

E

DEL CARDO

Guadiana

LAS MORAS LA QUINTA

CIELITO LINDO

JUAN DE DIOS PEZA

HERNANDEZ MACIAS

CODO

GUADIANA

BOCA NEGRA

QUEBRADA

PILA SECA

ANCHO DE SAN ANTONIO

INSURGENTES

PROL PILA SECA

ORIZABA

SAN ANTONIO

TINEJITAS

TO CELEYA
TO GUANAJUATO

INDEPENDENCIA

CANAL

UMARON

REFUGIO NORTE

REAL DE MINAS

IGNACIO ALLENDE

AV GUADALUPE

ZEFERIL

San Antonio

TESORO

SAN FELIPE

CALZ ESTACION

N HEROES

TO BUS AND
TRAIN STATION

LIBRAMIENTO (BYPASS)

0 SCAL

1 KILOMETER

1 MILE

ROAD ━━━ HIGHWAY

N

The streets of Centro (downtown) are always bustling and lively. Only during the two hottest and driest months, April and May, does the tempo seem to slow. Boutiques and restaurants are numerous and do a vigorous business, especially on weekends when large crowds of visitors from Mexico City, three hours south, overrun the town. Shopping in San Miguel is sheer delight for all who appreciate handmade crafts.

The best way to see and discover the nooks and crannies of San Miguel is to walk. A friend of ours calls San Miguel "one of the most sensual towns I know." Strolling around town is a pleasure—as long as you look where you are stepping and avoid falling off a high curb or into one of San Miguel's ubiquitous street holes, which a friend lovingly calls gringo traps! The town is densely packed, so everything is nearby and within easy reach. Usually, a five- to ten-minute walk will get you to an art opening or theater.

For those who live here, walking downtown to pick up the mail or meet someone for lunch or a cappuccino can be slow going. It is almost impossible to walk anywhere in Centro without bumping into friends on every other street corner. Steep and hilly parts of town outside of Centro are easiest to reach by car or cab, unless you are in great shape and love to walk.

June through September is the rainy season. Rains can be spectacular, preceded by lightning and thunder and then a heavy semi-tropical downpour, which usually lasts for an hour or two. After a rain, the town and countryside have a fresh scent of ozone and flowers. Outside of the rainy season, humidity is low.

Winters can be surprisingly cold—far colder than tourists expect—with occasional light frosts (the first heavy freeze in memory occurred in 1997). Most residents have fireplaces and electric or gas space heaters. There is neither air-conditioning nor central heating, and, except for a few really hot and cold nights, they are not needed. But warm sweaters, socks, and jackets are definitely required in winter. Still, winter in San Miguel is a great deal warmer than in most parts of the United States and is rarely gray or overcast. Many days in mid-winter you can wear shorts and light cotton shirts, but by evening it is time to bundle up a bit.

San Miguel is a town of fiestas. They happen so often that it can begin to feel like a holiday or saint's birthday is being celebrated almost daily. During these celebrations, incredibly loud, heart-stopping fireworks explode unexpectedly, day and night. People new to town think they are witnessing the beginning of a revolution. But most old-timers get used to the booms in the night. The family dog, on the other hand, lies quaking under the bed, head between paws.

San Miguel has a large—and quirky—retirement community, which lives in harmony with a tolerant and accepting Mexican population. The town has a long history of attracting writers, artists, and black sheep. But, like so many other gems that remained hidden to the outside world for decades except for a few pioneers, San Miguel has finally been discovered in a big way.

The effects are both positive and negative. As more foreigners have moved in, services have improved, new restaurants and bars have opened (some very good), and more cultural events are taking place. At the same time, real estate prices have begun to climb, making San Miguel among the most expensive small cities in Mexico. The boom has attracted developers and others looking to make a fast buck—driving prices even higher. Foreigners have certainly improved the economy of the town, but they have also bought up some of the best real estate in the center of town.

Rents are still reasonable, but if you think you can move to San Miguel, live very cheaply, and find low-priced real estate, you may be disappointed. Still, even San Miguel is less expensive than most of the United States.

History

The village of San Miguel was founded by Friar Juan de San Miguel in 1542. By 1555 San Miguel was a safe stop along the road between Mexico City and the rich silver mines of Zacatecas. Before that the original village, called San Miguel de los Chichimecas, was a Spanish outpost in hazardous Chichimeca Indian country. Later the name became San Miguel El Grande, in deference to its growing weaving and leather trade. The College of San Francisco de Sales was founded in San Miguel in 1734.

On September 8, 1810, the little town of San Miguel was catapulted into Mexican history. A small group of men from San Miguel, led by Ignacio de Allende, Juan Aldama, and Colonel Narciso Maria Loreto de Canal, had been plotting to overthrow the Spanish government of Mexico. Conspiring with them was Father Miguel Hidalgo, from the nearby town of Dolores. When he learned that the Spanish viceroy had discovered the plot, Father Hidalgo made his famous speech, the Grito de Dolores—the Mexican Declaration of Independence—and inspired a poorly armed ragtag band of rebels to march to San Miguel. Along the way, others joined in, and the revolution was under way. Within a year, Hidalgo, Aldama, and Allende were all betrayed and beheaded. It took 10 more years to end the Spanish rule of Mexico.

After the revolution, San Miguel became San Miguel de Allende. The first outsider known to move to San Miguel was Sterling Dickinson, who arrived in 1937. Dickinson, who died in San Miguel in 1998, was a pioneer who helped found the Instituto Allende. After World War II, American soldiers on the GI Bill began coming to the Instituto Allende to study Spanish. Around that time, artists and writers also began arriving to join the small but growing expatriate community.

How to Get There

It takes more than a little effort to get to San Miguel. The closest airport is in Leon, Guanajuato, about one and a half hours away by car. American, Continental, Aeromexico, Air California, and other airlines offer regular daily flights into Leon. Taxis run to and from the airport and San Miguel for about $50 each way. Those living in San Miguel usually drive to the airport and leave their cars if they are making a short trip out of Mexico.

Another option is to fly into Mexico City and then take a bus to San Miguel. Flights into Mexico City's airport are more frequent and generally less expensive. Just outside the airport is a plush Aeroplus bus, which travels nonstop to Queretaro in three hours, for about $15. From Queretaro, it is easiest to take a taxi to San Miguel, a 40-minute trip, for $10 to $15. You can take a bus as well.

From the States by car, it is easiest to cross the border at Laredo, Texas, even if you are coming from as far west as Albuquerque, New Mexico. Laredo is a 10-hour drive from San Miguel, most of it on four-lane toll roads. The route south, through El Paso and Chihuahua, is a slower and more difficult drive.

Driving from the far west, you'll travel down Mexico's west coast on Route 15. Expect several customs and *Federale* (federal police) stops along this route. These can be intimidating but are generally harmless if you keep your sense of humor. At Tepic, head for Guadalajara, then on to San Miguel. This trip can be done in three long days, but you'll wish you had slowed down, taken at least four, and enjoyed the beautiful countryside.

A comfortable first-class bus is the least expensive way to get to San Miguel from the States. Passenger train service to San Miguel has been discontinued.

The Foreign Community

Four to six thousand foreign residents live in San Miguel year-round. Another 1,000 to 2,000 snowbirds move to town for three or four months each winter. Add to these the foreign tourists who pass through town and those who come to study at one of the local art and language schools.

Mexicans in San Miguel are accepting of foreigners. The town has one of the oldest expatriate communities in Mexico; locals have had foreigners living in their midst for generations. The long inter-action has helped create an acceptance of foreigners and some long and very warm friendships. Nevertheless, most relationships between foreigners and Mexicans tend to be polite and good natured, but somewhat formal.

The majority of full-time foreign residents are retired, many in their fifties and sixties. Among them are writers and artists, ex-business people, rich and poor. Though they come from a variety of backgrounds—some very "straight"—together they seem to create a bohemian community, maybe because once they move to San Miguel, they let their hair down.

A small number of expatriates own businesses or work. Others, with more time on their hands, involve themselves in the local arts, theater, film, or literary scene. Volunteer organizations offer a way to socialize and, at the same time, help the community. Beyond the small circles of friends, there is the common link among people who live in a foreign land. San Miguel has a U.S. consular agency that can help you deal with passport and immigration problems that crop up. A local Mexican immigration office makes it relatively easy for foreigners to obtain residency documents.

In 1997, a series of articles appeared in a number of widely read magazines, travel newsletters, and newspapers in the United States. The articles claim San Miguel as the top travel destination, the top place to retire, and the best foreign town for real estate investment. The publicity has attracted a wealthier and more conservative crowd.

Ken Luboff

Shops in San Miguel de Allende's *portal*

Some longtime foreign residents worry that San Miguel will go the way of Aspen, Carmel, and Santa Fe. But we don't think that's likely, in a town with such a relatively small number of foreigners.

Real Estate

The heart of San Miguel is its historic downtown (Centro). In Centro, most homes are restored colonial-style structures, some 350 years old or more. Centro is where the action is, and it is one of the most sought-after living areas. With the exception of a few other coveted parts of town, the closer you are to Juarez Park in Centro, the more expensive the real estate. Views of the Parroquia (main cathedral) and other downtown churches, as well as the sunset, can greatly increase the price of property. You'll usually find a wide assortment of homes on the market, but those wanting to build downtown will find that good lots are few and far between.

The neighborhoods surrounding Centro are called *colonias*. The majority of foreign residents live in Centro and the colonias of Balcones, Atascadero, San Antonio, and Guadiana, which all have a mix of Mexicans and foreigners. Most other colonias, which are poorer, are predominantly Mexican, although some foreigners live in every part of town.

Most expensive houses in San Miguel are designed and laid out in the traditional colonial manner. From the street, you see their brightly painted walls with baroque facades and intricately carved doors. What is behind the walls is a mystery. The door of a colonial home usually enters into an interior courtyard—sometimes a magical garden—or a covered entrance area (loggia). Other architectural features include local stone (*cantera*) around most doors and windows, arches (often Moorish-looking), tile or brick floors, colorful tile kitchens, fireplaces, brightly painted interior walls, and high ceilings covered by either wood beams or brick domes (*bovedas*). Homes often have small guest houses, or casitas, on the property.

In many poorer parts of town, houses are run down and small, with walls of unplastered brick and very plain front doors. Even here, though, you might enter interior courtyards, with trees and flowering bushes, colorful potted plants, and songbirds in cages. Unlike houses in the United States, these traditional Mexican houses are sometimes more like family compounds, with many small rooms for parents, grandparents, brothers and sisters, and cousins. Recently, foreigners have been buying these homes and renovating them.

Real estate prices in San Miguel have been going up steadily for many years, but the ascent seems to have slowed. Is there a top in sight?

Centro

A recent ad in *Atencion San Miguel* listed a two-bedroom, one-bathroom fixer-upper on a small lot in Centro for $85,000. At the other end of the spectrum was a colonial villa with a pool, magnificent views, and gardens for $1.8 million. Another listing described a three-bedroom, three-bathroom colonial, with views and a garage, for $425,000. This price is somewhat high. Overall, the average price of a colonial in Centro is in the $175,000 to $350,000 range.

Atascadero

Atascadero is on a hill on the east side of town. Most houses in this area are large, built on good-sized lots, and relatively new (built within the last 40 years). Often, they have swimming pools and spectacular views of downtown and the sunset. A lot or house in this area can be expensive. For instance, a large three-bedroom, three-bathroom house, with guest casita and views, can sell for $750,000. Nevertheless, it is possible to find smaller homes and lots selling for around $100,000.

Los Balcones

Los Balcones is a prime residential area, on the next hill north of Atascadero, with extraordinary views to the west and to Centro. Balcones is the only area in town where you cannot find a home for less than $175,000. All the homes in the area are colonial-style, and built within the last 30 years. Some are very large. They are light on the inside and colorfully painted on the outside. An advantage to this area is its close proximity to the Cante botanical garden, a

A Single Woman in San Miguel Allende
by Kendal Dodge Butler

"Why do you want to leave California?" my Uncle Arthur asked. "Why do you want to abandon your friends and family and go to some godforsaken Mexican hill town where you don't have a job and nobody knows your name?"

"That's why, Arthur," I said.

What I should perhaps have explained is that San Miguel Allende is not exactly your average godforsaken Mexican hill town. San Miguel isn't even really Mexico, the gringo old-timers will tell you ruefully, acknowledging the fact that this famous artist's colony is hardly representative of the whole.

What it is for me and the many gringas like me—widowed, divorced, gay, or whatever, but unequivocally single and happy about it—is a place to reinvent ourselves, to wade shallowly or plunge deeply into the arts, to have massages or facelifts or affairs, or maybe just to watch the bananas ripen and ponder the curious courses of our own lives.

Like Mexico itself, San Miguel is a mixed-up juxtaposition of cultures, peoples, incomes, religions, lifestyles, and philosophical outlooks. And what's nicest about San Miguel is that these outlandish life forms live peaceably side by side. Burros and RVs, Indians and yuppies, mariachis and Mormon missionaries, painters and peasants and priests hang out companionably in the *jardín*. We get to know each other, smile, murmur *buenas tardes*, and go about our business.

And there are certainly a lot of businesses to go about in San Miguel. Restaurants for every taste and pocketbook, handsome *artesanías* and upscale art galleries, cheap pensiones and luxury B&Bs, discos and devil dancers, *horchata* and *tamarindo* and tamales for a few pesos on the corner and bourbon and filet mignon in the ritzy joints.

And everywhere are the fiestas for which San Miguel is famous. There's Saint Michael's Day, of course. There's Cinco de Mayo and 16 de Septiembre. There's Corpus Christi and Semana Santa and the Day of the Dead. There are the transvestite *locos* who take over the town on the feast of San Antonio. There's the *pamplonada*, when the bulls are let loose in the streets to pursue the thousands of young mexicanos and occasional intrepid *turista* who get loaded and prove their manhood the old-fashioned way by tempting death.

It's possible, of course, to insulate yourself from all this messy, pullulating life if you wish. In the golden gringo ghettoes on the hills above the old town, you can hide at your leisure from all things Mexican except the cheap labor and the glorious view, trekking occasionally into Querétaro to pick up supplies direct from *los Estados Unidos* at Sam's or WalMart.

For many of us, though—and I'm thinking particularly of the single women—San Miguel offers the chance to explore corners of our psyches left unvisited during lives devoted to careers, children, and husbands. It's our turn now. Women marry younger and live longer, and so are more often left alone in life. We bear widowhood better, I have read, find greater consolation in solitude, learn to live on our own and like it. Well, we'd damn well better, hadn't we?

And San Miguel gives us ample opportunity to explore ourselves. For the artistic, there are the Instituto Allende and Bellas Artes. For the linguistic, there are Spanish schools on every corner. For the hedonistic, there are wine, song, and— I am told—fantastically cheap drugs. For the altruistic, there are unlimited opportunities to heal and to help. And for the fatalistic, there is that unmatchably practical philosophy that is the Mexican outlook on death. So that's what I should have told my uncle. I get to be myself here, Arthur.

peaceful place for a walk, with trails that run along a spectacular canyon and past one of San Miguel's dams.

Guadiana

Guadiana is a popular colonia next to Centro and near the Instituto Allende. This area used to be funky, but it has changed quickly. You can still find some good deals on fixer-uppers and lots, but most newly built or renovated colonial-style homes are going for big bucks. A small two-bedroom, two-bathroom home with a garden in this area might sell for about $150,000 to $175,000. A lot with a view could cost $50,000 or more.

Other Colonias

The other colonias that surround Centro, including Guadalupe, Olimpo, Valle de Maiz, and Independencia, are poorer and not as picturesque as the ones that have already been gentrified. Though they are a little farther away, they are still within walking distance of downtown. These areas have fewer foreign residents, though foreigners living here, for the most part, are easily accepted. These colonias will probably be the next to fall to gentrification, because deals can still be found here.

A residential street in San Miguel de Allende

Ken Luboff

Los Frailes

Just 10 minutes from downtown by car or bus, you'll find the completely separate subdivision (*fraccionamiento*) of Los Frailes. Mostly wealthy and middle-class Mexicans and foreigners live in this cobblestoned, country village. Homes here run the gamut from attractive to grotesque, modest to palatial, modern to colonial—anything goes! This area is quieter than San Miguel and has slightly milder weather. Because it is "out in the country," lots tend to be larger and prices lower. Many of the houses and lots have great views of the lake (really a dam).

A new house in Los Frailes with a view of the lake, three bedrooms, four bathrooms, a pool, and a large garden sells for about $190,000. A large two-bedroom, three-bathroom house, with separate guest house or studio, sells in the $140,000 range.

Rentals

You can find rentals through classified ads, bulletin boards, or one of the many property management companies in town. During high season, December through April, the price of rentals increases. More expensive properties always include servants.

Long-term rentals cost less. A house renting long-term for $500 per month could rent for $500 per week during the high season. Long-term rentals in Centro might be as low as $300 a month or as high as $1,500 or more, depending on size, location, views, and condition. We know of one spectacular house that rents for $4,000 a month.

In the colonias where fewer foreigners live, or out in the country, long-term rentals can be as low as $150 a month. In the "rico" areas like Balcones, the same size property might cost that much per day! Recently, a seven-bedroom, seven-bathroom house in Atascadero, with a heated pool, was advertised for $1,500 per week. In the same paper, a three-bedroom, two-bathroom furnished house with a garage in Colonia San Antonio was advertised for $600 a month.

Arts and Entertainment

Culturally, San Miguel is like a mini-San Francisco (without the bay). A person could go nuts trying to keep up with the music festivals (classical and jazz), art openings, poetry readings, theater offerings, films, volunteer activities, and social gatherings. People even have to hide out at times to get some rest from the social whirl.

San Miguel has been an art colony for decades, and it still attracts artists and art students from all over the world. The art scene is vibrant and colorful. Galleries are perpetually having openings, attended by hundreds of art enthusiasts. Artists tell us, with some reserve, that the market is good. The Bellas Artes and the Instituto Allende are well-known art schools. They, as well as local artists, attract students who want to immerse themselves in San Miguel's artistic atmosphere.

Music is everywhere too. You'll hear ranchero music played by campesinos dressed almost in rags. In the main plaza every Sunday night, a local oompah band plays in the gazebo, as people dance around. Occasionally two bands (sometimes electrified) set up in one of the plazas and play right next to one another at the same time!

The Angela Peralta Theater presents concerts and music festivals throughout the year. Major events include three separate chamber music festivals (two in winter, one in fall) and a jazz festival. All boast top-name, internationally known talent—and all are a joy. What's more, the price of admission to an entire two-week festival costs about what it would for a nightly ticket at the same festival in the States.

San Miguel is one of the few cities in Mexico where you can get all the major U.S. cable-TV channels, in English. A package including the three networks, plus Fox, CNN, A&E, the History Channel, TNT, PBS, and a few others costs about $30 per month.

Two movie theaters in the local mall show films that were first run about six months earlier. Movies also show nightly at the Hotel Villa Jacaranda, where the price of admission also gets you a margarita and a bowl of popcorn. There are art-film clubs at the Bellas Artes, the library, and the Universidad del Valle. About 40 minutes away in Querétaro you'll find several very modern malls, with multiple-screen movie theaters, one with 12 screens. Apart from the normal video rental shops, found all over town, one specializes in classic and art films in English.

Fiestas

The fiestas, festivals, and celebrations of San Miguel are the craziest, most solemn, noisiest, and most frequent of any held in a small town in Mexico. Ask my dog—this is, if you can find one that's not hiding under a bed. At certain times of year, including almost all of September and about two weeks around Easter, the celebrations are continuous and awesome. There are fireworks just about every night and parades on most days. During Independence Day celebrations in September, a reenactment of the Grito—the speech that started the revolution—is followed by small firecrackerlike bombs thrown over the heads of the large crowd for about three hours in the middle of the night. To stand in the throngs celebrating El Grito is to be transported to another time and space—like being in the revolution itself.

During Semana Santa (Holy Week), people create altars and sand paintings on the floors of their homes, in rooms facing the street so passersby can see their creations. Solemn processions are an almost-daily event.

In the days leading up to Day of the Dead (November 2, near our Halloween), hundreds of booths suddenly appear, selling sugar candy in the shape of skeletons and coffins. Day of the Dead and other fiestas mark the bizarre marriage of Catholic rituals and ancient Indian ceremonies.

Newspapers and Books

Of the two local English-language newspapers, *Atencion San Miguel* is the most widely read. A weekly publication of the San Miguel Biblioteca (public library), it contains articles of local interest, an arts and culture supplement, advertisements, and complete listings of upcoming events. The last pages carry classified ads listing real estate for sale, apartments and houses for rent, business opportunities, services, classes, and personals.

El Independiente is a fine bimonthly newspaper with sections in both English and Spanish. It has editorial features on culture, food, travel, health, community events, and international news. It also contains classified advertisements. *Juarde* (*Who Are They?*) is a directory containing the names, addresses, and telephone numbers of most permanent foreign residents in San Miguel. It is updated and published annually.

The Biblioteca Publica is located in a beautiful colonial building that used to be a slaughterhouse. Its patio is a serene spot where foreigners and Mexicans get together to practice Spanish and English. Language teachers sometimes meet with students here. The library plays a central role in the life of the foreign community of San Miguel. It has one of the largest collections of English-language books in Mexico and an entire room devoted to books about Mexico. It operates a computer center, with classes for foreigners, as well as Mexican kids and adults. Its weekly house and garden tour and weekly flea market attract large crowds. It operates a quiet café, located inside the library, that provides an ideal atmosphere for a relaxed lunch or a cappuccino and a read. It also provides space for poetry readings and group meetings. In January 1999, the library proudly opened its newest addition, a state-of-the-art theater.

The town's two English bookstores each have modest collections of books. El Tecolote has a good selection of titles about Mexico and a variety of new titles, both fiction and nonfiction. The store will order any book you want, and it operates a book exchange. El Colibri specializes in mysteries, art books, and magazines and sells art supplies. English books are available at a few other stores in town, and occasionally the library has great used-book sales. Lagundis, a good art supply store, sells art books.

Community Organizations

There is probably more for expatriates to do here than in most average-sized U.S. cities—most of it within walking distance. Like anywhere, circles of friends form around interests, age groups, and idiosyncrasies.

Established schools like the Instituto Allende, Bellas Artes, and Academia Hispano Americana have been offering art, music, and language classes since we were youngsters. These days, at least 10 additional language and art schools operate in San Miguel. Add to this classes given by individual instructors in disciplines as varied as jazz dance, flamenco, yoga, art for kids, aerobics, tai chi, meditation, holotropic breath work, horseback riding, Mexican cooking, and a few others we can't even pronounce.

With time on their hands, many retirees give their energy freely to volunteer organizations. Some groups like the Center for San Miguel Adolescents, Save the Children, and the Audubon Society work to help solve poverty and health problems in the countryside. Many foreigners volunteer at the orphanage, the home for disabled children, or groups that assist the elderly. Foreigners also stack books in the library, set type for the local gringo newspaper, act with one of the three theater groups in town, and help out with the chamber music festivals and the jazzfest.

San Miguel has so many grandly impressive Catholic churches that you might want to become a Catholic. But those not so inclined have other choices: Baptist, Episcopal, Jewish, Mormon, Unitarian, Friends of Unity, Baha'i, Jehovah's Witnesses, Friends (Quaker), as well as a Buddhist Meditation Center.

Congregations and individuals offer lectures, retreats, and workshops on all sorts of esoteric subjects, given by local and visiting spiritual teachers, some internationally known. The town also has a spiritual bookstore. Alcoholics Anonymous holds daily meetings.

Recreation and Relaxation

There is nothing for weary bones and muscles like soaking in a thermal hot spring. There are at least 10 such springs within 10 minutes of San Miguel. The most popular are La Gruta, Escondido, and Taboada.

Cante, a cactus garden of about 150 acres, is a pleasant uphill walk from Centro. It is a relaxing place used by surprisingly few people. For longer hikes, visit the nearby Picacho Mountains, which you can reach by bus—or foot if you have the juice. It is best to take a car to visit the local pyramid or Canyon de Las Virgenes. Both are worth the trip.

In town, Walter Weber's are the main tennis courts. They are clay and nicely cared for. Ten minutes away by cab is the Club de Golf Malanquin, the local country club. Here you have to pay more to use the clay courts, but you will also get use of the pool and restaurant. The club's main feature is a very pleasant nine-hole golf course.

Dining and Nightlife

Most expats don't work, so every night can be Saturday night in San Miguel. It seems there is always something to celebrate. Going out on the town is easy and fairly inexpensive.

What's your pleasure? San Miguel doesn't have it all, but it does have a good selection of restaurants—Italian, French, Chinese, Argentinean, and Middle Eastern. Maybe you would prefer the vegetarian restaurant, one serving ribs, or the old-fashioned American place serving burgers and fries. There are even seafood restaurants in the desert.

Mexican restaurants range from fancy, with romantic atmosphere, excellent food, and high prices, to holes-in-the-wall with low prices and also great food. One restaurant serves Mexican food from Chiapas and another from the Chapala area. There are even a few greasy spoons—bad ones. Happily, there are no U.S. fast-food joints at all.

After eating, a walk around the dimly lit, romantic streets may be enough for you. If it's not, bars and restaurants offer after-dinner music and dancing, including salsa, jazz, blues, rock and roll, and disco. And a good cup of coffee, espresso, or cappuccino is easy to find any time of day or evening in small cafés and restaurants. Check out the Italian café in the Bellas Artes for an afternoon coffee.

Medical Services

Good, mostly bilingual local doctors can handle most general medical problems. The phonebook also lists a large number of specialists in private practice or associated with San Miguel's Hospital de la Fe. Local doctors and pathology labs can identify most common problems relatively quickly. They are especially astute at diagnosing stomach problems because they are so common in Mexico.

Some foreign residents with special medical situations feel safer seeing a doctor in the larger city of Querétaro, about 40 minutes away. There, the shiny new Hospital San Jose has a good reputation. Other people swear by the hospitals and doctors in San Luis Potosi, about 90 minutes away. It is widely agreed that the absolute best medical care in the country is found in Mexico City, about three hours away. The ABC (American-British-Cawdry) Hospital is considered top-notch.

Don't worry about bringing Spot to live in San Miguel. The town has many competent vets.

Money

Lloyd Asociados, where most foreign residents have accounts, probably offers the widest range of services, including paying utility bills when you are out of town. The bank is reliable and the best for international services such as bank-to-bank transfers.

However, even Lloyd can make you shake your head in amazement. On the occasional busy Friday afternoon, you might stand in line for half an hour, then arrive at the cage to find out that the bank has run out of money. "But," you are told, "the money truck is on its way!"

Other local banks are branches of larger Mexican banks. They operate pretty much the same as U.S. banks, with ATMs, checkbooks, and interest-bearing accounts. But it is important to note that few of the banks in Mexico have dollar accounts. Any money transferred to a Mexican bank account from a U.S. bank will be converted to pesos.

Most money-changing booths (*casas de cambio*) are open longer hours than banks and give as good a rate of exchange. Several will make special arrangements with foreign residents to cash personal checks from outside of Mexico.

Communications

In the past, telephones were at a premium in San Miguel. If you wanted to be sure to have a phone, you had to rent or buy a house that already had one. Now Telmex says it has added more phone lines and that getting a phone is not a problem. Still, if you want a phone it is a good idea to stop by the Telmex office and check avail-ability. Plans are afoot to overhaul the entire Mexican system and provide more lines and services. Cellular phones are always available, and cost is about the same as in the States.

San Miguel has two Internet service providers, both offering short- and long-term Internet service. Contact them at unisono@unisono .net.mx and mpsnet.com.mx. Unisono also maintains a complete San Miguel information Web site.

Sending and receiving mail through the Mexican postal system can be risky. Letters are slow to arrive, and packages may not arrive at all. More reliable are the private mail services (Border Crossings, Pack 'n' Mail, Mail Boxes, Etc., La Conexion) that operate in San Miguel. They provide patrons with a U.S. mailing address, from which mail is transferred daily by UPS to San Miguel. Letters from the States or Canada usually arrive in five or six days.

Books and other heavy objects can be very expensive to ship, due to import duties and overweight charges. We once ordered the Sunday *New York Times* and received it Tuesday. But when we saw the charges for the extra weight, we decided the paper wasn't worth it. We have since been told that La Conexion does not charge as much for weight. Please check this out yourself.

Market Basket

In the European style, many people shop for food daily at small mom-and-pop corner stores or at the stalls in one of two large pub-lic markets. No matter where people live in town, they always are within a block or two of a small grocery store, a pharmacy, and a knickknack shop. The large central markets are the most colorful and interesting places to shop and people-watch. Stalls display fresh fruit, produce, meat, chicken, flowers, and a few unrecognizables.

Food prices in San Miguel are more or less comparable to food prices in the other main retirement cities. The best deals are found at the markets in Centro, where you can still try to bargain. You may not get a lower price, but you might get a few extra bananas for the same price.

Organic produce is sold at the El Tomate market. Specialty shops sell fine cheeses, meats, and imported delicatessen items from the States, Europe, and South America. For more variety, locals head to San Miguel's one and only mall, just outside town, where the Gigante supermarket is located.

To enter a twentieth-century shopping experience, San Miguelitos drive 40 minutes to Querétaro, where they can shop at WalMart, Price Club, Sam's, Sears or Office Depot. Querétaro has one of the most beautiful colonial downtowns in Mexico. Once outside of Centro, though, it is modern "Mall City," with upmarket clothing and shoe stores, U.S. restaurant chains like KFC, and a new 12-plex movie theater. After a Querétaro Price Club shopping excursion, try a first-run movie before going back in time to San Miguel.

Cuernavaca

Cuernavaca has long been among the most desirable cities for foreign retirees. It is renowned internationally for its beauty and perfect climate. But in the last few years much of the press in the United States about Cuernavaca has been negative, giving the impression that the city is nothing more than a smaller version of sprawling, polluted, crowded, and crime-ridden Mexico City. The last time we visited Cuernavaca was almost 30 years ago, when it was still a small town with clear air. We seriously considered leaving it out of this book, but thought it only fair to go see the changes for ourselves. We were prepared for the worst!

As we approached Cuernavaca, we once again understood why so many expatriates have been attracted by its beauty. The city drapes over miles of a steep, broad valley, surrounded by layers of high mountain peaks. The highest and most imposing is the magnificent, 15,000-foot Mount Popocatepetl volcano, which dominates the horizon (when it is not shrouded in clouds).

Adding to the drama of the setting is a change in altitude from the upper end of town (6,000 feet) to the lower (5,000 feet), which doesn't sound like much but helps create pronounced differences in climate. At the upper end of town are mountain pine forests, where residents experience chilly nights and clear, dry days. Descending

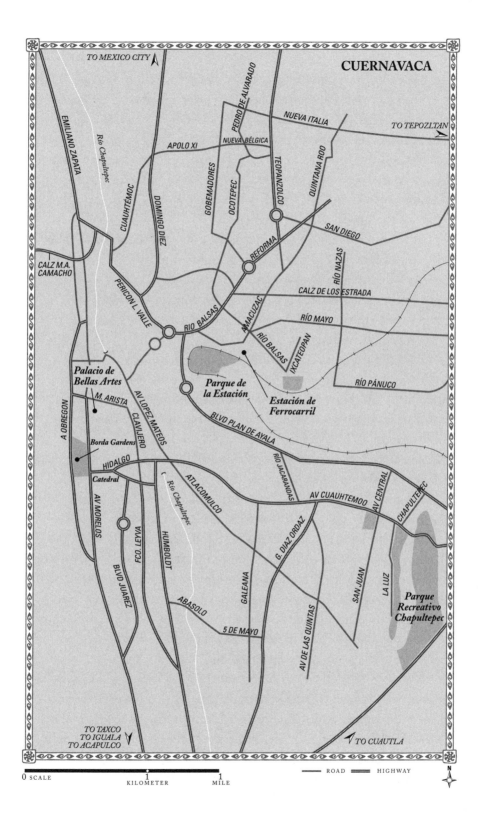

into the valley, the climate becomes warmer and more humid. At the lower end of town the climate is semitropical. Homes here have lush tropical gardens and swimming pools. Though the upper and lower ends of town are each only about 10 minutes away from the center, the change from one to the other is radical. We are told that some Cuernavacans live in the warmer, lower part of town and have second homes (weekend getaways) just 20 minutes away in the drier forests of the upper end.

Because of its near-perfect climate, Cuernavaca has been called "the City of Eternal Spring." Average year-round temperatures are between 70 and 90 degrees, with relatively low humidity, even at the lower end of town. The rainy season, in summer and early fall, brings sunny mornings and, usually, late afternoon or evening showers. Winter days are sunny and dry.

From the valley, the city radiates out onto hills, with canyons (*barrancas*) separating them. It is often impossible to cross from one barranca to another without first going back toward the center of town to connect with the road that goes up the barranca you want. With so many hills overlooking the valley below, residents have spectacular views from most parts of town.

Cuernavaca has definitely grown into a city of contradictions. The colonial downtown (Centro) is bustling, noisy, and traffic clogged, like any big city. It is a commercial and tourist hub of museums, markets, outdoor cafés, sidewalk balloon sellers, shops of all kinds, government office buildings, and streets bustling with people hurrying in every direction. Magnificent colonial buildings on quaint streets huddle next to ugly modern monsters. At first we found Centro intimidating. Once we got into its rhythm, we began to enjoy playing tourist, visiting museums, eating in great restaurants, and people-watching in the park.

When we left Centro and began exploring the city, we found sections that looked like they hadn't changed much in 400 years (except for overhead electric wires, TV antennas, and cars). We discovered old-fashioned winding streets, made narrow by beautifully hand-built stone walls. Small houses sit next to grand mansions with swimming pools and lush gardens. These streets are in direct contrast to the newer, less attractive, and humbler areas, where the majority of Cuernavaca's citizens live.

Since the time of the Aztecs, Cuernavaca has been a home and weekend getaway for Mexico's (and the world's) rich and famous. The Italian royal family chose Cuernavaca as its new home when it was forced out of Italy before World War II; many family members still live there. The city's normal population of 800,000 to 1 million often explodes by half again on weekends, with an invasion from Mexico City.

Though Cuernavaca is relatively close to the culture and amenities of Mexico City, it has plenty of culture of its own: universities, research institutions, movie houses, concerts, art galleries, spas, theaters, discotheques, sidewalk cafés, and modern shopping malls. It also has fine schools, first-rate medical facilities, and some of the best restaurants in the world.

Unfortunately, Cuernavaca's proximity to Mexico City has caused problems. Along with more people, crime, polluting industries, and a growing number of cars and buses have taken up residence in the city. Though not as bad as Mexico City, Cuernavaca's air pollution can be noticeable at times.

For several years Cuernavaca had the dubious distinction of ranking among the two or three top international kidnapping capitals. A few years ago, a kidnapping ring, which included top city and state officials, was exposed, and the governor of the state was forced to resign.

While they are concerned, locals don't seem preoccupied with crime. We talked to many residents who merely shrugged. Most increase security however they can, but live without fear. Some residents have moved to one of the smaller, more tranquil, and safer nearby villages, like Tepotzlan, Xochitepec, or Cocoyoc.

Each of these outlying towns is uniquely attractive. Tepotzlan, just 20 minutes away, is located in one of the most spectacular mountain settings in all Mexico. The town itself, built in a gently sloping valley, has interesting shops and restaurants that attract a tourist crowd from Mexico City on weekends. Views in every direction are breathtaking.

Ken Luboff

A busy downtown Cuernavaca street

Even with its problems, Cuernavaca has definite attractions as a retirement community. It has a great climate, a beautiful setting, a variety of cultural activities, and, maybe most important, a friendly, accepting, and interesting foreign community. It is easy to reach by air and only three hours from Acapulco by car. If you like the idea of living in a moderately large, active city, this might be the place for you.

History

The valley around Cuernavaca is so beautiful that it is easy to see why it attracted the Chichimecans in the 1200s and then the Aztecs. Before cars, when it was a small town, it must have been a restful paradise. At 7,000 feet, Mexico City can get pretty chilly in the winter, and the Aztec emperors were no fools. They would escape the cold, moving to the year-round springlike climate of the town they called Cuauhnahuac—"place of great trees."

After the conquest of Mexico in 1521, it didn't take long for Hernán Cortés and his buddies to discover the climate and beauty of the town whose name they mispronounced as *cuerno de vaca*—"horn of the cow." Cuernavaca was one of 30 Mexican cities awarded to Cortés by the Spanish crown, and it was his favorite. Cortés began building his palace in the city in 1530. *Palace* is not quite the right word to describe Cortés's home. The building in downtown Cuernavaca looks more like a small castle or fortress.

In 1529 Cortés founded the St. Francis Cathedral, one of the oldest churches in Mexico and known for its mariachi masses. Eventually Cortés retired to Cuernavaca to live in his fortress and at a sugar plantation he owned on the outskirts of town.

Cuernavaca remained a haven for the rich of Mexico City and the surrounding areas. Jose de la Bordo, Taxco's silver baron, built a palace there, as did Emperor Maximilian and Empress Carlota. Maximilian even had a home in Cuernavaca for his mistress, La India Bonita.

In nearby Cualtla, in 1911, Emiliano Zapata signed his famous Plan de Ayala, calling for land reform. A large statue of Zapata on horseback at the top of a major boulevard pays tribute to him.

North Americans first became aware of Cuernavaca in the 1930s, when Dwight Morrow was the U.S. ambassador to Mexico. Morrow and his family loved the city and spent as much time there as possible. After Dwight's daughter married Charles Lindbergh, Cuernavaca became widely known to people in the States.

Still, Cuernavaca remained a relatively small, quiet city until the Mexico City earthquake of 1985. The quake caused so much destruction and fear in the city that, to escape future quakes, people who could afford to began buying land and building in Cuernavaca. The population has continued to grow rapidly ever since.

How to Get There

It is fairly inexpensive to fly directly into the Cuernavaca airport from the larger cities in Mexico. From Guadalajara or Monterrey, a one-way flight costs about $40. From Tijuana it's about $100. From most points in the States, you'll fly into Mexico City's Benito

Juarez International Airport and then take the direct bus to Cuernavaca (ask a porter in the airport to show you to the bus). Buses leave frequently, but on an erratic schedule. Shared vans depart for Cuernavaca every two hours or so.

Buses also head to Cuernavaca on a regular basis from the Terminal de Autobuses de Sur in Mexico City. A taxi from the airport to the bus station costs just a few dollars, but a taxi directly to Cuernavaca costs about $80.

If you are driving from the north or west and have time for a detour, avoid driving through Mexico City. Instead, head toward Toluca on autopisto 55D, which originates in Guadalajara, where it is called 15D. You can also connect with it driving south from Querétaro. From Toluca, you will head south to Cuernavaca on a wonderfully picturesque road that eventually goes on to Taxco. A good map will help you get through Toluca.

Driving down from Texas, it is easier to "bite the bullet" and drive through Mexico City. Be sure not to drive in the city on the wrong license-plate number day (see Chapter 9: "Travel and Transportation"). We recommend that you go to AAA for a map and detailed instructions for traversing Mexico City.

Foreign and Local Communities

In the old days, Cuernavaca had a number of diverse foreign communities. It must have felt a little like the colony of a foreign power, what with the British Club, the American Club, the Canadian Club (not the drink), and various other national groups. The clubs functioned as meeting places and clearinghouses for each group. Very little social interaction occurred between the different foreign nationals, except among the very rich.

These days, the various clubs have dissolved into one large English-speaking club, which includes Europeans, Canadians, British, Americans, and English-speaking Mexicans (mainly those married to foreigners). We were surprised to find that the foreign community keeps pretty much to itself. Most foreigners don't speak much Spanish, except what is needed for normal daily interaction with Mexican employees, shopkeepers, and the like. Wealthy Mexicans, who circulate in the same society as wealthy foreigners, belong to the same country clubs, eat in the same restaurants, and attend the same parties, usually speak some English.

On our trips to Cuernavaca we have met many wonderfully down-to-earth and friendly foreign residents. We noticed there is a more defined and stratified social order there than in most other Mexican expatriate communities.

Real Estate

In Cuernavaca, you can have your choice of neighborhoods (*colonias*) with diverse geological features, ethnic makeups, and climate zones. Real estate runs the gamut from million-dollar mansions to modest two-bedroom homes for less than $75,000. In purely Mexican neighborhoods, the price of a home can be even less. Here are a few examples of what is available:

- An elegantly furnished colonial house with three large bedrooms, terraces, a guest house, pool, great view, gazebo, phone, and cable TV for $600,000, in an area of elegant homes, south of Centro, called Chipitlan
- A two-bedroom condo on a quiet street on the north side of town, with a garden, pool, studio, and doorman for $65,000
- A beautiful five-bedroom, seven-bathroom house in Tlaltenango, one of the oldest, most picturesque parts of town, with a guest house, pool, and large beautiful garden, walled and on a very large city lot, for $350,000

Communities near Cuernavaca are also attracting foreigners. These towns are all lush and beautiful, with many colonial buildings. In most cases, prices are far less than those for similar properties in Cuernavaca. Towns like Jiutepec, just south of Cuernavaca; Tepotzlan, about 20 minutes away; Xochitepec, to the south; and Cualtla, 45 minutes to the east, are more peaceful and crime free. If you can live without the action of the city, these towns may be for you. We saw a mini-hacienda, 15 minutes south of Cuernavaca, with five bedrooms, six bathrooms, two phones, and a very large lot with a great garden for only $140,000. What a great deal!

Rentals

Nice furnished houses and one-bedroom apartments rent for $400 to $600 per month in town. A two-bedroom, one-and-a-half-bathroom furnished house, only one block from Plaza Cuernavaca, recently rented for $500 per month. A two-bedroom house with a pool and garden in a nice area rented for $1,000 per month.

Arts and Entertainment

The city's social life revolves around dinners and parties among friends, nights out at one of Cuernavaca's famous restaurants, or activities at local clubs, galleries, and museums. The Robert Brady Museum, tel. (73) 18-8554 offers a classic film club, a lecture series, conferences, and events like the annual Day of the Dead celebration. The museum (known as the Casa de la Torre) is the former home of Robert Brady (1928–1986). It houses his collection of more than 1,300 objects of art, including Mexican colonial furniture, pre-Hispanic figures, primitive art of Africa, Asia, America, and India, and paintings by Diego Rivera, Frieda Khalo, and Rufino Tamayo among others. Other museums in town are the Xochicalco Museum, exhibiting indigenous baskets, and the Ethnobotanical Museum, with a collection of traditional herbal medicines and native Mexican plants.

Music, theater, and dance are widely available. Organizations like the Cuauhnahuac Museum, Amigos de la Musica, Jardin Borda, the University Center Gallery, and the Instituto Regional de Bellas Artes sponsor regular classical concerts, theater, and dance events. Musical events from the famous Cervantino Festival are performed in Cuernavaca every October. Teatro Ocampo also holds regularly scheduled musical, dance, and theatrical events.

The Borda Gardens, opposite the Cuernavaca Cathedral, is part of the residence built by Jose de la Borda, who came to Mexico from France in 1716 and made a fortune mining silver. Both the gardens and house were used by Emperor Maximilian and Empress Carlota for weekend getaways and parties. The Palace of Cortés, now known as the Museo de Cuauhnahuac, was built by Cortés in 1530. Among other treasures, the palace owns a number of murals by Diego Rivera. Both the Borda Gardens and the Palace of Cortés are used for cultural events.

When we last visited Cuernavaca, the Ballet Folklorico de Xochiphilli and the Danza Flamenca were both performing. A flute and harp concert was offered the same night. Every night you can hear live music at Sanborns or another club or restaurant in town. And remember that Mexico City, with its infinite variety and big-name performers, is only one hour away.

Cable TV is widely available, with a good selection of U.S. stations, including CNN and Fox. For movie fans, many theaters offer the latest U.S. releases, in English with Spanish subtitles. (By the way, reading those Spanish subtitles on the big screen is great way to

Ken Luboff

Borda Gardens

study Spanish.) The Brady Cine Club and the Cine Club Morelos show art films.

Newspapers and Books

The one and only English-language newspaper in town is the *Cuernavaca Lookout*. It is relatively new and small but will give you important insights into life in Cuernavaca. The paper can be reached by phone at (73) 13-2102.

A useful little book, *Cuernavaca, A Guide for Students & Tourists* by James Horn, gives information about life and services in the city. It is worth reading if you are considering a move to Cuernavaca. Contact Educational Travel Service at 716/637-6983 for a copy.

The Guild Library, (73) 12-5197, is a lending library with a selection of used books for sale. It is part of the Guild House, which raises money for charity through monthly thrift and bake sales. For more information call Jan Sloan at (73) 15-2239 or Jean Molina at (73) 15-3053. The library at the University of Morelos has a reading room, and the Cemanahuac Educational Community also runs a library. The only bookstores in town selling new books in English are Sanborns (two locations) and the American Book Store, (73) 11-3910.

Community Organizations

The Newcomers Club welcomes all English-speaking residents, regardless of nationality, even if they are old-timers. It provides information for new arrivals in town and organizes a wide variety of annual events. For information call Sue Schutt at (73) 82-0372 or Sue Romo at (73) 16-3434. The Creative Arts Center sponsors English-language plays, craft and fine arts fairs, concerts, and ongoing cultural celebrations such as an annual Christmas party. It also publishes a bilingual newspaper. For more information call (73) 11-7914, (73) 13-8115, or (73) 17-1790. The American Society of Cuernavaca is currently being organized. For information call Yvonne Flores, (73) 13-2905 or (73) 13-0632. The Navy League holds monthly luncheons with a variety of speakers. Call (73) 13-2768 for information.

The Cemanahuac Educational Community provides regular guided tours of Cuernavaca, Latin American studies courses, field trips to local archaeological and historical sites, lectures, workshops, and videos. It also has a small library of English books. Call (73) 18-6407 or (73) 12-6419 for more information.

People come to Cuernavaca from around the world to study Spanish and immerse themselves in Mexican culture. Many live with a Mexican family. These visits are arranged by schools like the Center for Bilingual Multicultural Studies, tel. (73) 17-1087, the Cuernavaca Language School, tel. (73) 17-5151, the Tlahuica Spanish Learning Center, 800/746-8335, and the Universal Centro de Lengua y Comunicacion Social, tel. (73) 18-2904 or (73) 12-4902.

Cuernavaca is also an academic center, with fine universities and research institutions. The Instituto Tecnologico y de Estudios Superiores de Monterrey, for instance, operates twenty or so research institutions in fields such as physics, electrical engineering, traditional medicine, solar energy, biotechnology, genetic engineering, marketing, and anthropology. These and other fine facilities draw a large number of Ph.D.s, M.D.s, scientists, and researchers to the city.

Families with young kids will be pleased to know that Cuernavaca has several bilingual schools. These include the Instituto Suizo-American, grades K–12, tel. (73) 16-0400, Discovery School, grades K–12, tel. (73) 18-5721, Colegio Marymount, grades 7–12, tel. (73) 13-1602, Centro Educativo Bilingue, grades K–12, tel. (73) 13-0911, and the Colegio Porter, grades K–6, tel. (73) 13-4070.

For after-school activities, La Vecindad offers dance, photography, painting, art, science, and theater courses, with special courses for children with Down's syndrome. Casa de la Ciencia offers workshops in science, physics, math, and chemistry for children three years old and up.

Catholic, Protestant, Baptist, Episcopal, and Orthodox Jewish congregations are represented in town. Services are held in English. Esoteric and metaphysical workshops and courses add another dimension to the spiritual community. The Camino Real Sumiya, formerly the Barbara Hutton estate and now a restaurant, offers something of a combination spiritual and gastronomic experience. The restaurant has a Zen meditation garden and a prayer temple.

An English-speaking Alcoholics Anonymous group meets Monday, Tuesday, and Thursday at 5:30 p.m. at Privada Chilancingo, Colonia Teopanzolco. For more information call (73) 13-7831

Market Basket

No place in Mexico has more shopping variety than Mexico City. You can get anything you want there, and it is just an hour away from Cuernavaca. Cuernavaca also has its share of shops and galleries selling clothes, jewelry, pottery, antiques, leather, and native crafts.

For more practical items, the city has several shopping centers and malls, the largest of which is Plaza Cuernavaca. These malls contain a variety of supermarkets, shops, and mega-stores like Aurrera, Commercial Mexicana, Morelos Sur, Woolworth, K-Mart, Sears, and Sam's Club. Of course, every neighborhood has food markets and specialty shops.

By far the lowest food prices in town are at the Adolfo Lopez Mateos Market in Centro. This is where most people shop when they don't mind fighting the crowds and the traffic. Alternatives are the mega-stores like Aurora and Commercia Mexicana and large supermarkets like Superama La Selva and Super Morelos. The best place to find items from the United States is Sam's Club. When you need a few eggs, some bread, or milk, there is always a local store nearby.

Golf or Tennis, Anyone?

Tennis players will find at least half a dozen places to play, ranging from free public courts to the Villa International de Tenis, the Tennis Palace, and the elegant Cuernavaca Raquet Club.

Golfers can choose among at least seven well-maintained 18-hole courses. A few are the Hacienda San Gaspar Golf Club, the Santa Fe Golf Club, the the Tabachin Country Club on the Mexico–Acapulco road, and the Club de Golf de Cuernavaca.

Gyms, fitness centers, and hotels offer other sports options, including swimming, weight training, aerobics, tai chi, dance, and yoga classes. Cuernavaca even has a bowling alley.

Dining and Nightlife

You'll find some excellent restaurants in Cuernavaca. Probably the most well known is Las Mananitas, said to have the best food in Mexico. Meals are served in an exquisite garden setting, complete with wandering peacocks and flamingos. The ambiance and service are first class. Las Mananitas is also a small and very exclusive hotel.

For good food served amid formal Japanese gardens, try Casa Real Sumiya. It's located about 15 minutes south of town and worth the trip. Other notable fine restaurants include Ex-Hacienda de Cortez, Maximillian's, Centro Castellano, and Hosteria Las Quintas, to name just a few.

You don't have to spend big money to get a good meal. You'll find restaurants in all price ranges and types, including Chinese, Italian, German, Japanese, seafood, Mexican, and some decidedly U.S.-style fast-food joints like VIPS.

The bar scene includes everything from quiet, romantic lounges to discos, complete with strobe lights and loud canned music. Clubs feature salsa, rock and roll, and piano music. Discos come and go, so ask at the Newcomers Club for the latest "in" places.

Getting Around in the City

Cuernavaca, like every Mexican city, has an extensive and very inexpensive bus system. Look for blue-and-white signs with a picture of a bus and the word *parada* (stop). Buses are slow and crowded, but at least they are cheap.

Taxis cost more (but are still reasonable), are plentiful in good weather, and are convenient. Ask what the fare will be before you get in.

Medical Services

Reputedly, the best hospitals in the country are in nearby Mexico City, but Cuernavaca has its own excellent medical facilities. Four public hospitals provide high-quality care. Hospital Cuernavaca was recommended to us, as was Hospital de Nino Morelence for children. One of the largest medical clinics is the Grupo Medico Rio Mayo, which has a large staff of specialists and excellent lab facilities. The Dental Specialty Clinic has on-staff specialists in pediatric dentistry, reconstructive surgery, general dentistry, and orthodontics. The local phone directory lists pages of dentists and doctors, who represent most medical and psychiatric specialties.

Communications

The Cafe San Jeronimo advertises that it "Bytes the Bagel," whatever that means. The café, which offers bagels, coffee, and Internet access, is located in Tlaltenango. Another Internet café is the Axon Cyber Cafe, tel./fax (73) 12-8525, e-mail: webmaster@axon.com.mx.

Local Internet service providers are Infosel Cuernavaca in Chapultepec, tel. (73) 22-7300 or (73) 22-7300, infocuernavaca @infosel.net.mx or andy@infosel.net.mx, and ciberic@infosel.net.mx. For international mail, foreign residents usually use a private mailing service such as Mail Boxes, Etc.

Consulate and Immigration

The nearest office dealing with U.S. passport problems is the U.S. embassy in Mexico City, Paseo de la Reforma 305, tel. (5) 209-9100. The Mexican immigration office in Mexico City is at the corner of Chapultepec and Insurgentes.

Mazatlán

Our first few trips through Mazatlán were quickies made 27 years ago, on the way from the States to beaches farther south. Our memories of Mazatlán were of a crowded, brassy, tourist resort town. When this book became a reality, we decided to return to Mazatlan to see if it, or we, had changed and if it now qualified to be included in this book. Here is what we found:

Mazatlán is really two cities in one, stretched out along beautiful beaches on the Pacific Ocean. At the southern end is the old city and the port of Mazatlán. In Old Town, also called Centro, you get the sense of a city that has seen better days. Here we found tattered and worn-out colonial buildings sitting alongside humble dwellings. Some run-down mansions have been, or are in the process of being, restored. Many are still in ruins. With some love and money, they could be bought cheaply and resurrected.

Mazatlán's Centro has the feel of many other mid-sized Mexican towns, with high-energy hustle and bustle around the shopping areas, main market, and grand cathedral in the center of town. Old Town has some pretty good restaurants and an archaeological museum, but it is made up mostly of blocks of poor-looking, but very clean, residential streets.

Mazatlán's only hills tower over Centro, Mexico's largest Pacific

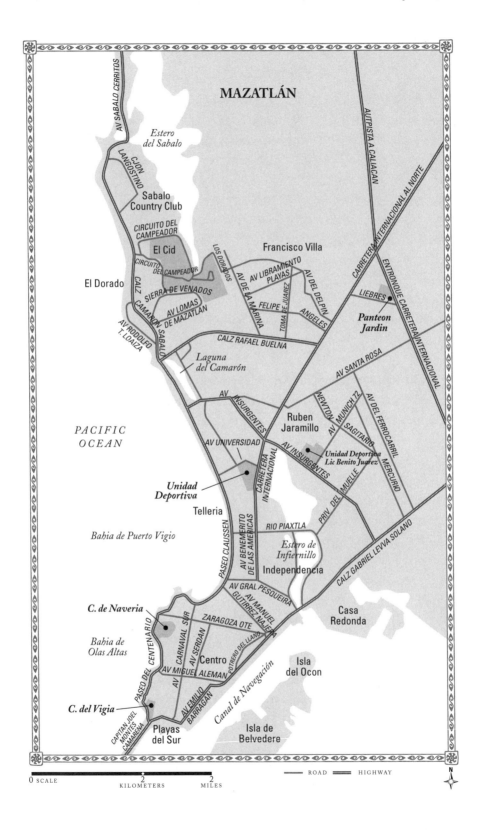

MAZATLÁN

AV SABALO CERRITOS

AUTPISTA A CALIACAN

Estero
del Sabalo

CARRETERA INTERNACIONAL AL NORTE

ENTRONQUE CARRETERA INTERNACIONAL

CJON
LANGOSTINO

Sabalo
Country Club

CIRCUITO DEL
CAMPEADOR

El Cid

Francisco Villa

El Dorado

CIRCUITO DEL CAMPEADOR

LOS DORADOS

AV LIBRAMIENTO
PLAYAS

AV DEL DELPIN

LIEBRES

CALZ
CAMARON SABALO

SIERRA DE VENADOS

AV DE LA MARINA

AV LOMAS
DE MAZATLAN

FELIPE

TOMA DE JUAREZ

ANGELES

Panteon
Jardin

AV RODOLFO
T. LOAIZA

CALZ RAFAEL BUELNA

AV SANTA ROSA

Laguna
del Camarón

AV INSURGENTES

Ruben
Jaramillo

NEWTON

AV MUNICH TZ

AV SAGITARIO

AV DEL FERROCARRIL

MERCURIO

PACIFIC
OCEAN

AV UNIVERSIDAD

CARRETERA INTERNACIONAL

AV INSURGENTES

Unidad Deportiva
Lic Benito Juarez

PRIV. DEL MUELLE

Unidad
Deportiva

Telleria

RIO PIAXTLA

CALZ GABRIEL LEVVA SOLANO

Bahia de Puerto Vigio

PASEO CLAUSSEN

AV BENEMERITO
DE LAS AMÉRICAS

Estero de
Infiernillo

Independencia

AV GRAL PESQUEIRA

C. de Naveria

ZARAGOZA OTE

AV MANUEL
GUTIRRE NAJERA

Casa
Redonda

Bahia de
Olas Altas

PASEO DEL CENTENARIO

AV CARNAVAL SUR

AV SERDAN

Centro

AV MIGUEL ALEMAN

SOTRERO DEL LLANO

Isla
del Ocon

C. del Vigia

CAPITAN JOEL
MONTES
CAMARENA

AV EMILIO
BARRAGAN

AV

Playas
del Sur

Canal de Navegación

Isla de
Belvedere

0 SCALE

2
KILOMETERS

2
MILES

ROAD   HIGHWAY

N

port, and the city's sprawling commercial and residential districts. The views from these hills are fabulous. The highest is called Ice Box Hill; in the early twentieth century, ships unloaded ice into a cave, called El Diablo, cut into the hillside. The cave is still there, on the ocean side of the hill. Nearby is Cerro del Creston, where the El Faro lighthouse sits 500 feet above the sea.

About eight miles north of downtown, along a four-lane beach-front avenue called the Malecon, is the main tourist area of Mazatlán—the Zona Dorado, or Golden Zone. This is where the majority of Mazatlán's large hotels, restaurants, bars, fast-food joints, galleries, and real estate offices are located. Crowds invade this part of town during the main tourist season (fall and winter) and especially during the famous Mazatlán Carnival, one of the largest Mardi Gras celebrations in Latin America.

To the east and north of the Golden Zone are the residential areas and marinas, where the majority of Mazatlán's 3,000 to 5,000 foreign residents live during the winter high season. This number includes people living in RVs and the 200 to 300 who live on boats

Ken Luboff

Mazatlán's beaches beckon.

in the marinas. The number of foreigners in residence drops radically at other times of year, especially during the hot summer. Almost all foreigners come from the States and Canada.

Even though Mazatlán has 500,000 to 600,000 residents, it felt smaller to us, despite the densely populated downtown. It doesn't have the "sophisticated" feel of some other retirement cities. It isn't pretentious, probably one of the factors helping to keep prices down. Mazatlán is a port of call for the "Love Boat." Well, not *the* Love Boat—but almost the same thing. Four cruise lines stop here regularly, on what they call "Mexico's Riviera." These are big babies, with one ship bringing as many as 2,200 passengers! And they all hit the Golden Zone together. Can you imagine!

Retirees choose Mazatlán for its proximity to the States, its great climate (with an average 82 degrees year-round), its low cost of living, and its relatively low crime rate (the city has robberies, but little violent crime). It is also physically beautiful, with long, wide beaches running from one end of town to the other. To the north and south of the city are many miles of deserted beach. Mountains frame the horizon to the east.

But not everything we learned about Mazatlán was positive. An expatriate who has lived here for many years told us that the town is changing in some unpleasant ways. He says that drugs have come to the schools, and graffiti is showing up on walls. He believes that the young are showing less respect for older people (by the way, he is not an "older" person). He is also upset that development has slowed to a crawl, compared to Puerto Vallarta and Cabo San Lucas, because of political infighting. Maybe he's just a grump!

This is not a community with New Age, arty, or intellectual pretentiousness. Though the town has a small theater group and a small art school, its has no large English-language libraries or language schools to attract serious students. To us, Mazatlán's foreign community felt very middle American, and not like a place for the black sheep of the family.

History

Even though Mazatlán had been known to Spanish sailors since 1531, when Spanish explorer Nuno de Guzman founded the town, it took the Germans to really get the place going. Until a group of German immigrants moved here in the 1830s, Mazatlán was fairly uncivilized. The Germans developed the port as a way of importing agricultural equipment. Then they left their mark on the town in the form of Pacifico beer, which is manufactured in Mazatlán.

Long before the arrival of the Spanish or the Germans, Mazatlán was called Mazatl—"Place of the Deer"—by the Nahuatl Indians who lived here. Indeed, it is not hard to imagine huge herds of deer roaming the plain between the ocean and the mountains to the east.

In the early 1600s, almost one hundred years after the town was officially inaugurated by Spain, gold and silver were mined in nearby mountain towns, transported to the bay, and loaded into Spanish galleons for the trip back to Spain. Stories abound of famous pirates attacking these ships, stealing the treasure, and burying it along the coast.

During the short reign of French Emperor Maximilian in the 1860s, Mexican troops fighting French troops in Mazatlán seized a large quantity of gold from the mines, helping to bring about Maximilian's defeat.

By the beginning of the twentieth century, Mazatlán's port was thriving, and its tourist industry was beginning to develop. Early visitors were especially attracted to the weather and the good hunting and fishing in the region. Throughout the twentieth century, Mazatlán continued to attract sportsmen and vacationers looking for warm water, a great climate, and an enjoyable place to relax. Although the hunting isn't what it used to be, the fishing here is still first rate.

How to Get There

Mazatlán is easily accessible by car from the States, a feature that appeals to retirees. It is only 735 miles south of the U.S. border at Nogales (just south of Tucson)—the first large beach resort/port city you come to heading down Mexico's west coast. The drive from Nogales takes a day and a half (a day if you push hard) on good-quality, four-lane Highway 15.

It would be an even easier trip if it weren't for the harassment that some drivers receive from Mexican officials on this stretch of road. Immigration at Nogales usually goes pretty smoothly, but about 21 miles into Mexico you will come to an *aduana* (customs) inspection point. The officers have been known to harass travelers, with a threat to search cars until a tip (*mordida*) is paid.

To make matters worse, you may be stopped again at the Sonora/Sinaloa state line by the PGR, a bunch of thuggish-looking federal police searching for guns and drugs. (Drugs entering Mexico? Say what?) They often carry automatic weapons and .45s. Just the threat of having your car searched in high desert temperatures is enough to convince some to part with a few dollars. If you are stopped, just be polite and do as the officers say. Nobody has been hurt by these guys—except in the pocketbook. It is smooth sailing once you enter the state of Sinaloa, where Mazatlán is located.

South of Mazatlán, the road continues on to Tepic and Guadalajara and connects with the highway heading south to Puerto Vallarta. Heading north on this road, from Tepic to Mazatlán, you'll reach a checkpoint at which drivers must stop at an old-fashioned auto mechanic's pit for an inspection of the undersides of their cars. The inspection is done quickly with no aggravation, though the slow-moving line of traffic before you reach the checkpoint can drive you crazy. Have a book ready.

By bus, it is a pleasant and inexpensive trip from the States to Mazatlán. Several major Mexican bus lines run from Mexicali, Nogales, and other large border towns to Mazatlán and points south. We recommend top-of-the-line buses for long trips; check out prices for *lujo* and *executivo* buses, which are the most comfortable. Buses traveling both north and south of Mazatlán are pulled over and inspected.

The Pacifico and Sinaloense trains head south from Mexicali on the U.S. border and arrive in Mazatlán about 20 hours later. Each stops along the way at Nogales, Hermosillo, Culiacan, Obregon, and a few other places. We prefer the more comfortable Pacifico. As with buses, we recommend that you take first-class trains.

If you prefer to fly, many inexpensive flights arrive in Mazatlán daily from Los Angeles, San Francisco, Phoenix, Seattle, Vancouver, and points east.

The Foreign Community

Foreigners in Mazatlán seem to be down to earth and pretty laid back. Most retire here for the relaxed atmosphere, low prices, weather, fishing, and golf. Most are in their sixties and up, but we met a few working Americans and Canadians in their forties and fifties.

This is not a town where you will find much New Age thought, a strong literary guild, or a large community of foreign artists. In fact, the foreign community has a small-town, Midwest feeling. The people are conservative, but friendly. Most residential areas have a congenial mix of foreigners and Mexicans, even if there isn't too much social interaction between them.

Real Estate

The majority of Mazatlán's foreign residents live in the relatively new developments in the southern end of the Golden Zone. These areas are quiet, clean, and safe. Neighborhoods like Las Gaviotas and Sabalo Country Club (not really a country club) are popular because real estate prices are low, the areas are tranquil, and the beach and marinas are nearby. Even in gated communities on golf courses, marinas, or the beach, prices are reasonable.

A small number of foreigners prefer the more Mexican feeling of the old part of town. Some of the most expensive real estate is found on Ice Box and Lomas Hills, where the views of the city and harbor are spectacular.

We were surprised by the amount of prime, undeveloped land we saw in Mazatlán. Just north of town, along the beach, are large stretches of undeveloped property without a house in sight. Even in town, on the north side, we saw large undeveloped tracts. Such land provided a contrast to the densely packed Centro and the more developed coastal cities like Puerto Vallarta.

El Cid Resort

El Cid is the largest residential and commercial development in town. It includes a large hotel on the beach and, through a gated entrance to the rear, a residential area on a beautiful, 18-hole, par-72 golf course. Set around the course are both modest and opulent homes, including a $2 million home being built by a Mexican rock star. Among the private homes are groups of tennis villas built around several shared courts. These sell for $95,000 to $125,000 for a two-bedroom, two-bathroom home, and $135,000 and up for a three-bedroom, three-bathroom home.

All the homes in El Cid look newly painted, and the lawns are well clipped. Prices range from $78,000 for a small two-bedroom, two-bathroom house off the course to $100,000 for a two-bedroom, two-and-a-half-bathroom furnished town house on the eighth green. A three-bedroom, two-and-a-half-bathroom house on the 14th green, with a pool, costs about $135,000. Larger, more elegant homes sell in the $300,000 range. Most of the homes in El Cid are easily rented during summer. The area has a mix of Mexicans, Americans, and Canadians.

Ice Box and Lomas Hills

Ice Box and Lomas Hills are in the uptown part of Mazatlán. The views from the hills—both up and down the coast—can be breathtaking. Here you'll find a mix of large and small homes, older and new homes, and several with ultra-modern architecture.

Most homes on the hills are owned by Mexican families, with a few foreigners scattered around. Finding houses to buy or land for sale on the hills is difficult and expensive. There are few lots left and a limited number of homes. New houses here can sell for as much as $500,000.

Sabalo Country Club and Las Gaviotas

Sabalo Country Club and Las Gaviotas are non-gated, middle-class neighborhoods, two or three blocks from the beach. Clean and quiet, they contain mostly inexpensive houses and condos, with some larger homes. Sabalo Country Club is a little more expensive, with new three-bedroom, three-and-a-half-bathroom homes selling for $71,000 to $90,000 and some nice ocean-view apartments costing about $45,000. In Las Gaviotas we saw homes from $40,000.

North Side

Several small new gated beachside developments have sprung up north of town on the beach road. Prices in these developments vary. In La Paloma, about 12 miles north of town, beachfront homes start at $150,000. In another development, a new three-bedroom townhouse sold for $135,000.

Copala

Copala is a small mining town in the hills about 25 miles from Mazatlán. It is one of several nearby towns to which Mazatlán residents escape during the hot summer months. A small number of foreign residents from Mazatlán own second homes in Copala.

Renting

Finding something to rent at a low price is fairly easy here. We saw a 2,000-square-foot, three-bedroom apartment with a garden and a 16-by-40-foot living room that rented for $230 per month. In Las Gaviotas, an average two-bedroom house rents for around $500 per month. In El Cid, without much effort, we found a three-bedroom, two-bathroom house for $600 per month.

RV Parks and Marinas

Mazatlán attracts a quite a few RVers and sailors, especially during winter. RVers usually hang out with other RVers staying at the same park, sailors with other sailors. We counted eight RV parks with approximately 950 sites. They are:

- Las Palmas Trailer Camp, Cameron Sabalo, tel. (69) 13-5311
- La Posta Trailer Park, Centro, tel. (69) 83-5310
- Maravillas, on the beach, tel. (69) 14-0400
- Playa Escondida, North Side, tel. (69) 88-0077
- San Bartolo, Camaron Sabalo, tel. (69) 13-5765
- Holiday Trailer Park, Cerritos, tel. (69) 13-2578
- Las Canoas, Cerritos, tel. (69) 14-1616
- Mar Rosa Trailer Park, Camaron Sabalo, tel. (69) 13-6187

The average prices charged at these parks are $21 per day on the beach, $19 per day one row from the beach, $17 per day two rows from the beach, $15 per day three rows from the beach, $12 per day four rows from the beach, and $3 for each additional person.

Parking your boat at one of the three marinas will cost as little as $4.50 per foot per month without electricity and water; $6.50 per foot per month with both.

Getting Around in the City

Most expatriates own cars, which they drove down from the States. Many make the relatively short trip back to the States once or twice a year. Most also use their cars to get around town. Those who don't drive recommend taking buses, which are inexpensive and run often. Taxis are both convertibles and hardtops (convertibles cost more). With either, agree on the fare before you get in for the ride.

Community Life

What retirees in Mazatlán love most is fishing, golf, tennis, a good bullfight, and their Venados baseball team, the 1997–98 AAA champions of Mexico's Pacific League. A small number of "retirees" work in real estate or operate businesses. Many retirees belong to one of a few local service clubs.

Hands Across the Border is a loosely formed group of American and Canadian residents who meet once a month for breakfast. Their goal is to raise money for the Humane Society, and they sponsor several fund-raising events.

Friends of Mexico, a new American/Canadian organization, provides services to help expatriates cope in a foreign society. The group helps members deal with health insurance, burial, long-term illness, visas, and so forth. It meets monthly at the Costa de Oro Hotel and charges 100 pesos for a two-year membership. The organization also has monthly bingo parties.

Unlike San Miguel, Cuernavaca, and Puerto Vallarta, Mazatlán has no well-known language or art schools. This eliminates the youthful, intellectual energy that you find in these other retirement cities (and many other Mexican cities). Nevertheless, it is possible to study Spanish at the Centro de Idiomas, tel. (69) 82-2053, reputed to be a very good school, or with the Spanish Conversation Club, tel. (69) 16-7223.

You won't find anything very spiritually offbeat here. When it comes to the retirement community, Mazatlán is a mostly white-bread, Christian town. Churches include Lutheran, Apostalic, Seventh Day Adventist, Mormon, Christian Fellowship (offering bilingual services), and, of course, Catholic.

Newspapers and Books

The *Pacific Pearl* (yooper@red2000.com.mx, tel. (69) 13-0117, fax (69) 13-4411 is Mazatlán's one and only English-language newspaper. Its director is Michael Veselik. The paper is packed with stories and information of interest to English-speaking tourists and residents. Each issue includes good maps of Centro and of the Golden Zone. Issues also include a professional and service directory, a medical directory, a chart comparing shopping prices, schedules of coming events, and extensive display and classified advertisements. The paper sells 16,000 copies a month and is growing. It is a great source of information for those considering a move to Mazatlán. (By the way, check the bulletin board outside the *Pacific Pearl* office for home sales and rentals.)

The second floor of the library downtown has a small stock of English books. We weren't able to find an English-language bookstore, but all major hotels have gift shops that sell at least a few books in English.

Arts and Entertainment

Although the Golden Zone has a few art galleries, Mazatlán really has no art scene to speak of. However, it is very proud of its most famous artist, Antonio Lopez Saenza, who exhibits his works in town on special occasions.

This is a tourist town, so of course you'll find most entertainment in hotels, bars, and restaurants, especially in winter. There are live performances, piano bars, and rock and salsa music. Each year in November and December, Mazatlán hosts the Fall Festival of the Arts at the Angela Peralta Theater. Performances include regional dance groups, orchestras from various parts of Mexico, local performers, and chamber groups from the United States.

The biggest show in town is the Mazatlán Carnival, said to be the third largest in the world after Rio de Janeiro and New Orleans. It goes on day and night for five days and completely takes over Mazatlán with parades, music, dancing, fireworks, and many thousands of tipsy and happy tourists.

The area has seven movie theaters, some showing first-run U.S. films in English with Spanish subtitles. Local cable TV offers only four or five channels in English. People who like to watch TV install satellite dishes. There is a large Blockbuster video store in the Zona Dorado and several smaller video rental stores.

Sports

Mazatlán loves its tournaments. El Cid Golf and Country Club's annual Tournament for Amateurs is held in November each year. The year 1998 marked the 25th anniversary of the event. The tournament draws over 300 amateur golfers every year.

El Cid inaugurated the annual Team Tennis Challenge Tournament in November 1998. Also in November 1998, anglers competed in the fourth annual Marina El Cid Billfish Classic. Open to all anglers with boats, it is Mazatlán's largest tournament.

With such great weather, it is not surprising to find most of the 130 local tennis courts crowded during winter. Most courts are located in hotels and resorts, which charge for their use. The most popular courts are at El Cid, Costa de Oro, Hotel Hacienda, Club Reforma, and Gaviotas Tennis Club.

The Estrella Del Mar development (tel. 69-82-3300) was built more than 20 years ago by Art Linkletter and friends (we are told that Art is no longer involved). The development itself hasn't grown much over the years, but its 18-hole golf course, right on the beach, is spectacular and of championship level.

The 18-hole course at the El Cid resort was designed by Larry Hughes. In December 1998, El Cid opened a nine-hole course designed by Lee Trevino—his first architectural project in Mexico. Club Campestre has a smaller nine-hole course.

Commercially, Mazatlán is primarily a shrimp and tuna port, but sport fishermen ecstatically haul in a wide variety of fish, including marlin, swordfish, mahi-mahi, wahoo, and sailfish. Many retirees have fishing boats docked at one of the three marinas in town. Locals also get away to El Salto lakes, about 40 miles inland to the northeast, for bass fishing.

Trips Outside Town

To the east of Mazatlán is the Sierra Occidental range. Gold was first discovered in these mountains in the sixteenth century. Later, in the mid-1800s, the mining towns of Concordia and Copala were founded. A drive to these towns is a pleasant day trip. This is also a great area for hiking and exploring.

Dining and Nightlife

Mazatlán is jam-packed with restaurants, bars, and hotels. Dining choices are varied—from fast-food joints to elegant restaurants. Seafood (especially shrimp) and Mexican food are both widely available. Other restaurants specialize in steaks, Chinese, Cuban, or Italian food, or health food (one very pretty café). Some restaurants in the Zona Dorado are expensive, but it is easy to find inexpensive, non-touristy Mexican restaurants in any part of town.

Almost every hotel has at least one restaurant/bar. The bar scene also varies—from romantic beachfront bars with soft lights, dancing, and a mellow atmosphere to noisy, wilder scenes. There are sports bars, floor shows, places to rock and roll, and Happy-Hour-all-day-long bars. With the cruise-ship crowd coming ashore to get blasted, and the usual large number of tourists, restaurants and bars can get pretty rowdy late in the evening. Foreign residents may or may not take a bite out of this nighttime apple, but at least they know it's there if they get hungry.

Medical Services

The hospital of choice among expatriates is the Sharp Hospital, a sister of the Sharp Hospital in San Diego. The staff speaks English,

Expatriate Perspective

Bob and Lee Story tell us what attracted them to Mazatlán:

We knew that we wanted to be close to water, as we had been living aboard our 41-foot Gibson houseboat, *Revelry*, on the Mississippi River just north of St. Louis for almost 10 years. We were tired of the cold winters, and we liked the idea of retiring on the Gulf Coast of Alabama and northern Florida.

For many years, friends recommended that we check out Mazatlán, but we preferred to stay in the States. In February 1996, we had reservations to vacation in the Destin, Florida, area, but they were canceled due to hurricane damage. The only warm, sunny location that our time-share club had available on short notice was in Mexico.

We went and immediately fell in love with this country. The people are so friendly, the architecture is creative, the land is awesome, and the prices were so low that there was a chance we could retire early. We decided that this was the country for us. All we had to do was find our corner.

We began exploring Guadalajara, Lake Chapala,

and the hospital has an intensive-care unit, modern lab and radiology equipment, and emergency air service. The hospital also honors most U.S. and Canadian insurance policies. Ambulance services are provided by the Mexican Red Cross.

Mazatlán has the usual array of doctors, dentists, plastic surgeons, pharmacies, and medical clinics. We were surprised to find a branch of the Betty Ford Clinic here—called the Oceanica Clinic.

Manzanillo, Playa del Carmen, Cancún, and the coast of the Yucatan Peninsula. In January 1997, we gave Mazatlán "the acid test" and loved it. In June 1998 we left St. Louis with all our gear and arrived at our new hometown two weeks later.

We chose Mazatlán because it is not totally dependent upon tourism. Mazatlán has a mix of industries: shrimp and tuna fishing, freezing and canning, light manufacturing, commerce and port activities, plus tourism—which accounts for about half of the area's economic wealth. We wanted a medium-sized city, and Mazatlán fit that bill. We want to be able to easily merge with the locals, something Mazatlán also offered.

We are in the process of buying a new *casa* on a charming cul-de-sac of about 15 casas, with a mix of about half Mexicans and half Americans. We are happy and can tell pleasant stories of our life here. We have made friends with Mexicans, as well as Canadian and American expatriates.

It wasn't easy leaving family and friends in the States, but they look at it this way: We've moved to a great vacation spot for them. And they're coming to see us!

Money

Though some retirees have Mexican bank accounts, the majority get their pesos from ATMs for the best rate of exchange. Bital, Banamex, Bancrecer, Confia, and Serfin Banks all have ATMs operating 24 hours daily. Most banks are open 8:30 to 1:30 Monday through Friday. Some Americans use the American Express office to cash checks.

Internet

Red2000, run by Moises Romero, is a local Internet service provider. Its Web addresses are www.mazcity.com.mx and www.maztravel.com. E-mail addresses are moytoy@mazatlán.com.mx and moytoy@red2000.com.mx. Two other local Internet servers are Noroeste Net and AcNet. Both have the same e-mail address: ventas-mzt@acnet.net.

You can pick up e-mail at the Cyber-Cafe Mazatlán, across from Domino's Pizza, or the Netpool café in the Zona Dorado. At Netpool, you can shoot a game of pool and eat while you surf the Net.

Mail

Most expatriates use Mail Boxes, Etc. in the Zona Dorado rather than the Mexican postal system. Mail Boxes provides a stateside address and delivers mail to Mazatlán regularly by UPS. Domestic Mexican mail can be posted at Mail Boxes (an official agent of the Mexican Postal Service), in major hotels, or at the post office down-town.

Consulate and Immigration

The U.S. Consular Agency is located across from the Hotel Playa Mazatlán, tel./fax (69) 16-5889 or (69) 13-4444 ext. 285. Office hours are 9 to 4 Monday to Thursday. The consular agent is Geri Nelson de Gallardo. The Mexican immigration office (migracion) is located in Centro.

Shopping Cart

Because of Mazatlán's size and proximity to the States, its stores carry most anything shoppers could want. It is also one of the least expensive Mexican retirement cities for shopping.

For food and household goods, most foreign residents shop at either Gigante, Comercial Mexicana, or Plaza Ley. Prices at these mega-stores vary, with Comercial Mexicana usually the highest and Gigante the lowest, but the differences may be just a few pesos. The *Pacific Pearl* regularly publishes charts comparing the prices of selected items at the three stores.

If you are turned off by the cold, fluorescent-lit mega-stores, there are many small groceries and fruit stores throughout town. Or you can shop in Centro at the main *mercado* (always an adventure).

In Mazatlán, we spotted the only drive-into (not drive-in) liquor store that we have ever seen anywhere. Drivers pull into a large garagelike building, buy their booze at a long counter, and drive out through the back door!

Other Retirement Cities

This chapter describes a few other Mexican retirement possibilities. They are as different from one another as Seattle, Washington, is from Naples, Florida. There are literally hundreds of other towns in Mexico with at least a few foreigners that could easily have been included. Some are so remote that only the hardiest, nuttiest, or most adventurous outsiders live there.

Guadalajara, Jalisco

Our travels often take us through Guadalajara, Mexico's second largest city. Driving in, we ease onto wide, tree-lined boulevards, dotted with fountains. Guadalajara has more than 5 million people, collectively known as Tapatos. It is a modern, sophisticated city that has managed to retain much of its charm—due in part to an abundance of trees and brightly colored flowers and to the Old World grace of the colonial downtown.

Guadalajara, along with nearby Chapala and Ajijic, is home to the largest number of U.S. and Canadian retirees in Mexico—20,000 to 30,000 or more. The old, well-established retirement community is friendly and easy to break into. The town is rich with arts and culture, has first-class universities, first-rate hospitals and medical care, sports and recreational facilities, great restaurants, and plenty of nightlife. It is relatively inexpensive, with easy availability of goods and services. In our opinion, Guadalajara is much prettier than any U.S. city of its size.

Foreigners living in Guadalajara have only good things to say about the town. What's more, Guadalajara has an almost-perfect climate, with a year-round average temperature of 66 degrees, a normal maximum of 87 degrees, and a minimum of 41 degrees. Average annual rainfall is 34 inches.

The foreign population is made up of all ages and types, including young couples with kids, working people, and older retirees. They live in everything from apartments and stately homes in the beautiful downtown area to humble houses in various *colonias* a little away from downtown to the suburbs in both rural settings and gated retirement communities. Two colonias with large numbers of Americans are Chapalita and Providencia.

Residential areas are generally quiet and, in typical Mexican fashion, houses have lush, colorful gardens hidden behind walls, often on handsome tree-shaded streets. In some neighborhoods on the surrounding hills, homes have views of the city and the Valley of Atemajac below.

Retirees can find just about any modern amenity found in any large city in the United States. You'll find a Price Club, Sam's Club, Wal-Mart, Office Depot, Sirloin Stockade, McDonald's, KFC, and Burger King, just to name a few. There are English-language bookstores, libraries, and movie theaters. And to balance all these modern franchises is one of the largest and most interesting old-fashioned Mexican markets in the Western Hemisphere. El Mercado Libertad is a huge market with hundreds of stalls selling everything from food to leather goods, live birds to iron candelabras.

Guadalajara is easy to reach, with its international airport served by a large number of airlines. Many flights are direct from the States. What's more, Guadalajara is only a four-hour drive from Puerto Vallarta and its surrounding beaches.

During the past 30 years or so, modern buildings and skyscrapers have changed Guadalajara's skyline. The city has become a major

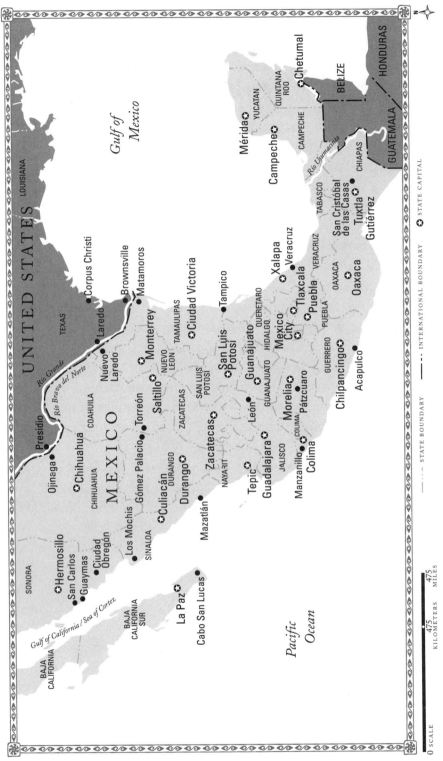

N

UNITED STATES

LOUISIANA

Gulf of
Mexico

TEXAS

Río Grande

Río Bravo del Norte

Presidio
Ojinaga

Corpus Christi

Brownsville
Matamoros

Laredo

Nuevo
Laredo

Chihuahua

CHIHUAHUA

MEXICO

COAHUILA

Gómez Palacio
Torreón

Saltillo

Monterrey

NUEVO
LEÓN

TAMAULIPAS

Ciudad Victoria

Tampico

Culiacán

Durango

DURANGO

ZACATECAS

SAN LUIS
POTOSÍ

San Luis
Potosí

QUERETARO

HIDALGO

Mazatlán

Zacatecas

NAYARIT

Tepic

León

Guanajuato

GUANAJUATO

Mexico
City

Xalapa

Veracruz

Hermosillo

San Carlos
Guaymas

Ciudad
Obregón

Los Mochis

SINALOA

SONORA

Guadalajara

JALISCO

Morelia

Pátzcuaro

COLIMA

Manzanillo
Colima

Chilpancingo

Acapulco

GUERRERO

Tlaxcala

Puebla

PUEBLA

VERACRUZ

OAXACA

Oaxaca

TABASCO

San Cristóbal
de las Casas

Tuxtla
Gutiérrez

CHIAPAS

Río Usumacinta

CAMPECHE

Campeche

Mérida

YUCATAN

QUINTANA
ROO

Chetumal

BELIZE

HONDURAS

GUATEMALA

Pacific
Ocean

Gulf of California / Sea of Cortez

BAJA
CALIFORNIA
SUR

BAJA
CALIFORNIA

La Paz

Cabo San Lucas

✪ STATE CAPITAL

- · - INTERNATIONAL BOUNDARY

---- STATE BOUNDARY

SCALE

0   475
    KILOMETERS

0   475
    MILES

business center and industrial giant. Along with these changes have come heavier traffic, urban sprawl, and occasional serious air pollution. Population increases have created poor, overcrowded, and unattractive new colonias, especially on the outskirts, where the city has spread into the surrounding countryside. Urban growth has engulfed nearby towns, like the still-very-picturesque town of Tlaquepaque, one of the main arts and crafts centers of Mexico.

Even with all of these changes, in many parts of the city you can still easily get a feeling of Guadalajara's romantic past. Maybe it's the flowers, the parks, the many public statues, or just the old movies we've seen that evoke a memory of gallant *caballeros* on horseback and beautiful dark-haired *señoritas* being serenaded by mariachi music.

If you want to learn more about Guadalajara, contact the American Society, San Francisco 3332, Col. Chapalita, tel. (3) 121-2395. It is a nonprofit clubhouse for American, Canadian, and European residents. Then check with the American Legion at San Antonio 143, Las Fuentes, tel. (3) 631-1208. Both organizations sponsor activities such as dinner-dances, Spanish classes, free blood-pressure checkups, and lunches. Each will gladly offer information to newcomers and will send brochures upon request. Check the appendix for the address of English newspapers in the city.

Guadalajara is too big for some retirees. Many people prefer to live 45 minutes away, in one of the peaceful towns on Lake Chapala, and make day trips to Guadalajara for shopping and cultural excursions. Yet new retirees arrive every day and love living here. Those who dream of retiring in a city with all the urban amenities, plus perfect weather and a low cost of living, may be able to realize their dreams in Guadalajara.

San Carlos, Sonora

San Carlos is a small coastal town that has it all for people who want to live in Mexico but are not interested in immersion into the Mexican culture. For a touch of Mexico, residents can drive about eight miles down the road to Guaymas, a city of 90,000.

Growing San Carlos now has about 5,000 residents, and a large number of them are from the States. But growth should not be unexpected in a beautiful seaside town, with a sense of safety and community, where English is spoken much more often than Spanish. San Carlos is more like an upscale southern California resort town than a Mexican fishing village. Housing prices are moderately high and going higher as new condominiums and developments are being built to meet expected demand. The cost of a two-bedroom house in a nice area ranges from $600 to $800 per month.

San Carlos is an easy drive of only about five hours from Nogales on the Arizona border. It is ideal for second or weekend homes, and even more ideal for retirees who like deep-sea fishing, scuba diving in warm Gulf waters, whale-watching, and golf. San Carlos also attracts wealthy Mexicans and a large number of RVers from the States. The Club Med, with its yacht marina, clubhouse, and golf course, is a preferred local hangout.

Weather here is very pleasant most of the year but hot in summer. Many locals don't mind the heat too much because of widespread air-conditioning. Restaurants are good, as are medical services and communications with the States. E-mail and Internet services are available in Guaymas.

No doubt that San Carlos is beautiful and has the amenities that can help make a move to Mexico hassle free. We personally prefer towns with more Mexican culture, but we can't see any reason why this town will not continue to grow rapidly in the future.

Pátzcuaro, Michoacán

The quiet colonial town of Pátzcuaro is located just a few kilometers above Lake Pátzcuaro, at an altitude of about 7,200 feet. The lake itself is located in a beautiful picture-postcard setting in the State of Michoacán, known for its pine-covered mountain landscape of rivers, lakes, and high volcanoes.

Adding to the romance of the setting is the island of Janitzio, which sits majestically in the middle of the lake. Pátzcuaro slopes up from above the lake to a relatively flat town center. Here you will find the Plaza Vasco de Quiroga, another of Mexico's magnificent colonial plazas. Adding to the picture-postcard setting are white-painted homes

Bob and Marybeth Macy

Shops line the streets of Cabo San Lucas.

with red-tiled roofs. Fanning out around the center are newer, less-picturesque areas of town.

Until recently, only a few foreigners had ever lived in and around Pátzcuaro. In the last year or two, the number of adventurous outsiders living in the area (mostly from the States) has grown to about fifty, out of a local population of about 75,000. Foreigners living here are attracted by the low cost of living, the still-very-low prices of real estate, and Pátzcuaro's beauty and relaxed atmosphere.

A very good friend bought 20 acres near the lake a few years ago and operates an organic and permaculture farm on the property. She says the soil is rich and the culture in the area even richer. We have seen her occasionally since her move to Pátzcuaro, and each time she seems ecstatically happy with her new life.

As quiet as it is, Pátzcuaro still has some amenities and activities for foreign residents. There is the *biblioteca* (library), with a good selection of English books; the local Teatro Emperador Caltzontzin, with its cultural events; the Center for Language and Ecotours of Pátzcuaro, a Spanish language and culture school; and a museum of popular arts. Aside from these facilities, the town's main activities revolve around shopping, sitting in one of the two town plazas people-watching, and eating at restaurants.

Pátzcuaro still retains some of the feeling of the Tarascan Indian village it once was. This is especially true at the Friday market, where locals display a variety of handmade crafts, including blankets, pottery, serapes (shawls), copper, and grotesque masks. It is also a great place to buy carved wooden doors and wooden furniture.

Throughout the year, a steady smattering of tourists visit Pátzcuaro. But tourism explodes during Christmas, Easter, and Dia de los Muertos—Day of the Dead—when thousands of mostly Mexican visitors come to watch ceremonial graveside activities of Pátzcuaro and Janitzios Purepecha Indians (descendent of the former Tarascan culture).

In the surrounding mountains are a number of very picturesque towns. Our favorites are Paracho, about 70 miles west, where hundreds of shops that manufacture and sell guitars and other stringed instruments line the streets, and Santa Clara del Cobre, about 12 miles south, where the manufacture of copper articles has been taken to a new artistic level.

The fact that Pátzcuaro is only about 45 minutes away from the large and culturally active colonial city of Morelia goes a long way in offsetting its small size and feeling of remoteness. Morelia, with about 500,000 residents, is the capital of the state of Michoacán. It has one of the most impressive and large colonial central plazas in Mexico. Morelia is also a university town, with a good variety of restaurants, several language schools, bookstores, and movie theaters.

For us, Pátzcuaro is a little too small and laid back. It is also a little too cold in winter, because of its altitude and relatively high humidity. The locals are pleasant but somewhat reserved. But for those looking for a relatively quiet small town, with low prices and spectacular beauty, Pátzcuaro would be a great place to live.

Oaxaca, Oaxaca

Barbara and I have always liked Oaxaca. We still have a brightly colored, hand-woven *huipil* (an Indian serape) that we bought many years ago from a tiny Indian woman on the *zocalo* (main square) there. It now hangs on a wall in our home.

In Oaxaca City, as in the entire State of Oaxaca, ethnic arts and crafts and Indian culture still flourish. Mexico's Indian heritage is very powerful in this southern state, where there are said to be 16 different indigenous languages and over 200 dialects spoken. Around Oaxaca City you can see wonderfully impressive ruins like Monte Alban and Mitla and many small villages, each dedicated to producing a particular craft.

Mexico's colonial past is also represented by the grand, six-teenth-century colonial architecture in and around the city's zocalo. It is here that both locals and tourists sit in outdoor cafés under shaded *portales* and watch the constant flow of tourists, vendors, musicians, and locals. The atmosphere has been improved by the closing of many streets leading into the plaza, a move that has turned it into a colorful pedestrian bazaar. Outside the center of town, Oaxaca looks like many other sprawling Mexican cities.

There are probably fewer than 200 foreigners living full-time in Oaxaca, out of a population of well over 300,000. In a way, this is a surprisingly small number, given the beauty of Oaxaca's setting, its warm dry climate, and its creative environment. It is also much less expensive than most other mid-sized, sophisticated Mexican cities.

Perhaps there are so few foreigners because of the city's remoteness. Oaxaca is 340 miles southeast of Mexico City and a long drive from the States. A new toll road makes driving the curvy roads through the mountains from Mexico City easier and cuts the driving time from 10 to about 6 hours. Still, getting to Oaxaca by car can be a real nuisance. It is difficult to avoid driving through Mexico City. Flying is also a bit of a hassle. There are no direct flights from the States, which means flying into Mexico City and changing planes. When we last tried, connections were difficult to make, and we wound up spending the night in Mexico City. There are now more airlines flying into Oaxaca from Mexico City, so maybe the situation is improving. Buses are inexpensive and make the trip from Mexico City often, but they are slow.

Of course, Oaxaca's remoteness, beauty, and relatively low cost of living are probably the major attractions to the expatriates who do live there. The foreign community tends to be artistically minded, another possible attraction. Oaxaca has several libraries and a few bookstores with English-language books. It has good language schools, museums, restaurants, coffee shops, and bars. There is also plenty of music, free on the zocalo and for a small cover charge at restaurants and cafés. There are even a couple of golf courses: Brenamiel Golf Club and Oaxaca Country Club.

Communication services seem good, and an electronic Oaxaca newsletter (published monthly by Stan Gotlieb at stan@mexconnect .com) offers opinions and information. There is a small newspaper in English and Spanish called *Oaxaca*.

As far as atmosphere is concerned, Oaxaca has plenty. Besides the European feeling of the zocalo, the huge open markets near downtown are breathtaking in the sheer quantity of hand-made rugs, jewelry, leather goods, hand-loomed cottons, pottery, wooden animals, and crafts on display.

Oaxaca may be the place to retire for artists and other expatriates who really want to immerse themselves in a unique blend of Zapotec, Mixtec, and Spanish cultures—and are not put off by the city's distance from the States.

Manzanillo, Colima

Manzanillo, a port town, has a kind of honky-tonk feeling that Barbara and I both enjoy. The city is a working town, not a slick tourist center like Puerto Vallarta. It does have some incredibly fancy tourist resorts and hotels, but they are located along the beaches to the north of town. The main zocalo, which faces the bay, is unpretentiously pretty, with a relaxed and open atmosphere.

From one side of the zocalo, you might see steel-gray ships docked at the local naval base or large cargo vessels at a loading dock. On the other three sides of the zocalo, you'll find restaurants, shops, and a few of central Manzanillo's better tourist hotels. For the most part, few of the shops are really touristy. Walk a few blocks farther into town and you will be caught up in the bustle of Manzanillo's business day. There is a certain funkiness about the town that may not be for everyone. For instance, one downtown street has a railroad track running down its center—easy to trip over.

We weren't able to get a reliable count of the Manzanillo area's permanent foreign community. We guess that there are no more than a few hundred expatriates, although the number of part-time residents swells during winter, when snowbirds arrive from the north.

Most foreigners live north of town along the beaches, from Las Brisas on Manzanillo Bay to Playa Santiago on Santiago Bay. This is also the main tourist area, with some enormous resorts like the famous Las Hadas. In some areas north of town, like Las Brisas, residential homes are scattered among small hotels and motels.

Santiago Bay is cleaner than Manzanillo Bay. The hills at the northern end are dotted with private homes, condominiums, restaurants, and hotels, most with fabulous views of the bay. Foreign residents live in this area and in gated communities like Club Santiago, located on the beach at the north end of the bay. Foreigners also live in small towns north of Manzanillo, including Barra de Navidad, 30 miles north, nearby San Patricio and Melaque, and La Manzanilla, just 13 miles north of that.

The very honky-tonk nature of Manzanillo probably draws some foreigners to the town. But more likely the semitropical climate, relatively low prices, and amenities, goods, and services are the greatest attractions. The area has some very good restaurants, good fishing, plentiful golf and tennis facilities, and fairly easy accessibility. A new four-lane highway from Guadalajara has cut driving time to Manzanillo to about three and one half hours. The Playa de Oro International Airport, about 20 miles north of town, has direct flights to Los Angeles via Aero California. Other airlines will have you change planes in Guadalajara or Mexico City.

Guanajuato, Guanajuato

We wanted to include Guanajuato because, though it and San Miguel de Allende are only about 50 miles apart, they are about as

Ron Mader

Sprawling hills surround Oaxaca City.

different from one another as two small colonial cities can be. Guanajuato is the jewel in the crown of Mexico's colonial cities. It is shaped like a humongous fruit bowl, with brightly painted houses climbing up its sides. The houses are not located along conventional streets, but are reached by way of steep narrow stairs and alleyways that snake up the sides of the bowl.

On the floor of the bowl, downtown Guanajuato has a series of wonderful Italianate plazas, with colonial hotels, outdoor cafés, and cobblestone streets. Located here are the greatest influences in the life of the city: the University of Guanajuato, government offices (this is the capital of the state of Guanajuato), and a unique atmosphere that attracts thousands of tourists.

What really sets Guanajuato apart for us is its youthful, cultural, and festive atmosphere. On typical nights during the school year, students crowd cafés and narrow streets around the university. On weekend nights, with thousands of tourists in town, is not unusual for mimes and other street performers to draw crowds in front of the Teatro Juarez, built in 1903 and a copy of the Paris opera house.

In the fall, Guanajuato hosts the Festival Cervantino, one of Mexico's biggest cultural events. First-rate performers from all over the world come to the city. Ballet, theater, and music occupy all the stages in town and overflow onto the stages of nearby towns like San Miguel and Dolores Hidalgo.

Services in and around Guanajuato are good. The Leon International Airport is only about a half-hour away. From there you can fly on American directly to Dallas, Aero Mexico to LA, or

Continental to Houston. The town has an Internet server and a large and colorful downtown market. In the city of Leon, about 45 minutes away, you'll find a Price Club and a few very fancy, decidedly uptown shopping malls.

Real estate and rental prices are lower in Guanajuato than in nearby San Miguel de Allende, although rentals in Centro are difficult to find. Surprisingly, there are very few foreigners living in Guanajuato, and you will rarely hear English spoken. The expatriates who do live in Guanajuato are mostly artists or those that love the culture of the city. Most live in either Valenciana or Marfil, both just outside the city center. We knew an American woman who started a bed-and-breakfast in Marfil, the Casa de los Espititus Alegres (House of the Spirits), a wonderful place that her husband now runs.

We love Guanajuato and continually wonder why we are not living there. Who knows—maybe someday we will.

Cabo San Lucas

Friends who have traveled extensively in Baja California describe it as one of the most magical places on earth. It is a thousand-mile-long tail hanging down from the bottom of southern California. With the Pacific Ocean on its west and the Gulf of Mexico (also called the Sea of Cortez) on its east, Baja has almost 2,000 miles of magnificent coastline and an arid, semi-mountainous center.

Cabo San Lucas, at the lower tip of Baja, has fabulous weather (average year-round temperatures of 75 degrees), great diving and fishing, and absolutely marvelous sunsets. It is the most developed and fastest-growing retirement community in Baja. This distinction has both pluses and minuses. On the plus side are regular flights to and from the States, five deluxe golf courses, and an extensive expatriate infrastructure that includes three local English newspapers: the *Gringo Gazette*, *Baja Sun*, and *El Tiempo Los Cabos* (English/Spanish). Explosive growth has brought high-end hotels, condos, apartments, and expensive private homes a la Beverly Hills. This is Southern California south!

On the minus side is the sheer quantity of development. A

recent article in the *Los Angeles Times* spoke of a clash of cultures due to rapid development. The article says that Los Cabos County has doubled its population since 1990, to 75,000. A significant number of newcomers are from the States. Billboards along the bay tell passersby: "Act Now—Only 24 Condos Available" and "Location, Location, Location." Of course, all of these signs are in English. Most of the Americans moving to this area do not speak Spanish, and few have any interest in learning the language.

While many Mexican residents of the area embrace the foreigners and their job-creating investments in real estate and construction, others are less sanguine. They complain that in creating gated communities, Americans are colonializing some of Mexico's most beautiful land and denying Mexicans access to their own beaches.

There is no getting around the natural beauty of this area, with its incredible white-sand beaches and desertlike rock formations jutting into a jade-blue sea. Fishermen and sailors here think they are in heaven. The same is true for golfers. But the cost of living in heaven is not cheap. Condominiums in some parts of town cost between $100,000 and $200,000. Private homes in the fanciest part of town, called Pedregal, can cost upward of a million bucks.

For those who want to be near the action, nightlife, and many restaurants of Cabo San Lucas —but not too near—San Jose del Cabo is just 20 miles away. It is a smaller, older town that has managed to maintain its sense of tranquillity and historic charm. Downtown, the mission and colonial square are reminiscent of older towns in the Mexican interior. But development is definitely coming to San Jose del Cabo, especially in the corridor between the two "Cabos," where the number of golf courses and resort developments has grown in recent years. In spite of all the development, inexpensive hotels and apartments can still be found. Trailer parks in both Cabo San Lucas and San Jose del Cabo attract large numbers of campers.

As we continue our travels around Mexico, we continue to scope out new towns with great retirement potential. In future editions of this book, we will be adding more choices to this chapter. If you run across a town that belongs here, let us know. Send us a note or an e-mail message in care of John Muir Publications. But we will understand if you decide to keep the place your own little secret!

Appendix

The States of Mexico

Mexico has 31 states and one federal district known as DF, much like our Washington, D.C. The states are Aguascalientes, Baja California, Baja California Sur, Campeche, Chiapas, Chihuahua, Coahuila, Colima, Durango, Guanajuato, Guerrero, Hidalgo, Jalisco, México, Michoacán, Morelos, Nayarit, Nuevo León, Oaxaca, Puebla, Querétaro, Quintana Roo, San Luis Potosí, Sinaloa, Sonora, Tabasco, Tamaulipas, Tlaxcala, Veracruz, Yucatán, and Zacatecas.

Newspapers

Atención San Miguel, a weekly newspaper in San Miguel de Allende, tel./fax (415) 2-3770; e-mail: atencion@unisono.net.mx

Independiente, a biweekly newspaper in San Miguel de Allende, tel./fax (415) 2-4515; e-mail: sareda@mpsnet.com.mx

Bargain Hunter, a monthly advertising paper in the Lake Chapala area, tel./fax (376) 2-0403

Colony Reporter, a weekly newspaper in the Guadalajara and Chapala area with a Puerto Vallarta supplement, tel. (3) 615-2177, fax (3) 616-9432, e-mail: reporter@informador.com.mx and reporter@infosel.net.mx

Cuernavaca Lookout, a biweekly newspaper with articles of local interest, advertising, and a calendar of events, tel. (73) 13-2102

El Financiero, a weekly national financial newspaper, tel. (525) 227-7600 (Mexico City), 800/433-4872 and 213/747-7547 (Los Angeles)

El Ojo Del Lago, a monthly newspaper in the Lake Chapala area with stories and advertisements of local interest, tel. (376) 5-3676 or (376) 5-2877, www.chapala.com

Gringo Gazette, a newspaper for southern Baja, 310/436-3433, fax 310/436-5080 (in the United States)

Mexico City Times, a daily national newspaper distributed throughout Mexico, tel. (5) 352-7593 or (5) 352-7654, fax (5) 352-5422, e-mail: mexcittm@infosel.net.mx

Oaxaca, a small local newspaper in English and Spanish, directed at tourists, with a small classified section, tel. (951) 587-64

The News, a daily national newspaper distributed throughout Mexico, tel. (5) 510-9623, (5) 512-5044, or (5) 512-4013, fax 521-8550, e-mail: thenews@ri.redint.com

Pacific Pearl, a monthly newspaper in Mazatlán, including stories of local interest, event and tourist information, and classified and display advertising, tel. (69) 13-0117 or (69) 13-4411, e-mail: yooper@red2000.com.mx

Vallarta Today, daily Puerto Vallarta newspaper, tel. (322) 4-2829 and (3232) 4-2928, fax (322) 4-1186

Newsletters

Adventures in Mexico, Apdo 31-70, 45050 Guadalajara, JAL, Mexico

Background Notes, published by the Department of State about countries around the world, Superintendent of Documents, U.S. Printing Government Office, Washington, DC, tel. (202) 512-1800 or (202)647-5225

Retiring in Guadalajara, Apdo 5-409, Guadalajara, JAL, Mexico

The Mexico File (free informational packet), tel. (800) 5-639-3453

The People's Guide to Mexico Travel Letter, P.O. Box 179, Acme, WA 98220, e-mail: mexico@peoplesguide.com

Mexico Real Estate and Travel, 800/501-0319 (in the United States)

Mexico Retirement and Travel Assistance, 6301 Squaw Valley Rd. #23, Pahrump, NV 89048-7949, tel. (523) 641-1152 (in Mexico), fax (523) 641-4555

Living in Mexico, 40 Fourth St., Suite 203, Petaluma, CA 94952

Magazines

Puerto Vallarta Lifestyles, a four-color quarterly, tel. (322) 1-0106, fax (322) 1-2255, e-mail: jgyserpr@zonavirtual.com.mx

Xcaret, a full-color magazine in English and Spanish focused on Cancún and the Yucatán Peninsula, tel. (98) 83-1539 or (98) 83-0623

Books

Best Rated Retirement Cities and Towns, Consumer Guide editors

Casa Mexicana: The Architecture, Design and Style of Mexico, Tim Street-Porter, Marie Pierre Colle

Invest and Retire in Mexico, Sidney Thomas Wise

Live Better South of the Border, "Mexico" Mike Nelson

Mexico, James A. Michener

Mexico Travel Book, distributed by AAA

Odyssey to Guadalajara, Griffith D. Lambdin

People's Guide to Mexico, Carl Franz

Recipe of Memory: Five Generations of Mexican Cuisine, Victor M. Valle, Mary Lau Valle

Tales of Retirement in Paradise, Polly G. Vicars (photographer)

Traveler's Guide to Mexican Camping, Mike and Terri Church

Internet Sites

Retirement and Foreign Travel

www.livingabroad.com—country-specific information for those thinking about relocating

www.travel.state.com—U.S. State Department information on foreign countries

www.aca.ch—American Citizens Abroad

Chapala

southmex@southmex.com

www.mexconnect.com

Cuernavaca
andy@infosel.net.mx
ciberic@infosel.net.mx
infocuernavaca@infosel.net.mx
webmaster@axon.com.mx
www.intersur.com

Mazatlán
moytoy@mazatlán.com.mx
ventasmzt@acnet.net
www.mazcity.com.mx
www.maztravel.com

Oaxaca
stan@mexconnect.com

Puerto Vallarta
info@pvallarta.icanet.net.mx
www.pvnet.com.mx
www.vallarta-online.com

San Miguel de Allende
mpsnet.com.mx
unisono@unisono.net.mx
www.infosma.com

U.S. Embassy and Consulates in Mexico

U.S. Embassy, Paseo de la Reforma 305, Colonia Cuauhtemoc, Mexico City, tel. (5) 209-9100

Consulate Guadalajara, Progreso 175, 44100 Guadalajara, Jalisco, tel. (3) 825-2998 or (3) 825-2700, fax (3) 826-6549

Consulate Hermosillo, Calle Monterrey 141 Pte. 83260 Hermosillo, Sonora, tel. (62) 17-2375 or (62) 17-2382, fax (62) 17-2578

Consulate Matamoros, Ave. Primera 2002 y Azaleas, 87330 Matamoros, Tamaulipas, tel. (88) 12-4402, fax (88) 12-2171

Consulate Merida, Paseo Montejo 453, 97000 Merida, Yucatán, tel. (99) 25-5011, fax (99) 25-6219

Consulate Nuevo Laredo, Allende 3330, Col. Jard'n, 88260 Nuevo Laredo, Tamaulipas, tel. (87) 14-0512, fax (87) 14-7984

Consulate General Tijuana, Tapachula 96, Col. Hipodromo, 22420 Tijuana, Sonora, tel. (66) 81-7400, fax (66) 81-8016

Consulate Ciudad Juarez, Avenida Lopez Mateos 924-N, Chihuahua, tel. (16) 11-3000

Consulate Monterrey, Avenida Constitucion 411 Poniente 64000, tel. (83) 45-2120

U.S. Consular Agents in Mexico

Acapulco—Joyce Anderson, Hotel Acapulco Continental, Costera
M. Alemyn 121, Office 14, 39580 Acapulco, Guerrero,
tel. (74) 81-1699 or (74) 69-0556, fax (74) 84-0300

Cabo San Lucas—David Greenberg, 1 Blvd. Marina y Pedregal #3,
Cabo San Lucas, B.C.S., tel./fax (114) 3-3566

Cancun—Carol Butler, Plaza Caracol Dos, Second Floor,
#320–323, Blvd. Kukulkan, Km. 8.5, Hotel Zone, 77500
Cancun, Q.R., tel. (98) 83-0272, fax (98) 83-1373

Ixtapa—Elizabeth Williams, Office 9, Plaza Ambiente, 40880
Ixtapa, Zihuatanejo, tel. (755) 3-1108, fax (755) 4-6276

Mazatlán—Gerianne Nelson Gallardo, Hotel Playa Mazatlán,
Rodolfo T. Loaiza 202, Zona Dorada, 82110 Mazatlán, Sinaloa,
tel./fax (69) 16-5889 or (69) 13-4444 ext. 285

Oaxaca—Mark A. Leyes, Macedonio Alcaly 201, #206, 68000
Oaxaca, Oaxaca, tel./fax (951) 4-3054

Puerto Vallarta—Laura A. Holmstrom, Vallarta Building, Plaza
Zaragoza 160, Piso 2-18, 48300 Puerto Vallarta, Jalisco, tel.
(322) 2-0069, fax (322) 3-0074

San Luis Potosí—Kathleen Reza, Francisco de P. Moriel 103-10,
96000 San Luis Potosí, S.L.P., tel./fax (48) 12-1528

San Miguel de Allende—Philip Maher, Hernandez Macias 72,
37700 San Miguel de Allende, Guanajuato, tel. (465) 2-2357, fax
(465) 2-1588

Mexican Government Tourism Offices in the United States

California—10100 Santa Monica Blvd. Suite 224, Los Angeles, CA
90067, 310/203-8191, fax 310/203-8316

Florida—2333 Ponce de Leon Blvd. Suite 710, Coral Gables, FL
33134, 305/443-9160, fax 305/443-1186

Illinois—70 E. Lake St. Suite 1413, Chicago, IL 60601,
312/565-2778, fax 312/606-9012

Texas—2707 North Loop West Suite 450, Houston, TX 77008,
   713/880-5153, fax 713/880-1833
New York—450 Park Ave. Suite 1401, New York, NY 10022,
   212/755-7261, fax 212/755-2874
Washington, D.C.—1911 Pennsylvania Ave. NW, Washington,
   D.C. 20006, 202/728-1750, fax 202/728-1758

Mexican Embassy in the United States

1911 Pennsylvania Ave. NW, Washington, D.C. 20006,
   202/728-1600, fax 202/728-1698

Mexican Consulates in the United States

Arizona—135 Terrace Ave., Nogales, AZ 85621, 602/287-2521
   Saguaro Savings Bldg. Suite 150, 700 E. Jefferson, Phoenix, AZ
   85034, 602/242-7398
California—331 W. Second St., Calexico, CA 92231, 619/357-3863
   905 N. Fulton St., Fresno, CA 93721, 209/233-3065
   125 Paseo de la Plaza, Los Angeles, CA 90012, 213/624-3261
   Transportation Center, 201 E. Fourth St., Oxnard, CA 93030
   805/483-4684
   9812 Old Winery Place Suite 10, Sacramento, CA 95814
   916/363-3885
   588 W. Sixth St., San Bernardino, CA 92401, 714/889-9836
   610 A St. Suite 100, San Diego, CA 92101, 619/231-8414
   870 Market St. Suite 528, San Francisco, CA 94102,
   312/392-5554
   380 N. First St. Suite 102, San Jose, CA 95113, 408/294-3414
   406 W. Fourth St., Santa Ana, CA 92701, 714/835-3069
Colorado—707 Washington St. Suite A, Denver, CO 80203,
   303/830-0601 or 303/830-0607
Florida—780 N. LeJeune Rd. Suite 525, Miami, FL 33145,
   305/441-8780

Georgia—3220 Peachtree Rd. NE, Atlanta, GA 30305, 404/266-2233

Illinois—300 N. Michigan Ave., Second Floor, Chicago, IL 60601, 312/855-1380

Louisiana—World Trade Center Suite 840, 2 Canal St., New Orleans, LA 70130, 504/522-3596

Massachusetts—20 Park Plaza Suite 321, Boston, MA 02116, 617/426-8782

Michigan—1515 Bood Blvd. at W. Grand River, Detroit, MI 48226, 313/965-1868

Missouri—1015 Locust St. Suite 922, St. Louis, MO 63101, 314/436-3233

New York—8 E. 41st St., New York, NY 10017, 212/689-0456

Pennsylvania—575 Philadelphia Bourse Bldg., 21 S. Fifth St., Philadelphia, PA 19106, 215/922-4262

New Mexico—Western Bank Building, 401 Fifth St. NW, Albuquerque, NM 87102, 505/247-2139

Texas—200 E. Sixth St. Suite 200, Austin, TX 78701, 512/478-2866

724 Elizabeth and Seventh Sts., Brownsville, TX 78520, 210/541-7061

410 North Tower, 800 N. Shoreline, Corpus Christi, TX 78401, 512/882-3375

1349 Empire Central Suite 100, Dallas, TX 75247, 214/630-7341 or 214/630-7343

1010 S. Main St., Del Rio, TX 78840, 210/774-5031

140 Adams St., Eagle Pass, TX 78852, 210/773-9255

910 E. San Antonio St., El Paso, TX 79901, 915/533-3644

4200 Montrose Blvd. Suite 120, Houston, TX 77006, 713/524-2300

1612 Farragut St., Laredo, TX 78040, 210/723-6360

1418 Beech St. Suite 102–104, McAllen, TX 78501, 210/686-0243

511 W. Ohio Suite 121, Midland, TX 79701, 915/687-2334

127 Navarro St., San Antonio, TX 78205, 210/227-9145

Utah—182 S. 600 E Suite 202, Salt Lake City, UT 84102,
    801/521-8502,
Washington—2132 Third Ave., Seattle, WA 98121, 206/448-3526

Mexican Trade Commission Offices in the United States

California—World Trade Center Suite 296, 350 South Figueroa St.,
    Los Angeles, CA 90071, 213/628-1220
Florida—New World Tower Suite 1601, 100 N. Biscayne Blvd.,
    Miami, FL 33132, 305/372-9929
Georgia—Cain Tower, 229 Peachtree St. NE Suite 917, Atlanta, GA
    30303, 404/522-5373
Illinois—225 N. Michigan Ave. Suite 708, Chicago, IL 60601,
    312/856-0316
New York—150 E. 58th St., 17th Floor, New York, NY 10155,
    212/826-2916
Texas—2777 Stemmons Freeway Suite 1622, Dallas, TX 75207,
    214/688-4096
    1100 N.W. Loop 410 Suite 409, San Antonio, TX 78213,
    512/525-0748

National Holidays and Celebrations

January 1—Año Nuevo (New Year's Day)
January 6 —Dia de los Reyes Magos (Three Kings' Day; children
    receive gifts on this day rather than on Christmas)
February 2—Dia de la Candelaria (candlelight processions and
    dancing
February 5—Dia de la Constitución (Constitution Day)
February 24—Dia de la Bandera (Flag Day)
Late February or early March—Carnaval (marking the beginning
    of Lent)
March 21—Dia de Nacimiento de Benito Juarez (birthday of
    Benito Juarez)
March or April—Semana Santa (Holy Week; the week beginning
    on Palm Sunday and ending on Easter)

May 1—Dia del Trabajo (Labor Day)

May 5—Cinco de Mayo (celebration of Mexico's victory over the French army at Puebla in 1862)

May 10—Dia de la Madre (Mother's Day)

September 16—Dia de la Independencia (Independence Day; commemorating Mexico's war of independence from Spain)

October 12—Dia de la Raza (Day of the Race; commemorating Columbus's discovery of the New World and the founding of the *mextizo*—Mexican—people)

November 1—Informe Presidencial (president's State of the Nation address to the legislature)

November 1—Dia de Todos Santos (All Saints' Day)

November 2—Dia de los Muertos (Day of the Dead; people bring food, drink, and flowers to cemeteries to commune with the departed)

November 20—Dia de la Revolucion (anniversary of the Mexican Revolution of 1910)

December 12—Dia de Nuestra Señora de Guadalupe (Day of Our Lady of Guadalupe, Mexico's national patroness)

December 16–24—Posadas (parades that commemorate the journey of Mary and Joseph to Bethlehem)

December 25—Dia de Navidad (Christmas Day)

Index

John Muir Publications' guides are available at your favorite bookstore

The 100 Best Small Art Towns in America 3rd edition
Discover Creative Communities, Fresh Air, and Affordable Living
U.S. $16.95

Healing Centers & Retreats
Healthy Getaways for Every Body and Budget
U.S. $16.95

Cross-Country Ski Vacations, 2nd edition
A Guide to the Best Resorts, Lodges, and Groomed Trails in North America
U.S. $15.95

Gene Kilgore's Ranch Vacations, 5th edition
The Complete Guide to Guest and Resort, Fly-Fishing, and Cross-Country Skiing Ranches
U.S. $22.95

Yoga Vacations
A Guide to International Yoga Retreats
U.S. $16.95

Watch It Made in the U.S.A., 2nd edition
A Visitor's Guide to the Companies That Make Your Favorite Products
U.S. $17.95

The Way of the Traveler
Making Every Trip a Journey of Self-Discovery
U.S. $12.95

Kidding Around®
Guides for kids 6 to 10 years old about what to do, where to go, and how to have fun in *Atlanta, Austin, Boston, Chicago, Cleveland, Denver, Indianapolis, Kansas City, Miami, Milwaukee, Minneapolis/St. Paul, Nashville, Portland, San Francisco, Seattle, Washington D.C.*
U.S. $7.95

JOHN MUIR PUBLICATIONS
P.O. Box 613 ◆ Santa Fe, NM 87504

For a catalog or to place an order call 800-888-7504.

About the Author

After living and working in Santa Fe, New Mexico, for more than 25 years, Ken and his wife, Barbara, decided to leave the rat race and move to San Miguel de Allende, Mexico. There, Barbara teaches yoga, and Ken writes and paints. Both enjoy life to the fullest.